The Amsterdam Town Hall in Words and Images

The Amsterdam Town Hall in Words and Images

Constructing Wonders

Edited by
Stijn Bussels, Caroline van Eck and
Bram Van Oostveldt

BLOOMSBURY VISUAL ARTS
LONDON • NEW YORK • OXFORD • NEW DELHI • SYDNEY

BLOOMSBURY VISUAL ARTS
Bloomsbury Publishing Plc
50 Bedford Square, London, WC1B 3DP, UK
1385 Broadway, New York, NY 10018, USA
29 Earlsfort Terrace, Dublin 2, Ireland

BLOOMSBURY, BLOOMSBURY VISUAL ARTS and the Diana logo are trademarks of
Bloomsbury Publishing Plc

First published in Great Britain 2021
Paperback edition first published 2022

Selection and editorial matter © Stijn Bussels, Caroline van Eck and
Bram Van Oostveldt, 2021
Individual chapters © their authors, 2021

Stijn Bussels, Caroline van Eck and Bram Van Oostveldt have asserted their right under
the Copyright, Designs and Patents Act, 1988, to be identified as Editors of this work.

For legal purposes the Acknowledgements on p. xii constitute an extension
of this copyright page.

Cover design by Toby Way.
Cover Image: The Citizens' Hall seen from the west. Courtesy Stichting Koninklijk
PaleisAmsterdam. © The Royal Palace of Amsterdam, photograph: Benning & Gladkova

All rights reserved. No part of this publication may be reproduced or transmitted in any form or by
any means, electronic or mechanical, including photocopying, recording, or any information
storage or retrieval system, without prior permission in writing from the publishers.

Bloomsbury Publishing Plc does not have any control over, or responsibility for, any
third-party websites referred to or in this book. All internet addresses given in this book
were correct at the time of going to press. The author and publisher regret any inconvenience
caused if addresses have changed or sites have ceased to exist, but can accept
no responsibility for any such changes.

A catalogue record for this book is available from the British Library.

Library of Congress Cataloging-in-Publication Data

Names: Bussels, Stijn, editor. | Eck, Caroline van, editor. | Oostveldt, Bram van, editor.
Title: The Amsterdam Town Hall in words and images : constructing wonders / edited by Stijn
Bussels, Caroline van Eck and Bram Van Oostveldt.
Description: London ; New York : Bloomsbury Visual Arts, 2021. |
Includes bibliographical references and index.
Identifiers: LCCN 2020046254 (print) | LCCN 2020046255 (ebook) |
ISBN 9781350205338 (hardback) | ISBN 9781350205345 (pdf) | ISBN 9781350205352 (epub)
Subjects: LCSH: Koninklijk Paleis (Amsterdam, Netherlands) | Campen, Jacob van,
1595–1657–Criticism and interpretation. | Architecture and fame–Europe. |
Curiosities and wonders–Europe. | Amsterdam (Netherlands)–Buildings, structures, etc.
Classification: LCC NA7751.A6 A47 2021 (print) | LCC NA7751.A6 (ebook) |
DDC 720.9492/352—dc23
LC record available at https://lccn.loc.gov/2020046254
LC ebook record available at https://lccn.loc.gov/2020046255

ISBN: HB: 978-1-3502-0533-8
PB: 978-1-3502-0537-6
ePDF: 978-1-3502-0534-5
eBook: 978-1-3502-0535-2

Typeset by RefineCatch Limited, Bungay, Suffolk

To find out more about our authors and books, visit www.bloomsbury.com
and sign up for our newsletters.

Contents

List of Illustrations	vi
List of Contributors	x
Acknowledgements	xii
1 Introduction *Stijn Bussels, Caroline van Eck and Bram Van Oostveldt*	1
2 The Palace of the Republic: Idea and Construction *Pieter Vlaardingerbroek*	29
3 The Amsterdam Town Hall: The Triumphant Statement of a Successor State *Caroline van Eck*	61
4 'Far More to Wonder, than to Fathom Completely': One Hundred Poems Devoted to the Town Hall *Stijn Bussels, Caroline van Eck and Laura Plezier*	83
5 The Portrait of a Building *Stijn Bussels*	117
6 The Exercise of Power: The Caryatids of the Town Hall's Tribunal *Frederik Knegtel*	143
7 Jacob's Trowels : The Construction of the Amsterdam Town Hall and Its Ceremonial Objects (1648–present) *Minou Schraven*	173
8 Under Discussion: Eighteenth-Century Reactions to the Town Hall *Freek Schmidt*	195
Index	231

Illustrations

1.1	The Citizens' Hall seen from the west.	3
1.2	The Tribunal.	3
1.3	Jurriaan Pool, silver medal commemorating the inauguration ceremony of the Amsterdam Town Hall, 29 July 1655.	8
1.4	Jürgen Ovens (?), *Entry of the Amsterdam Burgomasters*, c. 1662.	10
1.5	Gerrit Adriaensz. Berckheyde, *The Town Hall on Dam Square*, 1665–80.	12
1.6	Casper van Wittel (alias Vanvitelli), *View of St. Peter's Square*, c. 1700.	13
1.7	Hendrick Mommers, *View of the Louvre from the Pont-Neuf*, c. 1665.	13
1.8	Hendrick Mommers, *Market Scene before the Dam*, c. 1665.	14
1.9	Philips Galle after Maarten van Heemskerck, *The Temple of Diana at Ephesus*, 1572.	15
2.1	Salomon Jacobsz Savery, medieval Town Hall of Amsterdam as it appeared during the visit of Maria de' Medici in 1638.	30
2.2	The development of the building lot of the Amsterdam Town Hall, 1639–47.	31
2.3	Pieter Nolpe, unexecuted design for the Amsterdam Town Hall by SGL.	32
2.4	Jacob van Campen and Pieter Post, the interior of the Oranjezaal in Huis ten Bosch, The Hague.	34
2.5	Abraham Lutma, *Portrait of Jacob van Campen*, 1661.	35
2.6	Gerrit Adriaensz Berkcheyde, *The Amsterdam Town Hall*, 1672.	37
2.7	(a) and (b) Cornelis Danckerts, Ground plan of the Town Hall's ground and first floor, 1661.	39
2.8	View of Solomon's Temple and Palace, as published in Juan Bautista Villalpando, *In Ezechielem Explanationes et Apparatus Urbis ac Templi Hierosolymitani*, 1604.	42
2.9	Solomon's Palace.	43
2.10	Section of the north wing of the Amsterdam Town Hall, c. 1652.	44
2.11	Europe, as published in Cesare Ripa, *Iconologia of uijtbeeldingen des verstands*, 1656.	45
2.12	Edinburgh, Palace of Holyroodhouse.	51

3.1	Detail of chimney overmantle relief in Burgomasters' room, showing the triumph of Fabius Maximus Cunctator attributed to Artus Quellinus.	66
3.2	Passage from the Citizens' Hall leading to what are now the royal apartment and Salon of the English quarter.	67
3.3	Perugino, *Christ Giving the Keys to St Peter*, 1481.	69
3.4	Andrea Mantegna, *Triumphs of Caesar*, 1485–92.	70
3.5	Peter Paul Rubens and Erasmus Quellinus, *Free Copy after Mantegna's Triumphs of Caesar Canvas II and IX*, 1630s.	71
3.6	Title page of *Verscheidene Nieuwe Festonnen geinventeert door Iacob van Campen*, 1655–78.	72
4.1	Frontispiece of Joost van den Vondel, *Inwydinge van 't Stadthuis t' Amsterdam*, 1655.	88
4.2	Artus Quellinus and workshop, Medusa head in the Tribunal of the Town Hall, 1651–2.	101
4.3	Lieven Willemsz. Coppenol, calligraphic writing with Constantijn Huygens' Congratulations to the Noble Lords Rulers of Amsterdam, in its new Town Hall, 1657.	103
4.4	The Citizens' Hall of the Amsterdam Town Hall.	105
5.1	Jan van de Velde after Pieter Jansz. Saenredam, 'View on the Grand Square with Town Hall of Haarlem', 1628.	119
5.2	Johannes or Lucas van Doetechum after Hans Vredeman de Vries, 'View on a city with palaces and canal from a bird's eye perspective', 1601.	119
5.3	Gerrit Adriaensz. Berckheyde, *The Town Hall on Dam Square*, 1668.	120
5.4	Elias Noski, stone engraved with Huygens' poem, 1660.	125
5.5	Jacob van der Ulft, *Market on Dam Square*, 1653.	126
5.6	Hendrick Mommers, *Market Scene before the Dam*, c. 1665.	127
5.7	Jan Beerstraaten, *Ruins of the old Town Hall*, c. 1660.	128
5.8	Pieter Saenredam, *The Old Town Hall of Amsterdam*, 1657.	130
5.9	Willem van Nieulandt (II), *The Arch of Septimus Severus*, 1609.	133
5.10	Abraham de Verwer, *The Louvre Grande Galerie, view of Paris from the Barbier bridge*, c. 1640.	134
5.11	Abraham de Verwer, *Galerie du Louvre and the Porte Neuf*, c. 1640.	134
5.12	Abraham de Verwer, *The Louvre Grande Galerie, view of Paris from the Barbier bridge (upstream)*, c. 1640.	135
6.1	The Citizens' Hall seen from the West.	144
6.2	Marcantonio Raimondi, *Facade with caryatids*, 1502–34.	149

6.3	A caryatid from the Forum of Augustus, first-century CE copies of fifth-century BCE originals.	150
6.4	Cesare Cesariano, *Di Lucio Vitruvio Pollione de architectura libri dece* (Como: Gottardo de Ponte, 1521)	151
6.5	Hans Vredeman de Vries, plate 15 of 16, *c* 1565.	152
6.6	Jean Goujon, two of the four caryatids in the Salle des Caryatides, 1546–50.	153
6.7	Theodoor van Thulden after Peter Paul Rubens, *The Temple of Janus*, 1639–41.	154
6.8	Artus Quellinus, *The Judgement of Junius Brutus*, *c*. 1655.	157
6.9	Artus Quellinus, Interior of the Tribunal with a portion of the eastern wall visible on the right, *c*. 1655.	163
7.1	Johannes Lutma, silver trowel with inscriptions used at the foundation ceremony of the Amsterdam Town Hall, 28 October 1648.	174
7.2	After Johannes Lutma, silver medal issued at the foundation ceremonies of the Amsterdam Town Hall, 28 October 1648.	175
7.3	Rummer of green glass with inscriptions commemorating the foundation of the tower of the New Church, 26 June 1647.	177
7.4	Chamois apron used at the foundation ceremonies of the Amsterdam Town Hall, 28 October 1648.	179
7.5	Illustration showing the obverse and reverse of Lutma's silver trowel (7.1), 1849.	180
7.6	Gerrit Lambrets, drawing of a silver spoon given to the citizens standing on guard during the inauguration ceremony of the Amsterdam Town Hall, *c* 1810.	183
7.7	Jurriaan Pool, silver medal commemorating the inauguration ceremony of the Amsterdam Town Hall, 29 July 1655.	183
8.1	Daniel Marot, civil guard on Dam Square, presenting themselves to the Burgomasters of the city, on the occasion of the Amsterdam fair, 1686.	196
8.2	Martin Bernigeroth, portrait of Leonhard Christoph Sturm, 1707.	198
8.3	Dancker Danckerts (?) after Jacob Vennekool, ground plan of the main floor of Amsterdam Town Hall, 1661.	199
8.4	Leonhard Christoph Sturm, ground plan of the main floor of Amsterdam Town Hall, with Sturm's proposal for new external staircases, 1760.	200
8.5	Jacob Houbraken, *Portrait of Jan Wagenaar*, 1766.	201

8.6   Simon Fokke, *View of Amsterdam Town Hall with the New Church and the Weigh House on Dam Square,* c. 1770.   202
8.7   C. Bogerts after Hendrik Keun, *Interior of the central hall of Amsterdam Town Hall,* c. 1770–8.   203
8.8   Simon Fokke, *Dam Square with the Town Hall, New Church and Weigh House,* 1762.   204
8.9   Reinier Vinkeles, *Amsterdam Town Hall and Weigh House,* c. 1764–7.   205
8.10 Reinier Vinkeles, *Ball in Amsterdam Town Hall in 1768, on the occasion of the entry of Prince Willem V and Princes Wilhelmina,* 1771.   206
8.11 Reinier Vinkeles. *Portrait of Petrus Camper,* 1776.   208
8.12 Anonymous, *Tribunal in the Amsterdam Town Hall.*   209

Contributors

Stijn Bussels is Professor of Art History before 1800 at the Leiden University Centre for the Arts in Society, Leiden University. Until 2018, he was the Principal Investigator of the ERC Starting Grant project 'Elevated Minds. The Sublime in the Public Arts in Seventeenth-Century Paris and Amsterdam'. Together with Gijs Versteegen and Walter Melion, he is the editor of *Magnificence in the Seventeenth Century: Performing Splendor in Catholic and Protestant Contexts* in the *Intersections* series published by Brill (2020).

Caroline van Eck is Professor of Art History at Cambridge University and Fellow of King's College. In 2016, she was Slade Professor in Oxford. Her main research interests are art and architectural history and theory of the eighteenth century and early nineteenth century; classical reception; and the anthropology of art. She recently published *The Style Empire and its Pedigree: Piranesi, Pompeii and Alexandria, Architectural Histories* 6/1 (2018) and *Restoring Antiquity in a Globalizing World: Piranesi's Late Work and the Genesis of the Empire Style* (2019).

Frederik Knegtel is an Expert on Applied Arts at Venduehuis der Notarissen, The Hague. Until 2019, he was a PhD student at the Leiden University Centre for the Arts in Society. There, he wrote his thesis *Constructing the Sublime: The Discourse on Architecture and Louis XIV's Sublimity in Seventeenth-Century Paris*. His most recent essay, 'Transcending the Natural World: A Developing Sublime' in André Félibien's *Tapisseries du Roy*, is published in *Emblems and the Natural World*, ed. Karl Enenkel and Paul Smith (2017).

Bram Van Oostveldt is Professor of Theatre History at the Department of Art, Music and Theatre Sciences at Ghent University. His research interests focus on early modern and modern theatre and theatricality in France and the Low Countries. He has published on the early history of the sublime in the age of Louis XIV. His most recent book is *Tranen om het alledaagse: Diderot and the verlangen naar natuurlijkheid in het Brusselse theaterleven in de achttiende eeuw* (2013). Together with Caroline van Eck and Stijn Bussels, he is the editor of *Antoine Wiertz Revisited* (2020).

Laura Plezier is a PhD student at the Leiden University Centre for the Arts in Society. She is preparing a thesis on the seventeenth-century laudatory poems on the Amsterdam Town Hall and has co-authored an essay on the laudatory poems of Constantijn Huygens with Stijn Bussels and Marc Van Vaeck in *Spiegel der Letteren* (2017).

Minou Schraven is a Lecturer at the Amsterdam University College. She studies festivals and processions in early modern Italy, especially Rome. Together with Maarten Delbeke, she has edited *Foundation, Dedication, and Consecration in Early Modern Europe* (2012). Her most recent book is *Festive Funerals in Early Modern Italy: The Art and Culture of Conspicuous Commemoration* (2014).

Freek Schmidt is Professor of architectural history at the Vrije Universiteit Amsterdam. His most recent book, *Passion and Control: Dutch Architectural Culture of the Eighteenth Century*, was published in 2016. His research on the design, use and appreciation of the built environment in the early modern and modern age, makes use of insights of the history of art, culture and architecture, urban planning and heritage studies.

Pieter Vlaardingerbroek is Architectural Historian for the city of Amsterdam and Lecturer at Utrecht University. He studies architecture in the seventeenth century and has published widely on the Amsterdam Town Hall, the Portuguese Synagogue and the Canals. Amsterdam canal houses, their inhabitants and architects are his special interest. In 2011 he published *Het paleis van de Republiek. Geschiedenis van het stadhuis van Amsterdam*.

Acknowledgements

The European Research Council supported the research on the Town Hall as part of the Starting Grant Programme entitled 'Elevated Minds: The Sublime in the Public Arts in Seventeenth-Century Paris and Amsterdam'.

Further, the editors of the book would like to thank the Royal Palace Amsterdam Foundation for financing this publication and for all their practical help (especially Alice Taatgen), as well as all authors for their diligence and patience, Nora Naughton for her meticulous copy-editing, and everyone from Bloomsbury for all their support, especially Frances Arnold, April Peake and Anita Iannacchione, Lisa Carden and Merv Honeywood.

Stijn Bussels
Caroline van Eck
Bram Van Oostveldt

1

Introduction

Stijn Bussels, Caroline van Eck and Bram Van Oostveldt

Right in the heart of Amsterdam stands the Royal Palace, one of the most famous monuments in the Netherlands. In a typical year, the building has many visitors, from the leading international politicians received by the Dutch king to the hundreds of thousands of tourists buying tickets to enter. Even more visitors pose outside to immortalize themselves in front of this building. From the perspective of its founders – the citizens of Amsterdam, with the Burgomasters taking the lead – we could say almost four centuries after the start of its construction, the building still succeeds in its main aim of putting Amsterdam prominently on the world map.

In 1808, when Louis Napoléon ruled over the Kingdom of Holland, the building was transformed into a royal palace, but originally it was a town hall. Although the first plans were made in the late 1630s, construction did not start until 1648, in the wake of the Peace of Münster; the moment when the Dutch rebels were able to definitively – and victoriously – end their revolt against Spain and their Republic of the Seven United Provinces was recognized as an independent nation. At last, Amsterdam could fully invest in international trade. Although building works would continue until the early 1700s, the building was officially inaugurated in 1655. A few years prior to this, the building's predecessor, a dilapidated gothic town hall, had gone up in flames, so construction had to be expedited. There was, however, more going on than this mere practical problem. The old Town Hall had become a bigger and bigger thorn in Amsterdam's side. Long before it had burned down, the Burgomasters were so ashamed of their building that they had decided to have it replaced by a new one which could give the city and its inhabitants, as well as themselves, the dignity they felt they all deserved.[1]

At that time, Amsterdam had great political independence. It was an oligarchic city state in which the Burgomasters had supreme power. They came from a small number of mostly wealthy merchant families, such as Bicker, Backer, de Graeff, Huydecoper and Valckenier.[2] There were always four Burgomasters in order to not only share the administrative responsibilities, but also to represent the different factions in the civic elite. Each year, the sitting Burgomasters and Magistrates elected their successors from within their own ranks. There was a religious constraint, as only a Calvinist could become Burgomaster or Magistrate. Nevertheless, as trade had to be guaranteed by all means, a pragmatic and successful model of pluriconfessional society evolved in Amsterdam throughout the seventeenth century.[3] Because Amsterdam had become Europe's centre of trade, the Burgomasters had an important voice in the Republic. With the Town Hall, the Burgomasters wanted to visually represent their leading position in the city and the Republic, as well as their aspirations to world domination.

The new Town Hall also had to strengthen community spirit among the inhabitants of Amsterdam. As a result of international trade, the population of the city increased six times between 1575 and 1675.[4] The very high levels of immigration, as well as the emergent gap between extremely successful merchants, a group which included the Burgomasters, and the rest of the population, led to an eager search for a common identity. Many seventeenth-century poets praising the new building suggested that the construction of architectural splendour would bring people closer to each other, all rejoicing in Amsterdam's success. Such a shared sense of identity and civic pride was also strengthened by awe and admiration for the Town Hall, all the more as it was constructed at the legendary place of origin, a dam in the river Amstel (Amstel-dam) around which fishermen had once settled and which had led to the construction of Dam Square with its fish market. Here the new building was accompanied by three other iconic buildings, the New Church (Nieuwe Kerk), the Weigh House (Waag) and the Stock Exchange (Beurs).

Inside the building, citizens and their guests could also celebrate the prestige and civic coherence of Amsterdam, above all in the majestic Citizens' Hall (Burgerzaal) (Figure 1.1). After visitors had climbed the relatively modest stairs leading to the first floor, they suddenly came upon this public hall, the largest secular interior space in Europe at the time, made even more impressive through the many sculptures and huge maps in the marble floor. Another highlight in the building was the Tribunal (Vierschaar) that served only to proclaim the death penalty on felons (the trial and the actual execution were performed elsewhere), but was nevertheless the room that took central stage at the front of the building, taking up three floors and displaying the richest sculptures of the entire building (Figure 1.2). In this elaborately decorated Tribunal, the Burgomasters and

Figure 1.1 The Citizens' Hall seen from the west. Courtesy Stichting Koninklijk Paleis Amsterdam. © The Royal Palace of Amsterdam, photograph: Benning & Gladkova.

Figure 1.2 The Tribunal. Courtesy Stichting Koninklijk Paleis Amsterdam. © The Royal Palace of Amsterdam, photograph: Tom Haartsen.

Magistrates were able to exercise with full dignity their ultimate power, the decision over life and death, in order to protect their subjects by preserving order and discipline. The prominence of the Tribunal was evident from the earliest of plans. The architects competing to construct the new building had all reserved a central place for it and made it clearly visible from Dam Square, thus serving the old, respected tradition of public jurisdiction.[5]

Eventually, the Burgomasters gave the commission for the new Town Hall to Jacob van Campen (1596–1657),[6] rejecting a design by the experienced architect Philips Vingboons, who proposed a building with clear echoes of French palatial architecture, in favour of van Campen's Palladian approach.[7] The architect presented a design defined by rigorous proportions and a clear and hierarchical arrangement of the rooms. He had already acquired a reputation in Amsterdam as a fashionable architect through the façade he designed in 1625 for houses built for a wealthy merchant family, the Coymans, and even more through the construction of the city's first permanent theatre, begun in 1638. Van Campen had powerful family connections in the city himself; for example, his second cousin Nicolaas van Campen was a member of the city council,[8] but Jacob also maintained close ties to prominent figures connected to the Oranges, the dynasty of Stadholders. He designed Palace Noordeinde (1639) in The Hague for Frederick Henry, and he was very friendly with Constantijn Huygens (1596–1687), the poet, patron of the arts and secretary of the Stadholders. Together, they studied Vitruvius' treatise on architecture, and collaborated closely on the royal palace, Huis ten Bosch (1645–52). Throughout the construction of the Town Hall, Huygens would congratulate the Burgomasters in several poems on their excellent choice (see infra).

Moreover, as a talented painter, van Campen could also have important input into the Town Hall's rich decor.[9] He worked closely with the sculptor Artus Quellinus (1609–68), in whose house he lived for many months during the construction of the Town Hall. Quellinus came from Antwerp, where he had acquired international fame after studying in Rome with François Duquesnoy from 1635–9.[10] The Burgomasters persuaded him to come and work in Amsterdam with a very generous honorarium. In the end, the sculptor would work for the Burgomasters and their Town Hall for fifteen years (1650–65) and would complete his most important work there. Besides sculpture, there was also painting, most prominently in monumental canvases showing the Revolt of the Batavians against Roman rule in the galleries adjacent to the Citizens' Hall. These were painted from the early 1660s by Jan Lievens, Ferdinand Bol, Jacob Jordaens and Rembrandt van Rijn, among others.[11]

Challenges for the Town Hall

In the only English monograph on the building, *The Baroque Town Hall of Amsterdam* (1959), Katharine Fremantle argued that the collaboration of the Burgomasters with van Campen, Artus Quellinus and these eminent painters resulted in the magnum opus of the Dutch seventeenth century.[12] Later studies of the Town Hall, mostly written in Dutch, further develop the idea of the ultimate masterwork by relating the building to the complete oeuvre of van Campen, tracing the origins of the design and its use of ornament to Greco-Roman and Italian Renaissance architecture, as well as rigorously tracing the steps taken throughout the entire building process.[13]

This book wants to add to these studies by shifting the focus from the architectural and artistic aspects to the *impact* of the building. We start from the questions which the Town Hall raises for current architectural historiography. Thanks to studies on architecture in the early modern Low Countries, as well as Britain, it has become clear that the use of Greco-Roman and Italian Renaissance architectural tropes was not as self-evident as was previously accepted.[14] The new architectural style developed in cities such as Amsterdam and London was strongly associated with Catholic church architecture in Rome, but became interwoven with local traditions, idioms and values in complex manners. We will study these appropriations in the context of the Town Hall, as we can no longer simply assume an unproblematic taking-over of classical forms and models in the Dutch seventeenth-century context, as presented in traditional architectural history.[15] Because of its monumentality, which completely disrupted the existing medieval urban fabric, its conspicuous display of classical orders and harmonic proportions, as well as the use of rare and costly materials such as Carrara marble, the Town Hall shared striking similarities with the most prestigious buildings in papal Rome. Could the Burgomasters appropriate the architecture of their religious enemies in the centre of their city without any objection?

The cost of the building was also problematic. The merchants of Amsterdam had become extremely rich thanks to an unprecedented flowering of international commerce, but as exemplary burghers they were urged not to show their riches too openly.[16] From their pulpit, Calvinist preachers pressed the wealthy businessmen to consider carefully how to use their profits, more particularly to serve God and to help their less fortunate fellow townsmen.[17] An enormous building for which no equal could be found in the Republic – either in the shape of previous town halls, or city palaces – seems to be completely contrary to that ideal. How could an edifice that in design, size, wealth and costs was so unfamiliar to the Dutch be built by god-fearing burghers? How was it possible that Amsterdam dared to express its riches so openly?

To find answers to these questions, we can first look at how the advocates of the Town Hall succeeded in coping with two acute problems. First, there were the plans for a new tower for the New Church, situated directly adjacent to the location of the new Town Hall. Even within the group of Burgomasters, there were moves to drastically save money by constructing a less grand building, which would leave enough money to construct instead the highest tower in the Republic.[18] However, the debate was really about how closely the city administration had to be related to Calvinism. Were the Burgomasters allowed to fully display their power in this new building, or did they have to acknowledge the superiority of religious power by giving a substantial part of their finances to the construction of a new church tower? Eventually, the Town Hall obtained funding. Only the foundation and the first ten metres of the tower were built; after that, the plans were shelved once and for all.

A new (and costly) war was a second threat to plans for the Town Hall. Directly after the Dutch concluded peace with Spain in Münster, problems began with Britain. In the opinion of the British, Dutch trading overseas obstructed their own interests.[19] Between 1652 and 1654, the First Anglo-Dutch War was fought. These years were also crucial for the construction of the Town Hall. The war threw a spanner in these works, as the costs for the war ate into Amsterdam's budget extensively. The Burgomasters adapted their building project by removing two floors, but as soon as the war was finished, they completely reversed that decision and the construction of the Town Hall continued as originally designed.

The Burgomasters, supported by the majority of the civic elite, could thus fully execute their ambitious plans. In this book we ask, to begin with, how public support for the building was created and how the new style and high costs played in this. To answer these questions, the first essays in this book will look at new insights in the specific choices that the founders made in the design of the Town Hall, in the decorations on the façades and inside the building. Every building, and certainly the Town Hall, is more than a series of usable rooms, as a building can interact with its surroundings in expressing ambitions. In one of the tympana of the Town Hall, for example, the City Maiden sits enthroned as the ruler of the seas. On the floor in the Citizens' Hall, two enormous world maps, as well as a map of the heavenly firmament, proclaimed the belief that the city occupied the centre of the universe. Allegories appeared inside and on the façades to show the importance of peace and justice for Amsterdam, celebrating the actual impetus of the construction, the peace of Münster, as well as the most important function of the building: jurisprudence.

The Town Hall also urged its visitors to connect prosperous events in the present with Greco-Roman and Biblical precedents, and with a radiant future for the city. The many references to the Temple of Jerusalem, for instance, are surprising, because they are not used in a religious context for the construction of a church, but rather in the secular context of the Town Hall.[20] They served as a legitimization of the classical style, which here was presented as originating in Solomon's Temple; only subsequently would it be developed in Greco-Roman architecture. Moreover, by referring to Solomon, the Burgomasters could present themselves as the most competent leaders of God's new chosen people, the citizens of Amsterdam. Solomon was also present in a relief in the Tribunal as an *exemplum virtutis* for the magistrates.

Constructions before and beyond the construction

Besides the Town Hall itself, the authors of this book will look at what they call ritual, textual and visual 'constructions before and beyond the construction'. There is the building itself, the construction in the literal sense of the word, but there are also several ceremonies, as well as numerous poems, prints, drawings and paintings that continued to construct the identity of the building. Seventeenth-century writers were very conscious of its novelty and uniqueness, and the need to produce new constructions of it in different media that would give it a historical and civic context. Everard Meyster (1617-79), a country gentleman known to van Campen for example, wrote a play in which Jupiter summons all the great architects of history – from Vitruvius to Michelangelo – to give the Olympians some understanding of the building. Nevertheless, even Michelangelo has to admit that, for him, van Campen's architecture leads 'far more to wonder, than to fathom completely'.[21] The Italian architect mentions Joost van den Vondel (1587-1679) as the most appropriate person to help, as he wrote famous and influential poems celebrating the building. Inaugural rituals as well as countless texts and images began this work of interpretation and explanation, even before its construction had begun, as the Burgomasters performed ceremonies on the building site, poets wrote poems expressing their admiration for the building as it was being built and for its founders, and artists experimented in powerfully visualizing it.

The solemn public ritual celebrating the laying of the first stone amalgamated traditional Christian church-building ritual with civic rites into an artificial *novum* to mark such an important moment. It included the ritual itself and its celebrations in word and image. In the medal celebrating the inauguration in 1655, the building is made part of a classical allegory in which Mercury, the god of commerce, figures prominently (Figure 1.3). Amsterdam is likened to Thebes as Amphion is sitting in front playing the lyre with which he once made stones gather to form the Greek city's walls. The choice of a Palladian model is contextualized as part of the concerted attempt to make Amsterdam one of the successors of Greco-Roman antiquity. Thus, the inauguration ritual and its visual representations already prepared the public for the extraordinary character of the Town Hall and created public acceptance when the very first stones were laid. Its visual and textual representations enable us to connect its design with the aspirations of its founders and its broader civic context.

The texts and images celebrating the Town Hall are far from neutral. They give us a privileged insight in what the Burgomasters wanted their building to bring about. Poets often received handsome compensation for their efforts. For instance, the Burgomasters gave Vondel 'a silver cup or plate' (*een silvre kop of schaal*) for the extensive poem he wrote for the inauguration.[22] Often patrons and poets worked to mutual benefit. The equally comprehensive poem written for the inauguration by Jan Vos (1612–67) would have come as no surprise, given Vos was not only an extremely successful playwright of bloody tragedies, but a glass maker as well, who had received a huge commission as part of the Town Hall's completion.[23] In the case of Huygens, we can see his poems as a diplomatic

Figure 1.3 Jurriaan Pool, silver medal commemorating the inauguration ceremony of the Amsterdam Town Hall, 29 July 1655, d. 70 mm. Rijksmuseum Amsterdam, Public Domain.

means to strengthen his contacts with Amsterdam. After the sudden death of William II in 1650, whom he served as secretary, no new stadholder was appointed. This vacuum made the province of Holland, and certainly the city of Amsterdam, more powerful than ever before in the Republic. Huygens' attempt to charm the Burgomasters was well received, as his congratulations for their new building of 1657 were recited in the Town Hall at several occasions. They also had the poem engraved in black marble and gave it a prominent position in their chamber.[24]

Bringing magnificence to Amsterdam

Biblical and Greco-Roman antiquity interacted in the stylistic choices and the iconography of the Town Hall. So did magnificence or *ghrootdaadigheidt* (a literal translation of the Latin *magnificentia*, that is, performing great deeds), a prominent Greco-Roman concept used to defend the grand project. Laudatory poems often proclaimed this ancient virtue.[25] Dozens of authors, including Vondel, Vos and Huygens, present the Burgomasters as magnificent because they founded the Town Hall and, more precisely, because they spent extraordinary sums of money in a carefully considered way to increase the splendour of the city to an unprecedented degree and thus to serve the common interest of the citizens of Amsterdam. Poets present the founding Burgomasters as having the exceptional foresight, wisdom and courage to acknowledge that constructing a grand building was a bare necessity for the city.[26]

The Dutch poets refer to Solomon as the principal example of magnificence through building the Temple. Essentially, however, they fall back on Aristotle who developed the concept of *megaloprepeia* in his *Nicomachean Ethics*, which was subsequently taken up by Latin authors as *magnificentia* and which early modern Europe used gratefully to legitimize grand political projects.[27] The Greek philosopher presented magnificence as a virtue of the rich man who spends money abundantly. He deserves the fullest respect from his fellow citizens as his money serves the public good. In his ethics of big spending, Aristotle explicitly points up the difference with liberality. Everyone can be liberal, even if they give away only a small amount of money. By contrast, the virtue of magnificence is about being exceptional, since there one has to deal with spending extraordinary riches to support an outstanding project. Moreover, the enormous costs need to correspond with the public aims of the project. Because of these restrictions, Aristotle argues that performing magnificence is as hard as creating an excellent work of art. Like a talented artist, a magnificent person has to act in a well-considered and tasteful way.

In the imagery of the Town Hall, the magnificence of Amsterdam and her rulers is nowhere more explicitly visualized than in a drawing attributed to Jürgen Ovens (1623–78), an artist from the German city of Tönning who came to live in Amsterdam around 1640 (Figure 1.4).[28] On Dam Square, where the Town Hall is under construction, the Amsterdam City Maiden is seated on a triumphal wagon pulled by a pair of lions. A multitude of ancient gods and allegorical figures accompany her. We would relate these figures far more quickly to Counter-Reformatory Rome or the Southern Netherlands than to the Calvinistic Republic. Nevertheless, the artist explicitly connects the Baroque triumph of the City Maiden to the four Burgomasters at whom she looks. The Burgomasters are in full conversation while one of them ostentatiously holds a purse. Chained men and kneeling women beg Amsterdam's rulers for their attention. Between these supplicants, Abundance with her horn of plenty suppresses Envy and her serpent. Amsterdam luxuriates in her extreme wealth. Her rulers ensure that this wealth is spent carefully in their liberality and help for people in need. The Town Hall, which has already advanced to the first floor, from where people are looking at the triumphal parade through the windows, shows their magnificence.

Figure 1.4 Jürgen Ovens (?), *Entry of the Amsterdam Burgomasters*, c. 1662, black crayon, pencil in black and brown, d. 70.22 cm. Courtesy Hamburger Kunsthalle / bpk. © Hamburger Kunsthalle / bpk, photograph: Christoph Irrgang.

The Town Hall is situated on an idealized Dam Square with two prominent obelisks. In the early modern period, obelisks were not so much associated with Egypt as with Rome, where Pope Sixtus V had them resurrected throughout the city in the 1580s with impressive public ceremonies.[29] The obelisks lent splendour to the squares in front of the Lateran Palace and St Peter's Basilica, behind the Santa Maria Maggiore and on the Piazza del Popolo. In the background, there is a building whose roof statues resemble those of the Palazzo dei Conservatori on the Capitoline Hill. This drawing is not unique in connecting Michelangelo's design with the Town Hall. At the very start of its planning, the Burgomasters and some of the architects who submitted a design took the Roman building as its stylistic model. This connection takes us back to the Roman Kingdom and Republic, because the first political centre of ancient Rome was believed to be situated there. Dutch poets took this up immediately and claimed that Dam Square could be compared with the most famous of the seven Roman hills, precisely because the Town Hall was situated on Dam Square. For example, in his *Bouw-zang* of 1648, Vondel mentions Numa, the second king of Rome, famous for building the first administrative building on the Capitoline Hill, as well as for his peace-keeping, which was another important consideration for the Burgomasters: 'He planned to build the splendid Town Hall, the Capitol, high and proud on an arid rock.'[30]

But references to the Palazzo dei Conservatori largely disappeared from the building designs. Van Campen's final plans moved away from the Roman civic model to privilege the Biblical model of Solomon's Palace. Besides, in the visual arts, this drawing is the only one to suggest such a close identification between Rome and Amsterdam. The majority of the artists appeared to stay much closer to the reality on Dam Square, but nevertheless used innovative pictorial strategies to present the Town Hall as an example of pure magnificence. They employed perspective and colour, and manipulated the size of the figures in front of the building.

One of the most famous artists to explore these means is the Haarlem painter Gerrit Berckheyde (1638–98), who painted the front façade seen from Dam Square a dozen times. We can take a painting that is now in the Amsterdam Museum as an example (Figure 1.5). The painter uses a viewpoint in such a way that the two other prominent buildings on the square appear far less prominent than they were in reality. The Weigh House is placed far to the left side and the New Church pushed to the back. The façade is not perpendicular to our point of view, but twisted slightly, which gives a dynamism to the composition. The façade is bathed in sunlight, but shows a rich play of shadows as well. The clouds seem to float extraordinarily close to the cupola, suggesting it reaches into the skies.

Figure 1.5 Gerrit Adriaensz. Berckheyde, *The Town Hall on Dam Square*, 1665–80, oil on canvas, 75.5 × 91.5 cm. Loan from Netherlands Institute for Cultural Heritage (ICN), Rijswijk/Amsterdam on loan to Amsterdam Museum, Public Domain.

Many figures appear to look at the Town Hall, and are dressed in black, except the two men in the front who stand out with their colourful, exotic costumes. They illustrate that Amsterdam is a booming metropolis attracting varied, international visitors. The dark group seems to topple into a dark puddle of water, falling into nothingness in front of the monumental building.

Berckheyde was not unique in his development of these painterly strategies, but became one of their most influential practitioners.[31] Before long, they were adopted in the depiction of other buildings. As diverse as their political regimes might be, across Europe the buildings which rulers used to show their magnificence were represented carefully in images. Dutch artists were pioneers in visualizing grand buildings. The most notable, but rather late, example is Casper van Wittel (1653–1736) or Vanvitelli, a painter from Amersfoort whose *vedute* of ancient monuments and grand buildings became popular in Italy. In his *View on St. Peter's Square*, he uses the pictorial strategies Berckheyde had developed to great effect, highlighting the grand, embracing gesture of its colonnade (Figure 1.6). In Paris, decades earlier, a far less famous Dutch painter, Hendrick Mommers (1619–93), used related strategies in his paintings of the Grande Galerie of the Louvre and the Amsterdam Town Hall (Figures 1.7 and 1.8): light and dark effects emphasized the radiance of the buildings, contrasting with the everyday scenes in front of them, while the distortion of perspective

Figure 1.6 Casper van Wittel (alias Vanvitelli), *View of St. Peter's Square*, c. 1700, oil on canvas, 44.5 × 84.2 cm. Courtesy KHM-Museumsverband, Kunsthistorisches Museum Wien.

Figure 1.7 Hendrick Mommers, *View of the Louvre from the Pont-Neuf*, c. 1665, oil on canvas, 90 × 110 cm. RMN, Musée du Louvre. © 2020, photo Josse/Scala, Florence.

Figure 1.8 Hendrick Mommers, *Market Scene before the Dam*, c. 1665, oil on canvas, 84.5 × 120.7 cm. Dyrham Park, Gloucestershire, courtesy of the National Trust.

exaggerating their vastness. The Louvre becomes a revelation of the infinite because perspective is manipulated to make the Grande Galerie extend to the horizon. The Town Hall emerges in his hands as supernatural manifestation in the middle of human hustle and bustle.

Constructing wonders

Where visual artists emphasized the extraordinary nature of the buildings with the use of colour and perspective, writers linked the virtue of magnificence with the overwhelming effect of the Town Hall by presenting it as a pure wonder, thus placing it in Greco-Roman and Christian traditions.[32] These writers often drew on the topos of the seven Wonders of the World. Originally, these formed the highlights for travellers throughout the ancient world.[33] Eventually, however, only the list was preserved and the wonders themselves (with the exception of the Pyramid of Cheops) disappeared. In the early modern period, they were very popular, in the Low Countries among other images thanks to the prints of Maarten van Heemskerck (1498–1574) (Figure 1.9). Writers used them to praise a new building, and Dutch poets eulogizing the Town Hall were certainly no

Figure 1.9 Philips Galle after Maarten van Heemskerck, *The Temple of Diana at Ephesus*, 1572, engraving, hand-coloured, 211 × 258 mm. Rijksmuseum Amsterdam, Public Domain.

exception. Such praise became so popular that it was soon a fixed topos and even today figures in travel accounts of Amsterdam, such as those posted on TripAdvisor.[34] To give the topos maximal persuasiveness, poets exhausted themselves in creativity. In the lengthy laudatory poem that Vos made for the inauguration, he wrote 'This wonder that makes the eye of wonders wonder', using the rhetorical device of employing as many meanings and declensions of the same word as possible in one sentence.

A second tradition of wonders concerns the divine. In this case, the overwhelming effect is even more closely related to benevolence and thus to the virtue of magnificence. Since Greco-Roman antiquity, the concept of *sacer horror* is used to define the shattering impact of the close, physical presence of the divine.[35] *Sacer horror* indicates the religious consternation in which admiration goes together with complete astonishment and fear caused by the belief that the gods or cosmic powers are near, but that contact is at the same time presented as a sanctifying gift. From the sixteenth century onwards, the Jesuits in particular tried to evoke this set of conflicting emotions in their education, art and architecture.[36] Dutch Calvinist preachers often refer to the *Vreze Gods* (Fear of God) as well. The Amsterdam preacher Petrus Wittewrongel (1609-62), for example, devotes an extensive chapter of his influential *Christelicke Huys-Houdinge* to this concept. He defines it as a sensation that goes beyond mere anxiety, but a contrasted combination of it and awe, delight and consternation.[37]

Dutch poets wrote about feelings of attraction and repulsion, of joy and fear, thus playing on the tradition of *sacer horror*, when writing about the Town Hall. What makes the Town Hall stand out in this tradition, is that elements of that convention are deployed in a secular context. According to the poets, the visitors are completely overwhelmed because they want to be as close to the building as possible to enjoy its rich, beautiful, tasteful and ingenious characteristics to the fullest extent possible. They also sense that the building is so exceptional, it even becomes upsetting and frightening. The laudatory poems feature many personages – even ancient gods who once evoked *sacer horror* themselves – who are completely stunned by what they see and start to panic. After a while, they are able to control their feelings again, and begin to express their admiration for what Amsterdam and her magnificent rulers have achieved. An intriguing example can be found in a poem that Huygens dedicated to the enormous maps in the marble floor of the Citizens' Hall. He urged his readers to leave everyday feelings behind in order to be fully responsive to the contact with heavenly heights.

> Treedt vrij in 't gedruijs,
> Als vander aerd' geresen
> Op Sterr en Son en Maen;
> Hier werdt u in bewesen
> Hoe dat het eens naer desen
> Den saligen sal gaen.[38]

> *Enter freely in the bustle,*
> *As if you rise from earth*
> *Towards the Stars and Sun and Moon;*
> *Here it is demonstrated to you*
> *How, after [this life]*
> *The blessed will once fare.*

It is important to note that Huygens includes a careful 'as if' in his description of the overwhelming effect of the Citizens' Hall floor. It can be compared to the feelings aroused by divine contact, but not totally equalled. Thus, the appropriation of *sacer horror* to praise the Town Hall comes close to the sublime. Greco-Roman poetical and rhetorical treatises such as Longinus' *On the sublime* were read attentively in the academic circles of the legal theorist Hugo Grotius (1583–1645) and the classical scholar Gerardus Vossius (1577–1649), who were closely connected with the poets Vondel, Huygens and Vos.[39] The sublime evokes similar feelings as *sacer horror*, total shock as well as pure admiration going far beyond everyday experiences, but it is mainly associated with powerful, but human, means of persuasion. Thus, it could play an important part in the evaluation of the Amsterdam Town Hall.

A new view

To resume, this book starts from the question of how the Town Hall, a building unprecedented in scale and richness in the Republic, could be constructed in Amsterdam. How could the Burgomasters be sure that the public would accept it? In particular, the authors will consider how two problems were addressed. First, the problem of the evident associations of the building's classical style with papal Rome was solved by drawing attention to much earlier contexts, namely the Greco-Roman past and the Solomonic era, as well as by developing local varieties of that order. Second, the concept of magnificence was used to justify the huge costs. The Town Hall was presented as an indispensable means of strengthening the dignity of Amsterdam and her rulers. To discuss these strategies of legitimization, we will first focus on the building itself, its building process and decorations. Then we will look at the 'constructions before and beyond the construction', the ceremonies in and around the building, as well as the texts and images representing it.

In this book's first essay, Pieter Vlaardingerbroek provides new information regarding building models and processes. Where previous studies primarily referred to the influence of Vitruvius, Palladio and Scamozzi, Vlaardingerbroek argues for the great importance of the Temple and especially the Palace of Solomon as models for the Town Hall. By using these models, rather than the Capitoline buildings, the Burgomasters wanted to strengthen their public image as protectors of social cohesion in Amsterdam, and encourage the citizens to believe they were part of God's chosen people. At the same time, they neutralized associations with Roman architecture, both pagan and Catholic.

Caroline van Eck takes a different perspective: the Dutch Republic was a successor state, and had been recognized as a sovereign state at the Peace of Münster in 1648. This was unprecedented, and paradoxically made the search for precedents even more urgent. The Solomonic precedent is one of the strategies followed to create a pedigree for the young state, but as van Eck argues, van Campen and Quellinus also drew on two major and very widely used features of Roman art and the material culture of religion: the triumphal arch and the festoon. Both the interior and exterior display many features derived from the triumphal arch, and are covered in festoons of endless variety, carved with utmost care. The triumphal motif embodies the triumph, obviously, of the Dutch over the Spanish, and suggests a link to ancient Rome; the festoons embody notions of sacredness and festivities associated with this motif since the Minoan age. Thus, in a move typical of successor states from the Hellenistic period to the present, well-known elements from a regime with particular prestige are deployed in completely different political and cultural contexts.

In the second part of the book, we will turn to 'constructions before and beyond the construction' or how authors and visual artists experimented with capturing, in texts and images, the wondrous effect of the Town Hall and the magnificence of its founders. The Town Hall stands out because of the very large corpus of poems written in praise of it. As noted above, some of these are well known, such as those by Vondel and Vos, but the large majority have barely been studied before, let alone published in an English translation. We have, therefore, included a selection of these poems to show their richness and variety.

The genre of the poem in praise of a building or city goes back to classical rhetoric, where such praise was part of the tradition of *ekphrasis*.[40] This was eagerly echoed in early modern Europe, for example in Calderon de la Barca's *auto* (one-act religious play) in honour of the new palace of the Retiro (1634) and de Scudéry's praise of Versailles (1669).[41] In the Dutch Republic, laudatory poems about buildings enjoyed a true Golden Age thanks to the exceptional quantity and quality, with Constantijn Huygens's poem on his mansion *Hofwijck* as one of the most famous and striking examples.[42] Other highlights of this flowering are the more than 100 poems on the Town Hall.[43] The diversity of the laudatory poems on the building is considerable, ranging in length from the very first poem, a couplet by Mattheus Tengnagel in 1641, to Vondel's *Inwydinge*, comprised of no less than 1378 verses.[44] They are also distinguished by a surprising originality, twisting familiar themes and topoi into new shapes.

The counterpart of these laudatory poems are the countless seventeenth-century images of the Town Hall. In his essay, Stijn Bussels takes one of the earliest paintings Berckheyde painted of the building as his starting point for an exploration of how painters 'portrayed' grand buildings. A painter of portraits has to find a balance between depicting the individuality of a person and conveying their status and excellence. Similarly, painters portraying buildings had to do so in a way that made them directly identifiable, but also showed their greatness. We will even see that some seventeenth-century poets go one step further and praise painters such as Berckheyde because in their portraits, they have succeeded in giving life to the buildings.

As already mentioned, Quellinus played an important role in the decorations of the exterior and interior, which are of an unprecedented richness, opulence and variety. His astonishing white marble sculptures are present throughout the building, but play a very prominent role in the Tribunal. By placing Quellinus's caryatids of the Tribunal in a long and international history of the reception of antique models, Frederik Knegtel's essay argues that the exceptionally popular architectural topos was certainly not always slavishly imitated. A comparison with Goujon's caryatids in the Louvre and Rubens's for the ephemeral decorations of Don Ferdinand's entry into Antwerp in 1635, both important models, shows that the caryatids express many varied emotions, but also defines the uniqueness of the Amsterdam versions. Their effect on the public is documented in a series of poems, many of which have never been studied before.

Minou Schraven looks at the ceremonies that have contributed to the construction of the Town Hall in the mind of the public, and more particularly, the laying of the first stone in 1648 and the inauguration in 1655. Such rituals in and around the building have a very long and widely spread history in which they were used, both in the shaping of the actual ritual and its dissemination in word and image, to project the magnificence of the ruler or founder. The case of the Town Hall is no exception. Together with countless texts and images of the building, ceremonial performances strengthened its impact. Beside the broad historical perspective on the ceremonies of 1648 and 1655, Schraven also looks at the objects used during these rituals. The Burgomasters consciously used them to preserve memories of the ceremonial events. They certainly succeeded in this pursuit, for centuries later the objects, such as the silver trowel used for the laying of the first stone, are still displayed in the Rijksmuseum as a material reminder of the magnificence of the founders.

Finally, Freek Schmidt further adds to our knowledge of the impact of the building by studying how in the eighteenth century, the 'constructions beyond the construction' continued, but also changed fundamentally. There are many examples of eighteenth-century visitors who write about their admiration and complete astonishment, but there are also disapproving accounts. Critical visitors notice a striking discrepancy in what they are actually looking at and how they see the building represented in texts and images. Their critique is often fed by a change in taste due to new aesthetic ideals and architectural visions. Yet others disagree with such criticism, inspired by emergent nationalistic feelings that present the Dutch seventeenth century as the Golden Age and the Town Hall as its most important monument. Thus, appreciation of the building evolved from the admiration, mixed with awe and fear of the chief monument of the energetic city of commerce to a memory of an exceptional past.

Notes

1   Pieter Vlaardingerbroek, 'An Appropriated History: The Case of the Amsterdam Town Hall (1648–1667)', in *The Quest for an Appropriate Past in Literature, Art and Architecture*, ed. Karl Enenkel and Konrad Ottenheym (Leiden: Brill, 2018), 455–81.
2   For a broad view on the role of Amsterdam within the Republic and the world, see Jonathan Israel, *The Dutch Republic: Its Rise, Greatness, and Fall, 1477–1806* (Oxford: Clarendon Press, 1995).
3   Ronnie Po-Chia Hsia, 'Introduction', in *Calvinism and Religious Toleration in the Dutch Golden Age*, ed. Ronnie Po-Chia Hsia and Henk van Nierop (Cambridge: Cambridge University Press, 2002), 5.
4   Erika Kuijpers, *Migrantenstad. Immigratie en sociale verhoudingen in 17ᵉ-eeuws Amsterdam* (Hilversum: Verloren, 2005).
5   Pieter Vlaardingerbroek, 'Dutch Town Halls and the Setting of the *Vierschaar*', in *Public Buildings in Early Modern Europe*, ed. Konrad Ottenheym, Kirsta De Jonge and Monique Chatenet (Turnhout: Brepols, 2010), 105–18.
6   On van Campen, see esp. *Jacob van Campen. Het klassieke ideaal in de Gouden Eeuw*, ed. Jacobine Huisken, Koen Ottenheym and Gary Schwartz (Amsterdam: Architectura & Natura Pers, 1995).
7   Pieter Vlaardingerbroek, *Het paleis van de Republiek. Geschiedenis van het stadhuis van Amsterdam* (Zwolle: WBOOKS, 2011), Chapter 1.
8   Marten Jan Bok, 'Familie, vrienden en opdrachtgevers', in *Jacob van Campen. Het klassieke ideaal in de Gouden Eeuw*, 27–53.
9   Quentin Buvelot, 'Schilderkunst' and 'Ontwerpen voor geschilderde decoratieprogramma's', in *Jacob van Campen. Het klassieke ideaal in de Gouden Eeuw*, 54–120 and 121–54.
10 Frits Scholten, *Artus Quellinus. Beeldhouwer van Amsterdam* (Amsterdam: Rijksmuseum, 2010).
11 It is still open to interpretation why the latter's *Conspiracy of Claudius Civilis* was removed from the Town Hall only a few months after it was put up. Jan Blanc,

'Rembrandt and the Historical Construction of this *Conspiracy of Claudius Civilis*', in *Myth in History, History in Myth*, ed. Laura Cruz and Willem Frijhoff (Leiden: Brill, 2009), 237–53; Peter van der Coelen, 'Rembrandt's *Civilis*: Iconography, Meaning and Impact', in *Rembrandt 2006. Essays,* ed. Michiel Roscam Abbing (Leiden: Foleor Publishers, 2006), 31–56; Thijs Weststeijn, 'Rembrandt and the Germanic Style', in *Rembrandt and his Circle: Insights and Discoveries,* ed. Stephanie Dickey (Amsterdam: Amsterdam University Press, 2017), 44–66.

12 Katharine Fremantle, *The Baroque Town Hall of Amsterdam* (Utrecht: Haentjens Dekker & Gumbert, 1959). Cf. Jacobine Huisken, *The Royal Palace on the Dam in a Historical View* (Zutphen: De Walburg Pers, 1989).

13 M.G. Emeis, *Het Paleis op de Dam. De geschiedenis van het gebouw en zijn gebruikers* (Amsterdam: Elsevier, 1981); *Jacob van Campen. Het klassieke ideaal in de Gouden Eeuw*; Eymert-Jan Goossens, *Het Amsterdamse Paleis. Schat van beitel en penseel* (Zwolle: Waanders, 1996); Harry Kraaij, *Het Koninklijk Paleis te Amsterdam. Een beknopte geschiedenis van het gebouw en zijn gebruikers* (Amsterdam: Stichting Koninklijk Paleis te Amsterdam, 1997); Geert Mak, *Het stadspaleis. De geschiedenis van het Paleis op de Dam* (Amsterdam: Atlas, 1997); Pieter Vlaardingerbroek, *Het paleis van de Republiek. Geschiedenis van het stadhuis van Amsterdam* (Zwolle: WBOOKS, 2011).

14 See especially *Albion's Classicism: The Visual Art in Britain, 1550–1660,* ed. Lucy Gent (Yale: Yale University Press, 1996) and *Ambitious Antiquities, Famous Forebears: Constructions of a Glorious Past in the Early Modern Netherlands and in Europe,* ed. Karl Enenkel and Konrad Ottenheym (Leiden: Brill, 2019).

15 Wouter Kuyper, *The Triumphant Entry of Renaissance Architecture into the Netherlands: The Joyeuse Entrée of Philip of Spain into Antwerp in 1549, Renaissance and Mannerist Architecture in the Low Countries from 1530 to 1630* (Alphen aan den Rijn: Canaletto, 1994).

16 Simon Schama, *The Embarrassment of Riches: An Interpretation of Dutch Culture in the Golden Age* (London: Fontana Press, 1987).

17 E.g. Petrus Wittewrongel, *Oeconomia Christiana ofte Christelijke huyshoudinge* (Amsterdam: Abraham vanden Burgh, 1655).

18 Thomas von der Dunk, *Toren versus traditie. De worsteling van classicistische architecten met een middeleeuws fenomeen* (Leiden: Primavera Press, 2015) and Gabri van Tussenbroek, *De toren van de Gouden Eeuw. Een Hollandse strijd tussen gulden en God* (Amsterdam: Prometheus, 2017).

19 Israel, *The Dutch Republic,* 714–15.

20 Vlaardingerbroek, *Het paleis van de Republiek,* 54–6. For the references to Solomon and his Temple in a broader European religious context, see Anne-Françoise Morel, *Glorious Temples or Babylonic Whores: The Culture of Church Building in Stuart England Through the Lens of Consecration Sermons* (Leiden: Brill, 2019), esp. 66–72, with an extended bibliography.

21 Everard Meyster, *Hemelsch Land-Spel of Goden Kout der Amersfoortsche Landdouwen. Bevattende den buytensten Opstal van 't Nieuwe Stad-Huys* (Amsterdam: s.n., 1655), 21.
22 Geeraardt Brandt, *Het leven van Joost van den Vondel* ('s-Gravenhage: Frijhoff, 1932), 68. Cf. Marijke Spies, 'Minerva's commentaar: Gedichten rond het Amsterdamse stadhuis', *De zeventiende eeuw* 9, no. 1 (1993): 15.
23 Nina Geerdink, *De sociale verankering van het dichterschap van Jan Vos (1610–1667)* (Hilversum: Verloren, 2012), 54.
24 Stijn Bussels, Laura Plezier and Marc Van Vaeck, 'Amsterdam sierlijk verbonden met God. Het lofdicht op het Amsterdamse stadhuis van Constantijn Huygens', *Spiegel der Letteren* 59, no. 2/3 (2017): 261–90.
25 See Lodewijk Meyer, *Woordenschat in drie deelen ghescheiden* (Amsterdam: Weduwe van Jan Boom, 1669) 209 where 'magnificentie' is defined as 'heerlijkheidt, pracht, ghrootdaadigheidt'.
26 Cf. Stijn Bussels, 'Meer te verwonderen, als immer te doorgronden. Het Amsterdamse stadhuis, een overweldigende burgerspiegel', *Tijdschrift voor Geschiedenis* 126, no. 2 (2013): 234–48.
27 Nafsika Athanassoulis, 'A Defense of the Aristotelian Virtue of Magnificence', *Value Inquiry* 50 (2016): 781–95; Guido Guerzoni, 'Liberalitas, Magnificentia, Splendor: The Classic Origins of Italian Renaissance Lifestyles', *History of Political Economy* (1999): 332–78; Kornelia Imesch, *Magnificenza als architektonische Kategorie: Indiviuelle Selbstdarstellung versus ästhetische Verwirklichung von Gemeinschaft in den venzianischen Villen Palladios und Scamozzis* (Oberhausen: Athena Verlag, 2003); A.D. Fraser Jenkins, 'Cosimo de' Medici's Patronage of Architecture and the Theory of Magnificence', *Journal of the Warburg and Courtauld Institutes* 33 (1970): 162–70; F.W. Kent, *Lorenzo de' Medici & the Art of Magnificence* (Baltimore-London: Johns Hopkins University Press, 2004); *Magnificence and the Sublime in Medieval Aesthetics. Art, Architecture, Literature, Music*, ed. Stephen Jaeger (New York: Palgrave Macmillan, 2010).
28 Norbert Middelkoop, 'Een Amsterdammer in Hamburg en een Noord-Duitser in Amsterdam. Jürgen Ovens' portret van Dirck Kerckrinck', *Maandblad Amstelodamum* 97, no. 4 (2010): 163–69.
29 Anthony Grafton, 'Obelisks and Empires of the Mind', *The American Scholar* 71, no. 1 (2002): 123–27 and Michael Cole, 'Perpetual Exorcism in Sistine Rome', in *The Idol in the Age of Art. Objects, Devotions, and the Early Modern World*, ed. Michael Cole and Rebecca Zorach (Aldershot: Ashgate, 2009), 57–76.
30 "Hy voornam 't heerlijck Raetspalais,/ Het Kapitool, zoo hoog en trots/ Te bouwen op de dorre rots". Joost van den Vondel, 'Bouw-zang', in *Olyf-krans der Vreede*, ed. Reyer Anslo (Amsterdam: Tymen Houthaak, 1649), 391.
31 Leonore Stapel, *Perspectieven van de stad. Over bronnen, populariteit en functie van het zeventiende-eeuwse stadsgezicht* (Hilversum: Uitgeverij Verloren, 2000).

32 For an introduction to the concept of wonder as used in the medieval and early modern period, see *Wonders and the Order of Nature, 1150–1750,* ed. Lorraine Daston and Katharine Park (New York: Zone Books, 1998). For current and past work on the concepts of 'wonder', 'awe', and 'overwhelming emotions' in early modern literary theory going beyond the Dutch context, see among other publications David Sedley's discussion of Montaigne in *Sublimity and Skepticism in Montaigne and Milton* (Michigan: University of Michigan Press, 2005); James I. Porter, *The Sublime in Antiquity* (Cambridge: Cambridge University press, 2016); Deborah Shuger, *Sacred Rhetoric: The Christian Grand Style in the English Renaissance* (Princeton: Princeton University Press, 1988); James V. Mirollo, 'The Aesthetics of the Marvelous', in *Wonders, Marvels and Monsters in Early Modern Culture,* ed. Peter Platt (Newark: University of Delaware Press, 1999).

33 *The Seven Wonders of the World,* ed. Peter A. Clayton and Martin J. Price (London and New York: Routledge, 1988) and *The Seven Wonders of the World: A History of the Modern Imagination,* ed. by John and Elizabeth Romer (New York: Henry Holt & Co, 1995).

34 https://www.tripadvisor.be/ShowUserReviews-g188590-d244447-r403716730-Royal_Palace_Amsterdam-Amsterdam_North_Holland_Province.html (consulted 15 February 2020).

35 Rudolf Otto, *The Idea of the Holy: An Inquiry into the Non-Rational Factor in the Idea of the Divine and Its Relation to the Rational,* trans. John W. Harvey (London: Oxford University Press, 1980).

36 Ralph Dekoninck and Annick Delfosse, '*Sacer Horror:* The Construction and Experience of the Sublime in the Jesuit Festivities of the Early Seventeenth-Century Southern Netherlands', in the special issue 'The Sublime and Seventeenth-Century Netherlandish Art' of the *Journal of Historians of Netherlandish Art,* ed. Stijn Bussels and Bram Van Oostveldt, 2, no. 8 (2016), DOI: 10.5092/jhna.2016.8.2.9.

37 Stijn Bussels, 'Theories of the Sublime in the Dutch Golden Age: Franciscus Junius, Joost van den Vondel and Petrus Wittewrongel', *History of European Ideas* 7, no. 42 (2016): 882–92.

38 Constantijn Huygens, *Gedichten,* ed. by J.A. Worp (Groningen: Wolters, 1899) VI, 82–83 (our translation).

39 The three authors of this chapter were involved in the ERC starting grant project 'Elevated Minds: The Sublime in the Public Arts in Seventeenth-Century Paris and Amsterdam', where the reception of Longinus' *On the sublime* was related to expressions of wonder in poetry. Among others, the authors were involved as editors and contributors in two special issues: 'The Sublime and Seventeenth-Century Netherlandish Art' of the *Journal of Historians of Netherlandish Art* (see previous note), as well as 'The Sublime in Early Modern Theories of Art, Architecture and the Theatre', ed. Stijn Bussels, Bram Van Oostveldt and Wieneke Jansen, 2, no. 42 (2016).

See also: Wieneke Jansen, *Appropriating* Peri hypsous. *Interpretations and Creative Adaptations of Longinus' Treatise* On the Sublime *in Early Modern Dutch Scholarship* (Leiden: Unpublished PhD thesis, 2019).

40 On the rhetorical tradition of describing buildings or cities, see Christine Smith, *Architectural Principles in the Culture of Early Humanism* (Oxford and New York: Oxford University Press, 1992), 150–74; Ulrich Schlegelmilch, *Descriptio Templi. Architektur und fest in det lateinischen Dichtung des konfessionellen Zeitalters* (Regensburg: Verlag Schnell und Steiner, 2003); Robert Eriksen, *The Building in the Text: Alberti to Shakespeare and Milton* (University Park: Penn State University Press, 2001);

41 Pedro Calderon de la Barca, *El nuevo palacio del Retiro* (Madrid: Aguilar, 1952) (see Enrica Cancelliere, 'El nuevo palacio del Retiro' de Calderon: el Barroco come 'analysis situs' del cosmos', *Inicio* 12 (2019): 33+60) and Madeleine de Scudéry, *La promenade de Versailles* (Paris: Claude Barbin, 1669) (see Jörn Steigerwald, 'Les arts et l'amour galant. A propos de *La promenade de Versailles* de Madeleine de Scudéry', *Littératures classiques* 69 (2009), 51–63).

42 Research on the laudatory poem in the Dutch Republic is not extensive. For Huygens's country house poem, see Willemien de Vries, *The Country Estate Immortalized: Constantijn Huygens' Hofwijck* (Washington, D.C.: Dumbarton Oaks, 1990). Gregor Weber, *Der Lobtopos des 'lebenden' Bildes* (Hildesheim: Olms, 1991) starts from a long laudatory poem on painting by Jan Vos from 1654. Eddy Verbaan, *De woonplaats van de faam* (Hilversum: Verloren, 2011) concentrates on the *laudes urbium* in the seventeenth-century Republic.

43 This research is primarily done in Laura Plezier's PhD project as part of the ERC starting grant 'Elevated Minds'.

44 Matheus Gansneb Tengnagel, 'Op het toekomende Raedhuis', in: *Verscheyde Nederduytsche gedichten* (Amsterdam: Lodewyck Spillebout, 1648), 225 and Vondel, *Inwydinge van 't stadthuis t'Amsterdam*.

Bibliography

Athanassoulis, Nafsika. 'A Defense of the Aristotelian Virtue of Magnificence.' *Journal of Value Inquiry* no. 50 (2016): 781–95.

Blanc, Jan. 'Rembrandt and the Historical Construction of this Conspiracy of Claudius Civilis.' In *Myth in History, History in Myth*, edited by Laura Cruz and Willem Frijhoff, 237–53. Leiden: Brill, 2009.

Bok, Marten Jan. 'Familie, vrienden en opdrachtgevers.' In *Jacob van Campen. Het klassieke ideaal in de Gouden Eeuw, Jacob van Campen. Het klassieke ideaal in de Gouden Eeuw*, edited by Jacobine Huisken, Koen Ottenheym and Gary Schwartz, 27–53. Amsterdam: Architectura & Natura Pers, 1995.

Brandt, Geeraardt. *Het leven van Joost van den Vondel.* 's-Gravenhage: Frijhoff, 1932.
Bussels, Stijn. 'Meer te verwonderen, als immer te doorgronden. Het Amsterdamse stadhuis, een overweldigende burgerspiegel.' *Tijdschrift voor Geschiedenis* 126, no. 2 (2013): 234–48.
Bussels, Stijn. 'Theories of the Sublime in the Dutch Golden Age: Franciscus Junius, Joost van den Vondel and Petrus Wittewrongel.' *History of European Ideas* 7, no. 42 (2016): 882–92.
Bussels, Stijn, Bram Van Oostveldt and Wieneke Jansen (eds). Special issue, 'The Sublime in Early Modern Theories of Art, Architecture and the Theatre.' *Lias* 2, no. 42 (2016).
Bussels, Stijn, Laura Plezier, and Marc Van Vaeck, 'Amsterdam sierlijk verbonden met God. Het lofdicht op het Amsterdamse stadhuis van Constantijn Huygens.' *Spiegel der Letteren* 59, no. 2/3 (2017): 261–90.
Buvelot, Quentin. 'Schilderkunst' and 'Ontwerpen voor geschilderde decoratieprogramma's.' In *Jacob van Campen. Het klassieke ideaal in de Gouden Eeuw*, *Jacob van Campen. Het klassieke ideaal in de Gouden Eeuw*, edited by Jacobine Huisken, Koen Ottenheym and Gary Schwartz, 54–120 and 121–54. Amsterdam: Architectura & Natura Pers, 1995.
Calderon de la Barca, Pedro. *El nuevo palacio del Retiro*. Madrid: Aguilar, 1952.
Cancelliere, Enrica. 'El nuevo palacio del Retiro' de Calderon: el Barroco come 'analysis situs' del cosmos'. *Inicio* 12 (2019): 33–60.
Clayton, Peter A., and Martin J. Price (eds). *The Seven Wonders of the World*. London-New York: Routledge, 1988.
Coelen, Peter van der. 'Rembrandt's Civilis: Iconography, Meaning and Impact.' In *Rembrandt 2006. Essays*, edited by Michiel Roscam Abbing, 31–56. Leiden: Foleor Publishers, 2006.
Cole, Michael. 'Perpetual Exorcism in Sistine Rome.' In *The Idol in the Age of Art. Objects, Devotions, and the Early Modern World*, edited by Michael Cole and Rebecca Zorach, 57–76. Aldershot: Ashgate, 2009.
Daston, Lorraine, and Katharine Park (eds). *Wonders and the Order of Nature, 1150–1750*. New York: Zone Books, 1998.
Dekoninck, Ralph, and Annick Delfosse, 'Sacer Horror: The Construction and Experience of the Sublime in the Jesuit Festivities of the Early Seventeenth-Century Southern Netherlands.' In the special issue 'The Sublime and Seventeenth-Century Netherlandish Art', edited by Stijn Bussels and Bram Van Oostveldt. *Journal of Historians of Netherlandish Art* 2, no.8 (2016): DOI: 10.5092/jhna.2016.8.2.9.
Dunk, Thomas von der. *Toren versus traditie. De worsteling van classicistische architecten met een middeleeuws fenomeen*. Leiden: Primavera Press, 2015.
Emeis, Marinus Gerardus. *Het Paleis op de Dam. De geschiedenis van het gebouw en zijn gebruikers*. Amsterdam: Elsevier, 1981.
Enenkel, Karl, and Konrad Ottenheym (eds). *Ambitious Antiquities, Famous Forebears. Constructions of a Glorious Past in the Early Modern Netherlands and in Europe*. Leiden: Brill, 2019.

Eriksen, Robert. *The Building in the Text: Alberti to Shakespeare and Milton*. University Park: Penn State University Press, 2001.

Fraser Jenkins, A.D. 'Cosimo de' Medici's Patronage of Architecture and the Theory of Magnificence.' *Journal of the Warburg and Courtauld Institutes* 33 (1970): 162–70.

Fremantle, Katharine. *The Baroque Town Hall of Amsterdam*. Utrecht: Haentjens Dekker & Gumbert, 1959.

Geerdink, Nina. *De sociale verankering van het dichterschap van Jan Vos (1610–1667)*. Hilversum: Verloren, 2012.

Gent, Lucy (ed.). *Albion's Classicism: The Visual Art in Britain, 1550–1660*. Yale: Yale University Press, 1996.

Goossens, Eymert-Jan. *Het Amsterdamse Paleis. Schat van beitel en penseel*. Zwolle: Waanders, 1996.

Grafton, Anthony. 'Obelisks and Empires of the Mind.' *The American Scholar* 71, no. 1 (2002): 123–7.

Guerzoni, Guido. 'Liberalitas, Magnificentia, Splendor: The Classic Origins of Italian Renaissance Lifestyles'. *History of Political Economy* (1999): 332–78.

Huisken, Jacobine. *The Royal Palace on the Dam in a Historical View*. Zutphen: De Walburg Pers, 1989.

Huisken, Jacobine, Koen Ottenheym and Gary Schwartz (eds). *Jacob van Campen. Het klassieke ideaal in de Gouden Eeuw*. Amsterdam: Architectura & Natura Pers, 1995.

Huygens, Constantijn. *Gedichten*, edited by J.A. Worp. Groningen: Wolters, 1899.

Imesch, Kornelia. *Magnificenza als architektonische Kategorie: Indiviuelle Selbstdarstellung versus ästhetische Verwirklichung von Gemeinschaft in den venzianischen Villen Palladios und Scamozzis*. Oberhausen: Athena Verlag, 2003.

Israel, Jonathan. *The Dutch Republic: Its Rise, Greatness, and Fall, 1477–1806*. Oxford: Clarendon Press, 1995.

Jaeger, Stephen (ed.). *Magnificence and the Sublime in Medieval Aesthetics. Art, Architecture, Literature, Music*. New York: Palgrave Macmillan, 2010.

Jansen, Wieneke. *Appropriating* Peri hypsous. *Interpretations and Creative Adaptations of Longinus' Treatise* On the Sublime *in Early Modern Dutch Scholarship*. Leiden: Unpublished PhD thesis, 2019.

Kent, F.W. *Lorenzo de' Medici & the Art of Magnificence*. Baltimore-London: Johns Hopkins University Press, 2004.

Kraaij, Harry. *Het Koninklijk Paleis te Amsterdam. Een beknopte geschiedenis van het gebouw en zijn gebruikers*. Amsterdam: Stichting Koninklijk Paleis te Amsterdam, 1997.

Kuijpers, Erika. *Migrantenstad. Immigratie en sociale verhoudingen in 17e-eeuws Amsterdam*. Hilversum: Verloren, 2005.

Kuyper, Wouter. *The Triumphant Entry of Renaissance Architecture into the Netherlands: The Joyeuse Entrée of Philip of Spain into Antwerp in 1549, Renaissance and*

Mannerist Architecture in the Low Countries from 1530 to 1630. Alphen aan den Rijn: Canaletto, 1994.

Lodewijk, Meyer. *Woordenschat in drie deelen ghescheiden*. Amsterdam: Weduwe van Jan Boom, 1669.

Mak, Geert. *Het stadspaleis. De geschiedenis van het Paleis op de Dam*. Amsterdam: Atlas, 1997.

Meyster, Everard. *Hemelsch Land-Spel of Goden Kout der Amersfoortsche Landdouwen. Bevattende den buytensten Opstal van 't Nieuwe Stad-Huys*. Amsterdam: s.n., 1655.

Middelkoop, Norbert. 'Een Amsterdammer in Hamburg en een Noord-Duitser in Amsterdam. Jürgen Ovens' portret van Dirck Kerckrinck'. *Maandblad Amstelodamum* 97, no. 4 (2010): 163–9.

Mirollo, James V. 'The Aesthetics of the Marvelous.' In *Wonders, Marvels and Monsters in Early Modern Culture*, edited by Peter Platt, 24–44. Newark: University of Delaware Press, 1999.

Morel, Anne-Françoise. *Glorious Temples or Babylonic Whores. The Culture of Church Building in Stuart England Through the Lens of Consecration Sermons*. Leiden: Brill, 2019.

Ottenheym, Konrad, Krista De Jonge and Monique Chatenet (eds). *Buildings in Early Modern Europe*, 105–18. Turnhout: Brepols, 2010.

Otto, Rudolf. *The Idea of the Holy: An Inquiry into the Non-Rational Factor in the Idea of the Divine and Its Relation to the Rational*, trans. John W. Harvey. London: Oxford University Press, 1980.

Po-Chia Hsia, Ronnie. 'Introduction.' In *Calvinism and Religious Toleration in the Dutch Golden Age*, edited by Ronnie Po-Chia Hsia and Henk van Nierop, 1–7. Cambridge: Cambridge University Press, 2002.

Porter, James I. *The Sublime in Antiquity*. Cambridge: Cambridge University Press, 2016.

Romer, John, and Elizabeth Romer (eds). *The Seven Wonders of the World: A History of the Modern Imagination*. New York: Henry Holt & Co, 1995.

Schama, Simon. *The Embarrassment of Riches: An Interpretation of Dutch Culture in the Golden Age*. London: Fontana Press, 1987.

Schlegelmilch, Ulrich. *Descriptio Templi. Architektur und fest in det lateinischen Dichtung des konfessionellen Zeitalters*. Regensburg: Verlag Schnell und Steiner, 2003.

Scholten, Frits. *Artus Quellinus. Beeldhouwer van Amsterdam*. Amsterdam: Rijksmuseum, 2010.

Scudéry, Madeleine de. *La promenade de Versailles*. Paris: Claude Barbin, 1669.

Sedley, David. *Sublimity and Skepticism in Montaigne and Milton*. Michigan: University of Michigan Press, 2005.

Shuger, Deborah. *Sacred Rhetoric: The Christian Grand Style in the English Renaissance*. Princeton: Princeton University Press, 1988.

Smith, Christine. *Architectural Principles in the Culture of Early Humanism*. Oxford and New York: Oxford University Press, 1992.

Spies, Marijke. 'Minerva's commentaar: Gedichten rond het Amsterdamse stadhuis.' *De zeventiende eeuw* 9, no. 1 (1993): 15–34.

Stapel, Leonore. *Perspectieven van de stad. Over bronnen, populariteit en functie van het zeventiende-eeuwse stadsgezicht*. Hilversum: Uitgeverij Verloren, 2000.

Steigerwald, Jörn. 'Les arts et l'amour galant. A propos de La promenade de Versailles de Madeleine de Scudéry.' *Littératures classiques* 69 (2009): 51–63.

Tengnagel, Matheus Gansneb. 'Op het toekomende Raedhuis.' In *Verscheyde Nederduytsche gedichten*, 21. Amsterdam: Lodewyck Spillebout, 1648.

Tussenbroek, Gabri van. *De toren van de Gouden Eeuw. Een Hollandse strijd tussen gulden en God*. Amsterdam: Prometheus, 2017.

Verbaan, Eddy. *De woonplaats van de faam*. Hilversum: Verloren, 2011.

Vlaardingerbroek, Pieter. 'Dutch Town Halls and the Setting of the Vierschaar.' In *Public Public Buildings in Early Modern Europe*, edited by Konrad Ottenheym, Kirsta De Jonge and Monique Chatenet, 105–19. Turnhout: Brepols, 2010.

Vlaardingerbroek, Pieter. *Het paleis van de Republiek. Geschiedenis van het stadhuis van Amsterdam*. Zwolle: WBOOKS, 2011.

Vlaardingerbroek, Pieter. 'An Appropriated History: The Case of the Amsterdam Town Hall (1648–1667).' In *The Quest for an Appropriate Past in Literature, Art and Architecture*, edited by Karl Enenkel and Konrad Ottenheym, 455–81. Leiden: Brill, 2018.

Vondel, Joost van den. 'Bouw-zang.' In *Olyf-krans der Vreede*, edited by Reyer Anslo, 391. Amsterdam: Tymen Houthaak, 1649.

Vries, Willemien de. *The Country Estate Immortalized: Constantijn Huygens' Hofwijck*. Washington, D.C.: Dumbarton Oaks, 1990.

Weber, Gregor. *Der Lobtopos des 'lebenden' Bildes*. Hildesheim: Olms, 1991.

Weststeijn, Thijs. 'Rembrandt and the Germanic Style.' In *Rembrandt and his Circle. Insights and Discoveries*, edited by Stephanie Dickey, 44–66. Amsterdam: Amsterdam University Press, 2017.

Wittewrongel, Petrus. *Oeconomia Christiana ofte Christelijke huyshoudinge*. Amsterdam: Abraham vanden Burgh, 1655.

2

The Palace of the Republic: Idea and Construction

Pieter Vlaardingerbroek

The start of the construction of the Amsterdam Town Hall marked the end of a long period of political and religious turmoil in Western Europe. The Peace of Westphalia of 1648 ended the Thirty Years' War, which had brought death and destruction in the German Empire and surrounding countries. Part of this treaty was the Peace of Münster, in which the king of Spain recognized the Dutch Republic as an independent nation. The Amsterdam Town Hall was the ultimate expression of this peace. The new building was crowned by an allegorical statue of Peace not Justice, which was the usual adornment of a town hall, whose main function was as a court of law. The new building expressed the new hope that a long-lasting concord would bring even more prosperity to Amsterdam despite its already spectacular economic growth since 1600.[1]

Amsterdam's population had grown from 30,000 people in 1585 to 100,000 in 1620, reaching 200,000 in 1675. The expanding city needed a town hall that reflected its power and wealth as one of Europe's leading metropolises, equal to London, Paris or Naples.[2] Amsterdam, however, lacked the royal courts and the ancient histories of these cities, the roots of which could be traced back to Roman history, if not earlier. Amsterdam was founded in the thirteenth century as a village of fishermen and farmers. Its simple origins were still visible in 1638, when Maria de' Medici visited. Enormous festivities were held to celebrate her Joyous Entry into the city, and her visit was conceived as an implicit recognition of the Dutch Republic. Maria, as mother of the king of France, Louis XIII, and as mother-in-law to the kings of England and Spain, as well the Duke of Savoy, dignified Amsterdam with her visit. The Dutch rebel state was no longer regarded as an international pariah, but as a full partner in politics and trade, despite the fact that the official recognition of Holland would only occur in 1648 with the Peace of Münster.[3] Maria was entertained at different locations, and especially at the main hall of the Kloveniersdoelen, the gathering space of the local militia, which had been finished quite recently and for which Rembrandt's *Night Watch* was commissioned in 1642.[4] The minister and philosopher Caspar Barlaeus (1584–1648) was responsible for theatrical displays on the canals, as well as the subjects depicted on the ephemeral architecture, erected in honour of Maria, prints of which were published in his book *Medicea Hospes*.[5]

However, the visit presented the city with all its ambitions in the fields of international politics and world trade with a problem: the existing Town Hall was quite unfit for receiving any visitor of standing, let alone a queen such as Maria de' Medici. Barlaeus tried to turn the whole situation into something positive, saying that 'the antiquity and dilapidation give this building some dignity',[6] but in fact it was a run-down medieval building, consisting of a reused part of a convent, a dwelling and a mid-fifteenth-century tower with arcaded court of justice (Figure 2.1). This conglomerate of buildings was deemed unfit

Figure 2.1 Salomon Jacobsz Savery, the medieval Town Hall of Amsterdam as it appeared during the visit of Maria de' Medici in 1638, as published in Caspar Barlaeus, *Blyde Inkomst der allerdoorluchtighste Koninginne Maria de Medicis t'Amsterdam* (Amsterdam: Johan and Cornelis Blaeu, 1639). Rijksmuseum Amsterdam, Public Domain.

for the city in 1565, and plans had been made to construct a new Town Hall – but were never executed. Amsterdam, instead, focused on renewing all other kinds of public buildings and expanding the city. As Barlaeus put it: the city council preferred to spend money on the city rather than on themselves.[7]

The Burgomasters, however, must also have felt that they needed a new building that befitted the new status of Amsterdam as a metropolis. Four months after Maria's visit, they appointed a committee to investigate the condition of the building on the excuse that public safety was at stake. This decision demarcated the start of designing and constructing the new Town Hall.[8]

Towards a new Town Hall (1639–48)

The Burgomasters and Treasurers themselves participated in the committee of inquiry for building the new Town Hall. They employed civil servants to do the groundwork. City surveyor Cornelis Danckerts de Rij was sent to measure the area around Dam Square in the heart of the city and the location of the old Town Hall and its proposed replacement. At first, the committee drew up conservative plans to replace the old building by a new one on the same spot. The old Town Hall blended perfectly into the medieval urban fabric and it was a necessary exercise to demonstrate that the existing plot was too small and needed enlargement. The architect Philips Vingboons (1607–78) was commissioned to draw up a project that proved the committee right: no decent architecture could go ahead on the existing building plot, which was just 100 feet wide. In the end, all houses between the old Town Hall and the New Church, one of the two main churches in the city, were bought and eventually demolished. As a result, the ideas about the ground plan and its orientation were much less restricted by the existing urban fabric. Over the following nine years, seven different building plots were decided upon (Figure 2.2). The main problem was the relationship of

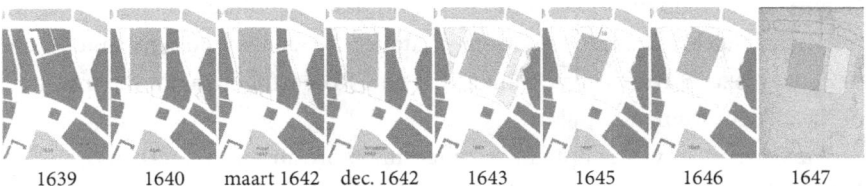

Figure 2.2 The development of the building lot for the Amsterdam Town Hall, 1639–47. In 1648, the building lot comprised both rectangles of 1647. Image by author.

Figure 2.3 Pieter Nolpe, unexecuted design for the Amsterdam Town Hall by SGL. Private collection.

the new building to Dam Square. At first, a close connection to the existing surroundings was sought, but during the process two changes of the central axis of the building plot followed, making the final Town Hall an entity in itself, perfectly oriented, but unrelated to the urban setting: a true monument to Amsterdam's glory and power. During this period of nine years, Vingboons supplied several other designs, as did the monogramist SGL and another unknown architect, who drew a design on a plan by the aforementioned De Rij (Figure 2.3). Vingboons' plans refer to the Roman Capitoline Hill and especially to Michelangelo's Palazzo dei Conservatori. The general idea behind these designs was to portray Amsterdam as the new Rome, following in the footsteps of the ancient Roman Republic.[9]

Amsterdam, however, opted for something more ancient than the Capitoline Hill or Rome. In the end, a building plot of 285 by 225 feet was reserved for the new building, designed by the painter-architect Jacob van Campen (1596–1657).

Jacob van Campen

The choice of van Campen as architect was not a surprising one. He had already designed some of Amsterdam's most iconic buildings. In 1625, he designed the first Italianate classical work of architecture in Holland, the Coymans' houses at the Keizersgracht. In 1633, he received the commission for the Girls' Courtyard of the Civic Orphanage, where he applied Ionic order on a colossal scale, and in 1638 he designed the first permanent theatre. Van Campen was a member of the gentry: originating from Haarlem, he had close family ties to Amsterdam's upper echelons. His mother descended from Willem Eggerts (c. 1360–1417), one of the richest and most powerful medieval merchants in Holland and also courtier at the court of Albrecht and William VI, Counts of Holland. Willem Eggerts had been responsible for founding and supporting the New Church at Dam Square. More than two centuries after his death, Eggerts was still a figure of enormous importance amongst Amsterdam's patricians. Van Campen was well aware of his background; he used Eggerts' coat of arms on his own epitaph in the Church of St George in Amersfoort. Van Campen had been Lord of Randenbroek, a title that had also belonged to Eggerts.[10]

Van Campen was the star architect of his day, working for Holland's greatest nobles.[11] He executed some of the most prestigious projects of the time. He was the unofficial court architect to Stadholder Frederick Henry of Orange-Nassau (1584–1647); he also supplied designs for the main courtiers in The Hague. Frederick Henry commissioned Palace Noordeinde (1639) that contained apartments for his son William II and his wife Mary Stuart, the English Princess Royal. Van Campen was also the mastermind behind the Oranjezaal in Huis ten Bosch (1647), the Dutch counterpart to Rubens' paintings of the Maria de' Medici Cycle for Palais du Luxembourg in Paris and his ceiling paintings for the Banqueting House in London's Whitehall Palace. The paintings in the Oranjezaal were done by painters from both Holland and Brabant, a way of symbolizing the unity of the Netherlands as a whole and glorifying the life and deeds of Frederick Henry (Figure 2.4). As Rubens was no longer alive, the main piece was done by his best surviving pupil, Jacob Jordaens.[12]

Van Campen designed for John Maurice of Nassau-Siegen the Mauritshuis (1633) in The Hague, generally regarded as one of best examples of Palladian architecture in Holland. In detailing the building, van Campen used Scamozzi's treatise *L'Idea della Architectura* (Venice, 1615). In 1634, he built a house in The Hague for Constantijn Huygens, the secretary of Frederick Henry and a central figure in Dutch cultural life of the Golden Age.[13] The poet Reyer Anslo recognized

Figure 2.4 Jacob van Campen and Pieter Post, the interior of the Oranjezaal in Huis ten Bosch, The Hague. Rijksdienst voor het Cultureel Erfgoed, Public Domain.

his great skills as an architect and praised some of his most important works – both the Hague houses, as well as the organ in Alkmaar and the New Church in Haarlem – in a poem:

> Zoo spreken zonder mondt de steenen van zijn lof.
> Dat tuig Graaf Maurits huis, dicht achter Hollants hof,
> En 't huis van Zuilichem, waar in Apol komt waren
> En t'Alkmaar orgelspel, en dan de kerk bij 't Sparen.[14]

> *The mouthless bricks speak his praise*
> *As witnesses Count Maurits' house, just behind Holland's court*
> *And the house of Zuilichem (Huygens), in which Apollo comes to be*
> *And the Alkmaar organ play, and the church at the Spaarne.*

Van Campen was trained as a painter and worked as both artist and architect. In 1614, aged around eighteen, he was registered as a painter in the Haarlem Guild of St Luke. His tender age might be an indication of his talent, but it is more likely that he was a gentleman-painter, who did not depend on his income as an artist. His patrician background has been splendidly described by Francesco Milizia in his *Memorie degli Architetti Antichi e Moderni*, stating that van Campen 'trattò l'arti liberali con vera liberalità, donando generosamente le sue pitture ed i suoi disegni. Bell' esempio per i ricchi e per i cavalieri'.[15] (Van Campen practised the Liberal Arts in a true and free spirit, generously donating his pictures and drawings. A great example for the rich and the nobility.) His training in the Liberal Arts probably made van Campen a master in geometry, the key mathematical

Figure 2.5 Abraham Lutma, *Portrait of Jacob van Campen*, as published in Jacob van Campen, *Afbeelding van 't Stadt Huijs van Amsterdam* (Amsterdam: Dancker Danckerts, 1661). Rijksmuseum Amsterdam, Public Domain.

discipline for any architect. The city chronicler of Haarlem Theodorus Schrevelius described him as a 'fast mathematician', referring to his ability in geometry and therefore architecture.[16] Does this simply mean that van Campen knew how to make the right proportions, as some authors think,[17] or do we have to see this remark in a more neoplatonic setting in which the heavenly or cosmic ideas could be transformed into worldly architecture by means of geometry? Or, to put it differently, did van Campen use geometry to produce architecture that reflects God's wisdom while designing the whole creation? There is a very intriguing portrait of van Campen, in which he is not depicted with a compass or other drawing instruments, nor with an architectural drawing or a depiction of a building, but rather with a cube-shaped block of stone (Figure 2.5).[18] For an architect or for any artist in general, this is a very particular attribute. Does this block of stone reference the fact that the new Town Hall would be built out of stone, or does it reflect the cornerstone of the building, the metaphor for Christ and the Temple? And might it be a reference to the perfectly cut block of stone, hewn out of the rough stone, representing a higher state of wisdom?

The design of the Amsterdam Town Hall

Van Campen had to incorporate the functions of a Town Hall into a design that would satisfy the statement of requirements of the Burgomasters and other city colleges that were to use the building. Therefore, it was essential to understand what the functions of the Town Hall were in seventeenth-century Amsterdam.[19] The Town Hall housed the city administration, in which the Burgomasters played the most important role. Several financial colleges assisted them: treasurers were responsible for the city's finances; the Treasurers Extraordinary were in control of collecting taxes for the Estates General with the college of accountants assisting them; the ancient and reverent Trustees of Orphans controlled the assets of orphans; the City Council was an advisory body and functioned as some kind of representative body of the patrician upper class. But despite the importance of these offices, they had little input into the design of the building.

The Town Hall also functioned as a courthouse, and this function exerted a far bigger influence on its design. The Town Hall was a public building in which people came to seek justice. The Magistrates dealt with the important cases (both criminal and civil), while less important civic cases were tried before the Commissioners of Petty Affairs. There also had to be a room for arbitration, an office for the Commissioners of Insurance and the Commissioner of Bankruptcy to deal with the many cases involving trade and economic court cases. In other words, for the general public, a Town Hall was primarily a courthouse.[20]

The new building needed to express both civic pride, as well as old privileges held by the city, and especially its highest right: the power over life and death. The local rulers were attached to the tradition of the Vierschaar, the Tribunal in which the accused was publicly condemned to death, being situated in an open space, adjacent to Dam Square, where the people of Amsterdam could gather to hear the verdict. This right determined the final form of van Campen's design. This function of the Town Hall as court of law was considered important enough that in this particular instance tradition triumphed over magnificence. The layout of the old Town Hall, with an open galleried Tribunal on Dam Square, in which people were publicly condemned to death (Figure 2.6), was chosen over a new design incorporating a monumental entrance.[21]

Figure 2.6 Gerrit Adriaensz Berkcheyde, *The Amsterdam Town Hall,* 1672, oil on canvas, 33.5 × 41.5 cm. Rijksmuseum Amsterdam, Public Domain.

But the outward appearance was of almost equal importance to the functional aspect of the building. Amsterdam was at the height of its power and wanted to express the new status, just as cities like Brussels, Antwerp and Augsburg had done before. And as the city had been an ardent advocate of ending the war against Spain, it wished to dedicate the new building to Peace.[22]

Van Campen designed a five-storey, rectangular building with projecting central and corner parts. The structure was defined by a central hall on the first floor, lit by two courtyards on the sides. Around these courtyards, galleries gave access to offices that were lit from the outer façades. The sandstone façades are adorned with a double order (Corinthian above, Composite below) set on an undecorated (Doric) ground floor. The pedimented front and back façades have enormous sculpted tympana, made of Carrara marble, depicting the oceans and continents of the world bringing tribute and treasures to the allegorical figure of Amsterdam. These tympana were an absolute novelty on this scale in Europe and set the standard for many subsequent public buildings. The pediment on the Dam side was adorned by three acroteria: a copper-bronze cast statue of Peace, set on a pedestal at the peak, and figures of Prudentia and Justitia at the angles. Crowning the front façade, a round, arcaded tower in the Corinthian order projected from the roof of the Dam Square elevation.

The ground floor was home to several functions. The Tribunal was located in the central bay of the façade, behind an entrance gallery. Left and right of the Tribunal were entrances to the building. An internal staircase behind the Tribunal led to the first or main floor. Around the northern courtyard were the prison cells, as well as the torture room and the jailers' living quarters. Additional cells were to be found in the cellar below. The Amsterdam Exchange bank had offices surrounding the southern courtyard, with cellars below to stock the account holders' gold. Another part of the ground floor was taken up by the living quarters of the concierge.

The first or main floor housed the most important space in the building, the Citizens' Hall (Figure 2.7). This enormous space was 60 by 120 feet and 90 feet high. It served as an extension of the public space of Dam Square, its sole purpose to symbolize the 'civitas' of Amsterdam, the foundation under and starting point of all governmental functions. This idea is made visible in the architecture of the Citizens' Hall, which has superimposed Corinthian orders, the most important classical order, that reflect the outside façades. The marble floors depicted large maps of the world, as well as a star chart, which was to be mirrored by another star chart in the ceiling, although this was never executed. The decoration of the walls had depictions of the elements and the four continents. Two U-shaped

The Palace of the Republic 39

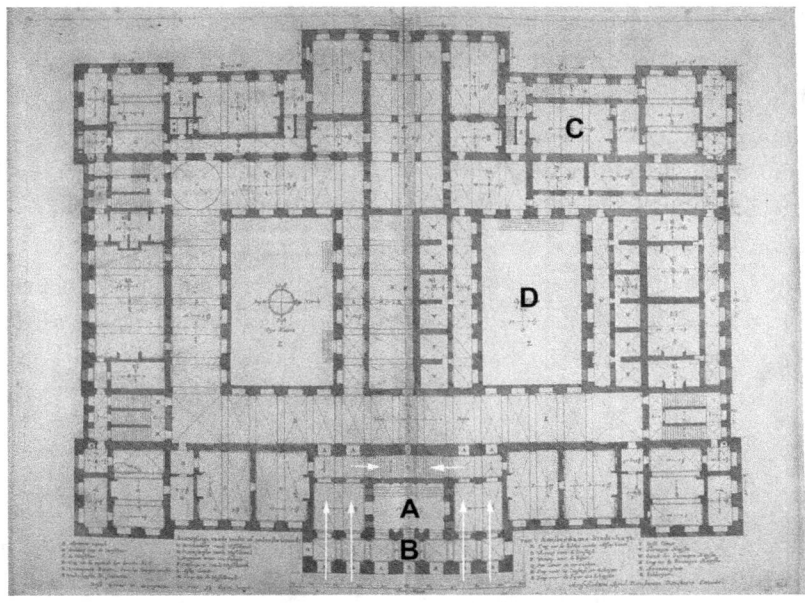

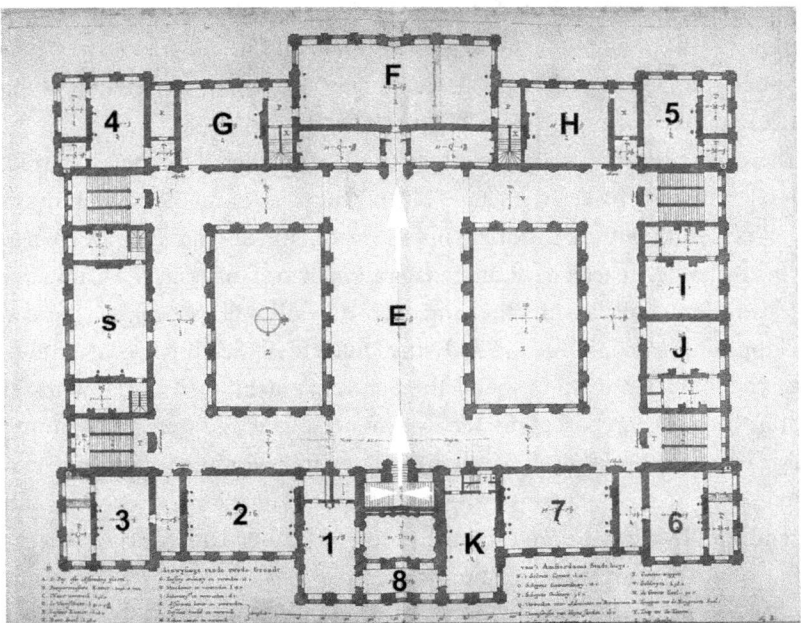

Figure 2.7 (a) and (b) Cornelis Danckerts, ground plan of the ground and first floor, as published in Jacob van Campen, *Afbeelding van 't Stadt Huijs van Amsterdam* (Amsterdam: Dancker Danckerts, 1661). The figures indicate offices of the administration, while the characters indicate rooms with a court function. The arrows indicate the route taken by visitors. Utrecht University Library, Public Domain.

galleries connected to the Citizens' Hall and served as monumental passageways to the offices. The division of functions was very much determined by the function of court of law. The largest room on the main floor was the Magistrates' Chamber, located at the end of the main axis of the building. All other administrative functions were set in less architecturally important places. The financial offices were situated at the corners, while the City Council and Burgomasters were located along the Dam Square side.[23]

The second floor held other offices, such as the marriage room, where people had to register their nuptials. The third and fourth floors were mainly used for storage and an armoury; the roof structure was kept mainly empty.

The origins of the design

What were the origins of van Campen's design? The history of the city did not supply many models on which to base a design. Amsterdam did not have a grand history to draw upon: as noted above, its origins were humble. In 1275, the first town privileges or city rights were granted, and Amsterdam grew to become the largest city in Holland in the 1500s, eventually surpassing all other cities in the Dutch Republic during the seventeenth century.

There was a strong competition between Dutch cities about being the oldest. Cities like Dordrecht, Haarlem and Leiden kept parts of medieval buildings as a way of underlining their historical importance.[24] Amsterdam did not try to win this losing battle. Instead of finding inspiration in local history, van Campen had to draw wider parallels with other and older times. Roughly speaking, there were two kinds of tradition present. Firstly, the Dutch identified themselves with their 'forefathers', the Germanic tribe of the Batavians mentioned in the writings of Tacitus. They lived in peace with the Roman occupants and were known for their courage and loyalty, as well as their qualities in swimming and horse riding. When some of the Batavians' privileges was withdrawn, they revolted, and in the end the Romans restored the tribe's former status. Dutch historians of the seventeenth century regarded the Batavians as a noble people that reminded the Romans of their sense of honour. As a result, the Batavians formed part of ancient Roman culture, which was incorporated into the Dutch history.[25]

A second and equally important parallel was drawn between the Dutch people and the Biblical people of Israel. It could only be through God's benevolence that a country without any natural resources, like the Netherlands, could thrive. As the Israelites were liberated from the Egyptian yoke, so the

Dutch were freed from Spanish tyranny. Holland was seen as the New Israel, the new chosen people. Important contemporary events and people were identified with biblical examples.

This identification with Israel also had an architectural component, which would have an enormous impact on the final design of the Amsterdam Town Hall. There is a general tendency to see Dutch classical architecture of the seventeenth century as wanting to copy the Vitruvian rules as closely as possible, especially by using several Italian treatises. Modern scholarship stresses the formal importance of Vincenzo's Scamozzi's *L'Idea della Architectura Universale* at the expense of other writers such as Palladio and Vignola.[26] But these sources may not accurately reflect the inspiration of seventeenth-century Dutch architecture, as another, and perhaps more profound debate on architecture was taking place at this time. In most influential Dutch architectural books of the seventeenth century, there is one dominant question: what was the origin of architecture?

According to most people in Holland, the answer to this question could be found in the Bible. The whole discussion was heavily influenced by the many reconstructions of the Temple of Jerusalem proposed by Spanish scholars. Many Dutch architects adopted the theory of the Spanish Jesuit Juan Bautista Villalpando found in the second volume of *In Ezechielem Explanationes et Apparatus Urbis ac Templi Hierosolymitani* (Explanations on Ezekiel and the Layout of the City and of the Temple of Jerusalem, 1604). He pointed to Biblical buildings and specifically Solomon's Temple as the origin of classical architecture, stating that Vitruvius was merely an exegete of the God-given architecture of the Old Testament. He imagined the temple to be an enormous building covered with Solomonic pilasters and raised on a huge platform with curving buttresses (Figure 2.8). This Solomonic architecture formed the base for all other classical orders, but most closely resembled the Corinthian order. According to Villalpando, the ancient Greek sculptor Callimachus had stolen the idea of the Corinthian capital from the Solomonic order.[27]

The few literary sources written by Dutch architects clearly refer to Villalpando's ideas. Salomon de Bray, in his introduction to the *Architectura Moderna*, informs us that the divine architecture of the Temple was older than Greek classic architecture. It is very likely that van Campen studied Villalpando alongside Constantijn Huygens, who borrowed and later owned a copy of this book. No writings by van Campen survive on this matter, but we do know that this subject had his attention. He and his good friend, the poet and botanist Johan Brosterhuijsen, collaborated on a book on architecture, which had to contain translations of Vitruvius, Wotton (*The Elements of Architecture*) and some passages of Palladio's *I Quattro Libri dell'Architettura* concerning temples

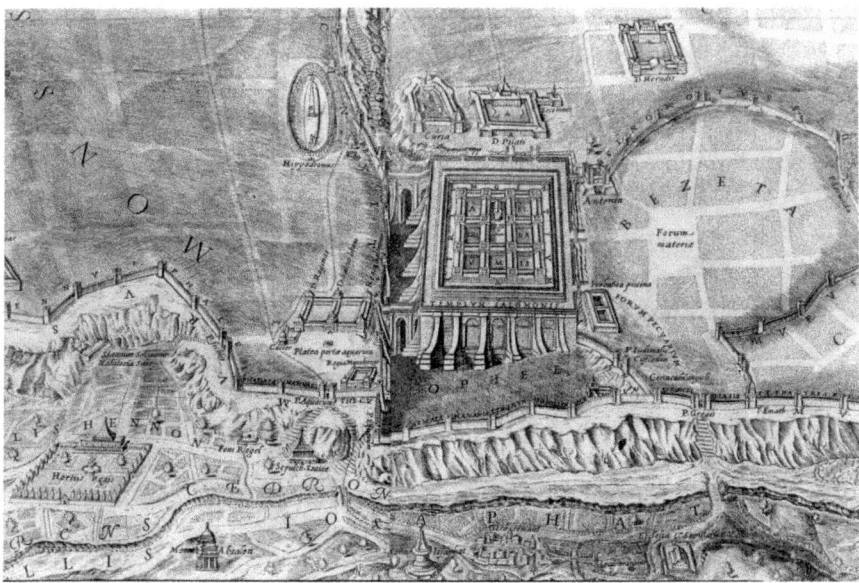

Figure 2.8 View of Solomon's Temple and Palace, as published in Juan Bautista Villalpando, *In Ezechielem Explanationes et Apparatus Urbis ac Templi Hierosolymitani* (S.l.: s.n., 1604). Utrecht University Library, Public Domain.

and public buildings. The book was to have an introduction by van Campen on the origin of architecture.[28] This origin probably refers to the architecture of the Temple of Jerusalem, for which God Himself had given the directions. An architect that knew the origins of true architecture in its highest (heavenly) form, would also be capable of recreating it, just as King Solomon had done while building the Temple and designing his own palace.

This combination of classical and divine architecture would prove very helpful for the design of the Amsterdam Town Hall. Van Campen chose Solomon's Palace as the inspiration for his design: Solomon was the great king-architect who brought peace to the country (Figure 2.9), and his Palace served as a government building, containing a court of law, a treasury and an armoury, all spaces found in a town hall. As described in 1 Kings 7, the Palace consisted of three architectural orders and was built of large, perfectly hewn blocks of stone. Solomon's Palace was described by Villalpando as well, and he indicated that its architecture was similar to that of the temple. However, according to his account, the structure was different. On the plan of Jerusalem we see the Palace as a rectangular building with two inner courtyards. It had tower-like structures on the corners and one tower in the middle. According to the description of Villalpando, the central hall was the House of the Forest of the Lebanon, a large

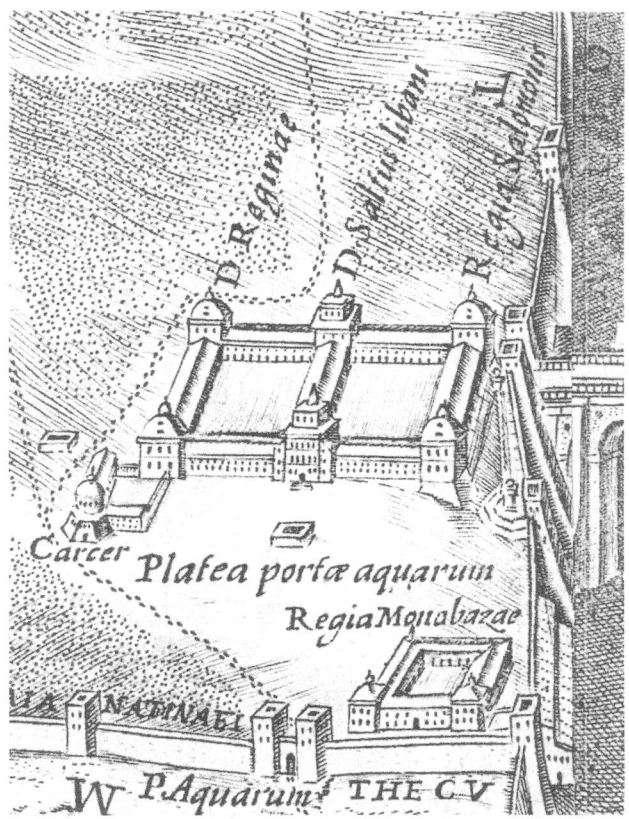

Figure 2.9 Solomon's Palace (enlargement of detail shown in Figure 2.8).

room on which Vitruvius had based his Basilica, measuring 120 by 60 feet. Van Campen translated this space into the Burgerzaal or Citizens' Hall, which shared the same measurements as the Basilica. In order to place all the necessary functions of cells and Tribunal on the ground floor, van Campen had to lift the Citizens' Hall to the first floor. He could justify his choice by referring to the aforementioned passage of Palladio about public buildings, in which he claimed that the Basilica was originally on the ground floor, but that modern basilicas – such as his own design in Vicenza – tended to be on the first floor and that an architect could freely omit galleries or redesign them in any way they saw fit.[29] In the case of Amsterdam, this freedom allowed van Campen to situate the galleries around the inner courtyards.[30]

For the elevation of the façades and the Citizens' Hall, van Campen wanted to use the Corinthian order exclusively. This can be concluded from the prints

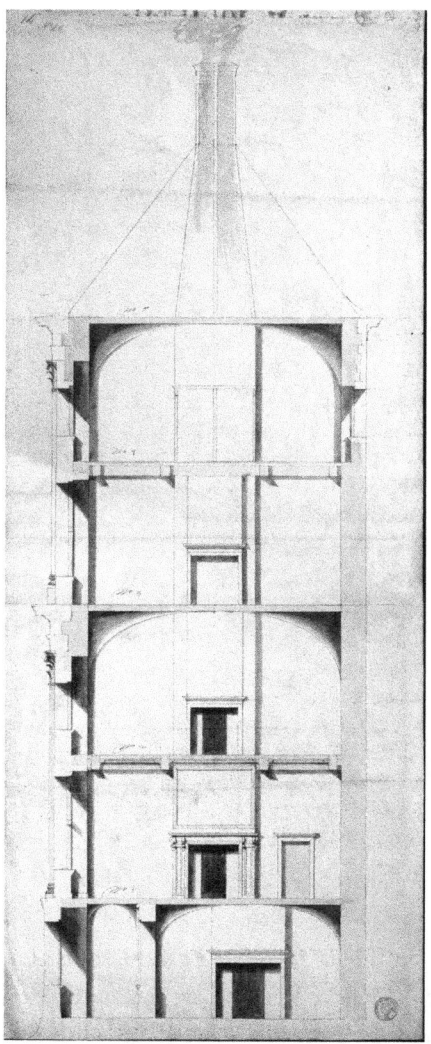

Figure 2.10 Section of the north wing of the Amsterdam Town Hall, c. 1652. Stadsarchief Amsterdam, Public Domain.

as well as from one of the very few surviving architectural drawings.[31] One of these shows an unexecuted design of the northern wing where the façade is adorned with two super-positioned Corinthian pilasters instead of the eventually executed Composite and Corinthian pilasters (Figure 2.10).[32] This fascinating drawing, dating from around 1652, shows the same kind of architecture as the internal façades of the Citizens' Hall, drawing upon Villalpando's interpretation of the design of the temple.

For the tower, van Campen used a cupola-shaped structure that also refers to the Temple of Jerusalem. During the eighty years of war with the Spanish, similar structures were used to indicate true faith, both by the Spanish and the Dutch. The origin for this shape is again the Temple of Solomon. In this case, it is not the historical Temple as described in the Bible, but the ancient tradition that the Dome of the Rock was regarded as a Temple.[33] Architects considered this centralized building as an evocation of the Temple. Many similar shapes were used as tabernacles on Roman Catholic altars, symbolizing the fact that these structures housed the consecrated bread or the body of Christ – therefore serving as the House of God. An excellent example can be found in the San Lorenzo in the Escorial.

The cupola was also an important element in Cesare Ripa's depiction of Europe (Figure 2.11). The Dutch translation of Ripa – which was edited in 1644 and became extremely influential in art in general and in the case of the

Figure 2.11 Europe, as published in Cesare Ripa, *Iconologia of uijtbeeldingen des verstands*, (Amsterdam: Cornelis Danckerts, 1656). Utrecht University Library, Public Domain.

Amsterdam Town Hall in particular – described the cupola as follows: 'The temple that she holds in her hand, signifies that in that place (Europe) is true and Christian, perfect religion, and that she with all her buildings extolls above the rest of the world.'[34] It was a wonderful element to add to the Town Hall, symbolizing not only a temple of peace, but also a country in which true religion rules.[35]

Jerusalem, Amsterdam and the cosmological programme of the interior

As discussed above, the Amsterdam Town Hall was a translation of Solomon's Palace, both in the way it functioned and in the way van Campen designed it. Amsterdam was considered the New Jerusalem: the heart of the world and the centre of the cosmos. Van Campen fortified this Amsterdam-centred vision by designing an interior programme in which the world and the cosmos turned around Amsterdam. This design evolved during the first years of construction. The evolution can be visualized by comparing the models, prints and drawings of the building. There are two very important series of prints, one edited by the city architect Daniel Stalpaert in 1650 and one published as a book by Dancker Danckerts in 1661 called *Afbeelding van 't Stadt Huys van Amsterdam* (Depiction of the Town Hall of Amsterdam). The earliest and rarest prints, however, date from 1648, and show the plans of the ground floor and first floor. The differences between the printed ground plans of 1648 and those of 1650 indicate that the decorative programme must have been invented in a later stage (around 1650). These changes can also be deduced from the original building model (1648), which was altered internally according to the later plans from 1650. The most prominent change was the introduction in the galleries of statues of classical gods that embodied the planets and therefore the universe. They enclosed the Citizens' Hall, where statues of the continents and of the four elements stood, out of which all things present on earth were supposed to be made. Two enormous coloured maps of the world were laid out in marble, as well as a central chart of the stars or heavens. Everyone could have the world at his or her feet and believe to be at the centre of creation.[36]

The overarching idea of combining classical and biblical antiquity had its effect as well on the choice of subjects of paintings and sculptures, that acted as historical exempla. The Tribunal contained depictions of Solomon's Judgment and of the Verdicts of Zeleukos and Lucius Junius Brutus, representing wisdom, impartiality and mercy. The City Council's room had a large painting of Solomon, praying for wisdom, while the Old Burgomasters' room had a painting by Govert Flinck depicting Manius Curius Dentatus, who preferred to eat turnips rather than the bribes offered to him by the Sabines.[37] In the case of the Magistrates' Court, biblical history was used to address a political theme. Ferdinand Bol's large painting of Moses bringing the Law was contrasted by the chimney frieze representing the erection of the Golden Calf under the high priest Aaron. The underlying idea was that the supervision of religion was better in the hands of a worldly leader such as Moses than with a religious leader such as Aaron, or to translate it to seventeenth-century Amsterdam, where the Burgomasters were better keepers of the true faith than ministers of the church.[38]

The large series of paintings in the galleries, depicting Batavian history, must be seen as an afterthought following van Campen's departure. Burgomaster Cornelis de Graeff was responsible for introducing this series, which was executed by Jan Lievens, Jurriaen Ovens and Jacob Jordaens.[39]

Building history and actors (1648–67)

Construction of the Town Hall started in 1648 and lasted until 1667. It proceeded rather slowly: it took over nine months to drive in 13,659 pine piles, each of which was 14.5 metres long. On 28 October 1648, the Burgomasters' sons and nephews laid the first stone, dressed in leather aprons, holding silver trowels and wearing gold medals on their chests. Brick foundations were laid and the building started rising up behind the old Town Hall, which remained in use until it burnt down in 1652. The northwest corner of the building rose first, while the construction ended in the northern wing. In 1652, only the cellars and the ground floor were ready. When the building was inaugurated in 1655 as the Town Hall, just half of it was finished. In 1659, the building was structurally completed with the exception of the tower, which was added in 1665. The large statues on the pediment at the back were put in place in 1667. Work on the interior continued well after 1667. Large works such as the decoration of the 'Krijgsraadzaal' (the large meeting room for the civic guard) were only completed around 1700. By that time, the building needed some major renovations. The undecorated and visible roof construction of the Citizens' Hall had to be renewed completely between 1700 and 1703. The new roof structure was finished with a barrel vault, decorated with an enormous painting celebrating 'the glorification of Amsterdam'.[40]

The city had an Office for Public Works responsible for maintaining city buildings, including bridges and other civil engineering structures. Building a new Town Hall required a separate and newly created organization. In order to organize the building campaign smoothly, Amsterdam employed a city architect. In 1648, the painter and broker Daniel Stalpaert (1615–76) was appointed to supervise the construction together with van Campen. The city architect was not employed for his artistic skills, but rather for his expertise in overseeing the building process, although he may have had a hand in detailing certain parts of the building, especially after 1654 or 1655, when van Campen left the construction site, probably after a row with Stalpaert and possibly about the change in the classical orders of the building's façade.[41] Plan changes made after 1655, however, must have been done by Stalpaert.

Willem de Keyser, son of the former city sculptor Hendrick de Keyser, was hired to oversee the execution of the enormous amount of stonemasonry and sculpture that adorned the building, which was partly done by the city officials themselves. A city smith was employed to oversee the ironworks which were needed to clamp together the sandstone blocks of the façades.

Most of work, however, was not done by the department for public works itself. A building project of this size could not be incorporated into the existing organization, which had its hands full with its regular work of maintaining city buildings, streets and water works. Contractors built most of the building. In his monumental chronicle on Amsterdam, Jan Wagenaar informs us of the fact that 'not only the rough building work was done by contractors, but also the statues, the copper doors, the paintings and the other ornaments'.[42] This decision created competition amongst the artists and labourers of the city, allowing high-quality work to be achieved more quickly and cheaply. The total costs were 8 million guilders, according to Wagenaar. This assertion cannot be checked, as practically all records concerning the building process were subsequently lost, but he was generally very well informed. It has been suggested that contests were held for the paintings that adorn the building. The city sculptor Artus Quellinus was not employed by the city, but worked as a privileged contractor, invited by the Burgomasters to live and work in Amsterdam. In his receipts, one of the few building records left to us, he specifically mentioned that works were tendered to him. From 1652 onwards, Rombout Verhulst was his competitor, as can be concluded from some sculptures clearly signed by his hand.[43]

Apart from the bricks, which were Dutch, materials were imported from all over the world: sandstone from Bentheim and Obernkirchen in present-day Germany, stone from Avesnes-le-Sec in France, coloured marble from the Southern Netherlands, over 700 cubic metres of white Carrara marble from Italy, Swedish sandstone, limestone and copper, as well as slate from England, to name the most important. The enormous variety in materials was needed not only to achieve a colourful design, but also to facilitate the execution of the building. For the construction of the Citizens' Hall, for instance, many types of stone were used. More costly stones were used for the parts of the architecture at eye level. For the pilasters and the parapets under the windows, white marble was used. For the upper part sandstone was employed, which was easier to work. Within the lower entablature, which consisted of a Bentheimer or Oberkirchener sandstone, the modillions were made of softer Gotland sandstone. The festoons inbetween the lower capitals were either in sandstone from Gotland (long façades) or limestone from Avesnes-le-Sec (end walls). The large entrance portals were constructed of Carrara marble, adorned with half columns in Rouge Royal, while the festoon on the marble was of Gotland stone; the statues on the portals were made of stone from Avesnes-le-Sec. The use of all these different materials was done out of economy. The limestone from Avesnes-le-Sec and Gotland sandstone were light and very soft stones, which were easy to carve. Sculpting marble was far more difficult and twice as expensive. To obscure the differences, van Campen applied finishing layers of faux marble in order to create a uniform building with a classical appearance.[44]

An intricate play of marble and classical orders defined the worthiness of each office. In Holland, white marble was considered the most classic, followed by Rouge Royal and variants of black Belgian marble. The most important office, that of the Burgomasters, thus received a fireplace with a white marble chimneypiece and Corinthian columns. The large room for the former Burgomasters, an extremely important advisory body, also contained a Corinthian chimneypiece, but with a combination of white marble and Rouge Royal used for the shafts of the columns. The chimneypiece in the Magistrates' Room was again in the Corinthian order, but with more red marble, both in the shafts, and in parts of the entablature. The City Council chamber received a chimneypiece similar to that of the Magistrates' room, but with a Composite capital, which according to Scamozzi, was a lower order than the Corinthian. The Treasurers were given a chimney with a fireplace in white marble, but in the Ionic order. Their 'rank', however, did not coincide with their real influence, working closely together with the Burgomasters. To make up for this, the shafts of the chimney columns were sculpted with plants by Quellinus, resulting in one of the most elaborately sculpted elements in the building. The chimneypiece of the office of the Bank of Amsterdam was executed in a black Belgian marble, while the Commissioners of Petty Affairs were given one in sandstone.[45] It is very likely that the finishing layers of the offices were differentiated in a similar way, giving the less prestigious offices an oak graining and more prestigious offices a walnut or rosewood graining.[46]

The Amsterdam Town Hall in its European context

The Town Hall was a prestige project aimed at lifting Amsterdam to an international level. Jacob van Campen did this by taking his inspiration from Solomonic buildings. This desire to identify with Solomon was not uniquely Dutch: similar movements existed in Spain, Great Britain, Denmark, Germany and France. The Danish king Christian IV was introduced by his father as a new Solomon. During a visit to his brother-in-law James I in England in 1606, Christian IV even appeared as Solomon in a masquerade written by Ben Jonson.[47] In France, Louis XIV had the Louvre extended and here also it has been suggested that Solomon's Temple had a strong influence on Charles Perrault's design.[48] This identification with Solomon certainly had an influence on other royal buildings. The best-known example is the Escorial by Philip II of Spain, who identified himself with Solomon. The Escorial is a combination of a church, a monastery and a palace and the archetype of a building based on the design of the Temple.[49] The focal point is the church, taking over the place of the Holy of Holies in the Temple. The courtyards around it reflect the courts of the Temple. Towers are positioned on the corners of the courtyards, as was the case in the Temple.

Great Britain had a long Solomonic tradition, particularly under the reign of the Stuart king James I, who saw himself as 'a spiritual descendant of the Hebrew kings'. As a king of peace, he also identified himself with Solomon, while his people regarded Great Britain as New Israel.[50] James's son Charles I took the Temple of Jerusalem as the model for the reconstruction of Whitehall Palace, and his own son Charles II did the same when enlarging the Palace of Holyroodhouse in Edinburgh, incorporating the sixteenth-century parts built by the Scottish king James V that resembled medieval reconstructions of the Temple (Figure 2.12).[51] Both the Spanish Habsburgs and the British Stuarts

Figure 2.12 Edinburgh, The Palace of Holyroodhouse. Image by author.

referenced the Solomonic tradition as a way of expressing their legitimacy: in both countries they had succeeded other royal families and wanted to present themselves as new Solomons who, with their wisdom and divine protection, brought peace and prosperity to the nation.

So while Amsterdam was not unique in referring to Solomon, it seems to be extraordinary that it happened in a Republican setting. Many town halls and other institutional buildings expressed allegiance to territorial lords, countries or provinces by adorning their façades with heraldic ornaments.[52] This reference to a higher earthly power is completely absent in Amsterdam, apart from the Imperial Crown on the head of the allegorical figure of Amsterdam in the front tympanum; a symbol that was granted to the city by Emperor Maximilian. Amsterdam regarded itself a free city and as the focal point of power and the centre of the world, and therefore referred only to itself and depicted itself in the decorative scheme of the new Town Hall. The city interacted on the level of territorial lords as if it were a person, as can be demonstrated by the fact that Amsterdam was the godfather of the oldest son of the Elector of Brandenburg. The exceptional thing about the Amsterdam Town Hall is the choice of Solomon's Palace as the inspiration for its ground plan and layout. The reason for this probably lies in the fact that the combination of functions of Solomon's Palace was rather like that of a town hall. The heart of the Palace was taken up by a large hall, followed by the Solomon's courtroom, a disposition which was clearly reflected in the Amsterdam Town Hall.

In the seventeenth century, the Town Hall appeared in many paintings. It is even one of the most portrayed buildings in the world, which underlines its great significance.[53] It was the most important building in the Netherlands: a true expression of a golden era in which Holland dominated the Republic and played an important role in international politics, while Amsterdam dominated Holland. The significance of the building was still recognized in the nineteenth century by the King of Holland, Louis Napoléon, brother of Napoleon Bonaparte, who was made king in 1806 and had to look for a building which befitted his status. The palaces of the stadholders were not considered to be grand enough. There was only one building in the former Republic worthy enough to serve as a palace: the Amsterdam Town Hall. In 1808, he asked the city to 'loan' the building until Louis had built himself a palace in Amsterdam. However, the new palace was never built. The city attempted several times to regain control over the building, but it failed. In the end, it was sold in 1935–6 for 10 million guilders to the state. The palace of the Dutch Republic became the palace of the Kingdom of the Netherlands.[54]

Notes

1 For the Amsterdam Town Hall in general, see: Katharine Fremantle, *The Baroque Town Hall of Amsterdam* (Utrecht: Haentjens Dekkers & Gumbert, 1959); Pieter Vlaardingerbroek, *Het paleis van de Republiek. De geschiedenis van het stadhuis van Amsterdam* (Zwolle: WBOOKS, 2011); Eymert-Jan Goossens, *Het Amsterdamse paleis. Schat van beitel en penseel* (Zwolle: Uitgeverij Waanders, 2010). This chapter is an excerpt of my 2011 book and owes much to Pieter Vlaardingerbroek, 'An Appropriated History: The Case of the Amsterdam Town Hall (1648–1667)', in *The Quest for an Appropriate Past in Literature, Art and Architecture*, ed. Karl A.E. Enenkel and Konrad A. Ottenheym (Leiden/Boston: Brill, 2019), 455–81.

2 Clé Lesger, 'De wereld als horizon. De economie tussen 1578 en 1650', in *Geschiedenis van Amsterdam 1578–1650. Centrum van de wereld*, ed. Willem Frijhoff and Maarten Prak (Amsterdam: SUN, 2004), 103–87.

3 Vlaardingerbroek, 'An Appropriated History', 455–58.

4 S.A.C. Dudok van Heel, 'The Night Watch and the Entry of Marie de' Medici. A New Interpretation of the Original Place and Significance of the Painting', *The Rijksmuseum Bulletin* 57 (2009): 5–41

5   Kasper van Baerle (or Caspar Barlaeus), *Medicea hospes, sive Descriptio publicae gratulationis, qua Mariam de Medicis excepit* (Amsterdam: Johan and Cornelis Blaeu, 1638). Published in Dutch as *Blijde Inkomst der allerdoorluchtighste Koninginne Maria de Medicis t'Amsterdam* (Amsterdam: Johan en Cornelis Blaeu, 1639).
6   In Dutch: 'D'ouderdom en bouwvalligheid geven dit gebouw eenige achtbaerheid'; Van Baerle, *Blijde Inkomst*, 47.
7   Vlaardingerbroek, *Het paleis van de Republiek*, 18–21.
8   Stadsarchief Amsterdam (Amsterdam City Archives), archive 5025 (Vroedschap), inv.no. 16, fol. 229–229v (28 January 1639).
9   Koen Ottenheym, *Philips Vingboons (1607–1678). Architect* (Zutphen: De Walburg Pers, 1989), 111–27; Vlaardingerbroek, *Het paleis van de Republiek*, 21–33.
10 Marten Jan Bok, 'Familie, vrienden en opdrachtgevers', in *Het klassieke ideaal in de Gouden Eeuw*, ed. Jacobine Huisken, Koen Ottenheym and Gary Schwartz (Amsterdam: Architectura et Natura, 1994), 27–52 (27).
11 For van Campen and his architectural works, see Koen Ottenheym, 'Architectuur', in *Jacob van Campen. Het klassieke ideaal in de Gouden Eeuw*, ed. Jacobine Huisken, Koen Ottenheym and Gary Schwartz (Amsterdam: Architectura et Natura, 1994), 155–99.
12 Quentin Buvelot, 'Ontwerpen voor geschilderde decoratieprogramma's', in *Het klassieke ideaal in de Gouden Eeuw*, ed. Jacobine Huisken, Koen Ottenheym and Gary Schwartz (Amsterdam: Architectura et Natura, 1994), 121–53.
13 Pieter Vlaardingerbroek, 'De stadhouder, zijn secretaris en de architectuur. Jacob van Campen als ontwerper van het Huygenshuis en de hofarchitectuur onder Frederik Hendrik', *Nederlands Kunsthistorisch Jaarboek* 51 (2000): 61–81.
14 Reyer Anslo, 'Het Gekroonde Amsterdam met het nieuw stadthuis', in *Olijfkrans der Vrede* (Amsterdam: Gerrit van Goedesberg, 1649), 406.
15 Francesco Milizia, *Memorie degli Architetti Antichi e Moderni* (Bassano: Remondini, 1785), 157.
16 Theodorus Schrevelius, *Harlemias, ofte, om beter te seggen, De eerste stichtinghe der stadt Haerlem* (Haarlem: Thomans Fonteyn, 1648), 383.
17 Koen Ottenheym, *Schoonheid op maat. Vincenzo en de architectuur van de Gouden Eeuw* (Amsterdam: Architectura & Natura Press, 2010), 104–05; Maaike Dicke, Koen Ottenheym, Wolbert Vroom, *VI. Vincenzo Scamozzi. De grondgedachte van de universele bouwkunst. Architect te Venetië. Klassieke zuilenorden* (Amsterdam: Architectura et Natura, s.a.).
18 Abraham Lutma, *Portrait of Jacob van Campen*, etching, published in Jacob van Campen, *Afbeelding van 't Stadt Huijs van Amsterdam* (Amsterdam: Dancker Danckerts, 1661).
19 Sjoerd Faber, Jacobine Huisken and Friso Lammertse, *Van Heeren, die hunn' stoel en kussen niet beschaemen. Het stadsbestuur van Amsterdam in de 17^e en 18^e eeuw. Of

Lords, who seat nor cushion do ashame. The government of Amsterdam in the 17th and 18th centuries (Amsterdam: Stichting Koninklijk Paleis te Amsterdam, 1987).

20 Pieter Vlaardingerbroek, 'Dutch Town Halls and the Setting of the Vierschaar', in *Public Buildings in Early Modern Europe*, ed. Konrad Ottenheym, Krista De Jonge and Monique Chatenet (Turnhout: Brepols, 2010), 105–18.

21 Katharine Fremantle, 'The Open Vierschaar of Amsterdam's seventeenth-century Town Hall as a setting for the city's justice', *Oud-Holland* 80 (1965): 65–111.

22 Eymert-Jan Goossens, 'De Vredestempel. Het Amsterdamse stadspaleis uit 1648', in *1648. Vrede van Munster. Feit en verbeelding*, ed. Jacques Dane (Zwolle: Waanders Uitgevers, 1998), 205–23.

23 Vlaardingerbroek, 'Dutch Town Halls'.

24 Vlaardingerbroek, 'An Appropriated History', 455; Konrad Ottenheym, 'The Mediaeval Prestige of Dutch Cities', in *The Quest for an Appropriate Past in Literature, Art and Architecture*, ed. Karl A.E. Enenkel and Konrad A. Ottenheym (Leiden/Boston: Brill, 2019), 418–54.

25 I. Schöffer, 'The Batavian Myth during the Sixteenth and Seventeenth Centuries', in *Geschiedschrijving in Nederland. Studies over de historiografie van de Nieuwe Tijd. Deel II: Geschiedbeoefening*, ed. P.A.M. Geurts and A.E.M. Janssen (The Hague: Martinus Nijhoff, 1981), 85–109; Sandra Langereis, 'Van botte boeren tot beschaafde burgers. Oudheidkundige beelden van de Bataven 1500–1800', in *Bataven. Verhalen van een verdwenen volk*, ed. Pieter Roelofs, Louis Swinkels and Edwin Buijsen (Amsterdam: De Bataafsche Leeuw, 2004), 72–106.

26 Ottenheym, *Schoonheid op maat*, 7, 104–105; Ottenheym, *VI. Vincenzo Scamozzi*, 15–17.

27 See for Villalpando: Tessa Morrison, *Juan Bautista Villalpando's Ezechielem Explanationes. A Sixteenth-Century Architectural Text* (Lewiston: The Edwin Mellen Press, 2009).

28 Leiden, University Library, special collections, inv.no. 37 (41): Johan Brosterhuijsen to Constantijn Huygens, Amersfoort 6 February 1642: 'Ick ben in 't oversetten van Vitruvius ghecomen tot in 't midden van het laetste boeck. De heer Campen, die sijn ootmoedighe ghebiedenisse aen UEd[ele] doedt, raedt mij daer nae het laetste boeck van Palladio, daer in hij handeldt van de tempels der oude, ende de laetste capittelen van sijn voorgaende boeck, daer hij van haer publike ghebouwen spreekt, oock over te setten, om achter Vitruvius te drucken, het welck ick oock meen te doen, t en waer dat UEd[ele] daer ijede teghen hadde. Mijn Wotton, die de voorlooper van Vitruvius moet weesen, is ghereedt om ghedruct te werden, maer hij heeft alleen ghewacht nae een verhael van den oorsprongh der bouwconst, dat de heer Campen ontworpen heeft ende, t en waer door belet van siecte, dese winter soude opghemaect hebben. Dan nu beter te pas sijnde, sal sijn E[dele] daeraen vallen.' See also Vlaardingerbroek, *Het paleis van de Republiek*, 71–2.

29 Andrea Palladio, *I Quattro Libri dell'Architettura* (Venice: Dominico de' Franceschi, 1570), book III, chapters 19 and 20.
30 Vlaardingerbroek, 'An Appropriated History'.
31 Of all the hundreds of drawings made for the construction, only a handful survives. Four of them are attributed to Van Campen. Three sketches show the general idea for a painting in the Citizens' Hall and the two pediments of the façades, upon which the painter or sculptor had to base his final design for execution. One architectural drawing was made for a reduced town hall (1653), which remained unexecuted (Stadsarchief Amsterdam, Collectie Bouwtekeningen, inv.no. G 20-12; Vlaardingerbroek, *Het paleis van de Republiek*, 56-8).
32 Stadsarchief Amsterdam, Collectie Bouwtekeningen, inv.no. I V.2.9; Vlaardingerbroek, *Het paleis van de Republiek*, 54-6.
33 William J. Hamblin and David Rolph Seely, *Solomon's Temple: Myth and History* (London: Thames & Hudson, 2007), 102-03.
34 Cesare Ripa, *Iconologia of uijtbeeldingen des verstands* (Amsterdam: Dirck Pietersz Pers, 1644), 602-03: 'De Tempel die zij op de hand houd, bediet, dat aldaer is de waere en Christelijcke volmaeckte Religie, en dat zij met haere gebouwen boven de geheele Werreld uijtblinckt.' English translation by the author.
35 According to the Dutch Creed the government was made responsible for upholding the true faith (article 36).
36 Fremantle, *The Baroque Town Hall*, 30-56.
37 One of the offered artefacts on the painting is the famous auricular ewer by Adam van Vianen, now in the Rijksmuseum. See also Reinier Baarsen, *Kwab. Ornament als kunst in de eeuw van Rembrandt* (Amsterdam: Rijksmuseum, 2018).
38 Albert Blankert, *Kunst als regeringszaak in Amsterdam in de 17e eeuw. Rondom schilderijen van Ferdinand Bol* (Lochem: De Tijdstroom B.V., 1975).
39 Marianna van der Zwaag and Renske Cohen Tervaert, *Opstand als opdracht/The Batavian Commissions* (Amsterdam: Stichting Koninklijk Paleis te Amsterdam, 2011).
40 Vlaardingerbroek, *Het paleis van de Republiek*, 149-61.
41 Vlaardingerbroek, *Het paleis van de Republiek*, 97.
42 Jan Wagenaar, *Amsterdam, in zyne opkomst, aanwas, geschiedenissen, voorregten, koophandel, gebouwen, kerkenstaat, schoolen, schutterye, gilden en regeeringe*, 3 vols. (Amsterdam: Isaak Tirion, 1760-7), vol. 2, 28. English translation by the author.
43 Vlaardingerbroek, *Het paleis van de Republiek*, 105-21.
44 Vlaardingerbroek, *Het paleis van de Republiek*, 128-29, 137, n. 493v.
45 Vlaardingerbroek, *Het paleis van de Republiek*, 137-38.
46 Pieter Vlaardingerbroek, 'Tussen concept en geschiedenis. Een analyse van de restauratie van het Koninklijk Paleis Amsterdam (2005-2011)', *Bulletin Koninklijke Nederlandse Oudheidkundige Bond* 112 (2013): 122-34.

47 Juliette Roding, 'King Solomon and the Imperial Paradigm of Christian IV (1588–1648)', in *Reframing the Danish Renaissance. Problems and Prospects in a European Perspective*, ed. Michael Andersen, Brigitte Boggild Johannsen and Hugo Johannsen (Copenhagen: National Museum, 2011), 235–42.

48 Campbell, 'The Paired Columned Entrance'; André Corboz, 'Il Louvre come palazzo di Salomone', in *Gian Lorenzo Bernini architetto e l'architettura europea*, ed. Gianfranco Spagnesi and Marcello Fagiolo, 3 vols (Rome: Istituto della Enciclopedia Italiana, 1983–4), vol. 2, 563–98.

49 John Bold, *John Webb. Architectural Theory and Practice in the Seventeenth Century* (Oxford: Oxford University Press, 1989) 107–125. For the Solomonic context of the Escorial, see R. Taylor, 'Architecture and Magic: Considerations on the Idea of the Escorial', in *Essays in the History of Architecture presented to Rudolf Wittkower* ed. Douglas Fraser, Howard Hibbard and Milton J. Lewine (London: Phaidon Press, 1967) 81–109.

50 Graham Parry, *The Golden Age restor'd: The Culture of the Stuart Court, 1603–1642* (Manchester: Manchester University Press, 1981) 21, 22, 23, 26–9, 31–2, 35. Quote taken from p. 23.

51 Ian Campbell, 'The Paired Columned Entrance of Holyroodhouse as a Solomonic signifier', in *The Architecture of Scotland in its European Setting: 1660-1750* (in print).

52 Christine Stevenson, *The City and the King. Architecture and Politics in Restoration London* (New Haven: Yale University Press, 2013), 4.

53 Numerous paintings were made from the 1650s onwards by Gerrit Berckheyde, Jan van der Heyden, Jan van der Ulft and Abraham Stork, some of which were sold abroad, such as the painting by Jan van der Heyden, bought by Cosimo de Medici and still in the Uffizi in Florence. See Jan Peeters et al, *Het Paleis in de schilderkunst van de Gouden Eeuw* (Zwolle: Waanders Uitgevers, 1997). For the leading role of the Netherlands with regard to architectural view painting, see the introduction of John Harris, *The Artist and the Country House: A History of Country House and Garden View Painting in Britain 1540-1870* (London: Sotheby Parke Bernet Publications, 1979).

54 Vlaardingerbroek, *Het paleis van de Republiek*, 221–2.

Bibliography

Anslo, Reyer. 'Het Gekroonde Amsterdam met het nieuw stadthuis.' In *Olijfkrans der Vrede*, edited by Reyer Anslo, 406. Amsterdam: Gerrit van Goedesberg, 1649.

Baarsen, Reinier. *Kwab. Ornament als kunst in de eeuw van Rembrandt*. Amsterdam: Rijksmuseum, 2018.

Baerle, Kasper van (or Caspar Barlaeus). *Blijde Inkomst der allerdoorluchtighste Koninginne Maria de Medicis t'Amsterdam*. Amsterdam: Johan en Cornelis Blaeu, 1639.

Blankert, Albert. *Kunst als regeringszaak in Amsterdam in de 17e eeuw. Rondom schilderijen van Ferdinand Bol*. Lochem: De Tijdstroom B.V., 1975.

Bok, Marten Jan. 'Familie, vrienden en opdrachtgevers.' In *Het klassieke ideaal in de Gouden Eeuw*, edited by Jacobine Huisken, Koen Ottenheym and Gary Schwartz, 27–52. Amsterdam: Architectura et Natura, 1994.

Bold, John. *John Webb. Architectural Theory and Practice in the Seventeenth Century*. Oxford: Oxford University Press, 1989.

Buvelot, Quentin. 'Ontwerpen voor geschilderde decoratieprogramma's.' In *Het klassieke ideaal in de Gouden Eeuw*, edited by Jacobine Huisken, Koen Ottenheym and Gary Schwartz, 121–53. Amsterdam: Architectura et Natura, 1994.

Campbell, Ian. 'The Paired Columned Entrance of Holyroodhouse as a Solomonic signifier.' In *The Architecture of Scotland in its European Setting: 1660–1750* (in print).

Campen, Jacob van. *Afbeelding van 't Stadt Huijs van Amsterdam*. Amsterdam: Dancker Danckerts, 1661.

Corboz, André. 'Il Louvre come palazzo di Salomone.' In *Gian Lorenzo Bernini architetto e l'architettura europea*, edited by Gianfranco Spagnesi and Marcello Fagiolo, II, 535–98. Rome: Istituto della Enciclopedia Italiana, 1983–4.

Dicke, Maaike, Koen Ottenheym and Wolbert Vroom (eds). *Vincenzo Scamozzi. De grondgedachte van de universele bouwkunst. Architect te Venetië. Klassieke zuilenorden*. Amsterdam: Architectura et Natura, s.a.

Dudok van Heel, S.A.C. 'The Night Watch and the Entry of Marie de' Medici. A New Interpretation of the Original Place and Significance of the Painting.' *The Rijksmuseum Bulletin* 57 (2009): 5–41.

Faber, Sjoerd, Jacobine Huisken and Friso Lammertse. *Van Heeren, die hunn' stoel en kussen niet beschaemen. Het stadsbestuur van Amsterdam in de 17^e en 18^e eeuw. Of Lords, who seat nor cushion do ashame. The government of Amsterdam in the 17th and 18th centuries*. Amsterdam: Stichting Koninklijk Paleis te Amsterdam, 1987.

Fremantle, Katharine. 'The Open Vierschaar of Amsterdam's seventeenth-century Town Hall as a setting for the city's justice.' *Oud-Holland* 80 (1965): 65–111.

Fremantle, Katharine. *The Baroque Town Hall of Amsterdam*. Utrecht: Haentjens Dekkers & Gumbert, 1959.

Goossens, Eymert-Jan. 'De Vredestempel. Het Amsterdamse stadspaleis uit 1648.' In *1648. Vrede van Munster. Feit en verbeelding*, edited by Jacques Dane, 205–23. Zwolle: Waanders Uitgevers, 1998.

Goossens, Eymert-Jan. *Het Amsterdamse paleis. Schat van beitel en penseel*. Zwolle: Uitgeverij Waanders, 2010.

Hamblin, William J., and David Rolph Seely. *Solomon's Temple. Myth and History*. London: Thames & Hudson, 2007.

Harris, John. *The Artist and the Country House. A history of country house and garden view painting in Britain 1540–1870*. London: Sotheby Parke Bernet Publications, 1979.

Langereis, Sandra. 'Van botte boeren tot beschaafde burgers. Oudheidkundige beelden van de Bataven 1500–1800.' In *Bataven. Verhalen van een verdwenen volk*, edited by Pieter Roelofs, Louis Swinkels and Edwin Buijsen, 72–106. Amsterdam: De Bataafsche Leeuw, 2004.

Lesger, Clé. 'De wereld als horizon. De economie tussen 1578 en 1650.' In *Geschiedenis van Amsterdam 1578–1650. Centrum van de wereld*, edited by Willem Frijhoff and Maarten Prak, 455–8. Amsterdam: SUN, 2004.

Milizia, Francesco. *Memorie degli Architetti Antichi e Moderni*. Bassano: Remondini, 1785.

Morrison, Tessa. *Juan Bautista Villalpando's Ezechielem Explanationes. A Sixteenth-Century Architectural Text*. Lewiston: The Edwin Mellen Press, 2009.

Ottenheym, Koen. 'Architectuur.' In *Jacob van Campen. Het klassieke ideaal in de Gouden Eeuw*, edited by Jacobine Huisken, Koen Ottenheym and Gary Schwartz, 155–99. Amsterdam: Architectura et Natura, 1994.

Ottenheym, Koen. *Philips Vingboons (1607–1678). Architect*. Zutphen: De Walburg Pers, 1989.

Ottenheym, Koen. *Schoonheid op maat. Vincenzo en de architectuur van de Gouden Eeuw*. Amsterdam: Architectura & Natura Press, 2010.

Ottenheym, Konrad. 'The Mediaeval Prestige of Dutch Cities.' In *The Quest for an Appropriate Past in Literature, Art and Architecture*, edited by Karl A.E. Enenkel and Konrad A. Ottenheym, 418–54. Leiden: Brill, 2019.

Palladio, Andrea. *I Quattro Libri dell'Architettura*. Venice: Dominico de' Franceschi, 1570.

Parry, Graham. *The Golden Age restor'd: The Culture of the Stuart Court, 1603–1642*. Manchester: Manchester University Press, 1981.

Peeters, Jan, *Het Paleis in de schilderkunst van de Gouden Eeuw*. Zwolle: Waanders Uitgevers, 1997.

Ripa, Cesare. *Iconologia of uijtbeeldingen des verstands*. Amsterdam: Dirck Pietersz Pers, 1644.

Roding, Juliette. 'King Solomon and the Imperial Paradigm of Christian IV (1588–1648).' In *Reframing the Danish Renaissance. Problems and Prospects in a European Perspective*, edited by Michael Andersen, Brigitte Boggild Johannsen and Hugo Johannsen, 235–42. Copenhagen: National Museum, 2011.

Schöffer, I. 'The Batavian Myth during the Sixteenth and Seventeenth Centuries.' In *Geschiedschrijving in Nederland. Studies over de historiografie van de Nieuwe Tijd. Deel II: Geschiedbeoefening*, edited by P.A.M. Geurts and A.E.M. Janssen, 85–109. The Hague: Martinus Nijhoff, 1981.

Schrevelius, Theodorus. *Harlemias, ofte, om beter te seggen, De eerste stichtinghe der stadt Haerlem*. Haarlem: Thomans Fonteyn, 1648.

Stevenson, Christine. *The City and the King. Architecture and Politics in Restoration London*. New Haven: Yale University Press, 2013.

Taylor, R. 'Architecture and Magic: Considerations on the Idea of the Escorial.' In *Essays in the History of Architecture presented to Rudolf Wittkower*, edited by Douglas Fraser, Howard Hibbard and Milton J. Lewine, 81–109. London: Phaidon Press, 1967.

Vlaardingerbroek, Pieter. 'An Appropriated History: The Case of the Amsterdam Town Hall (1648–1667).' In *The Quest for an Appropriate Past in Literature, Art and Architecture*, edited by Karl A.E. Enenkel and Konrad A. Ottenheym, 455–81. Leiden: Brill, 2019.

Vlaardingerbroek, Pieter. 'De stadhouder, zijn secretaris en de architectuur. Jacob van Campen als ontwerper van het Huygenshuis en de hofarchitectuur onder Frederik Hendrik.' *Nederlands Kunsthistorisch Jaarboek* 51 (2000): 61–81.

Vlaardingerbroek, Pieter. 'Dutch Town Halls and the Setting of the Vierschaar.' In *Public Buildings in Early Modern Europe*, edited by Konrad Ottenheym, Krista De Jonge and Monique Chatenet, 105–18. Turnhout: Brepols, 2010.

Vlaardingerbroek, Pieter. 'Tussen concept en geschiedenis. Een analyse van de restauratie van het Koninklijk Paleis Amsterdam (2005–2011).' *Bulletin Koninklijke Nederlandse Oudheidkundige Bond* 112 (2013): 122–34.

Vlaardingerbroek, Pieter. *Het paleis van de Republiek. De geschiedenis van het stadhuis van Amsterdam*. Zwolle: WBOOKS, 2011.

Wagenaar, Jan. *Amsterdam, in zyne opkomst, aanwas, geschiedenissen, voorregten, koophandel, gebouwen, kerkenstaat, schoolen, schutterye, gilden en regeeringe*. Amsterdam: Isaak Tirion, 1760–7.

Zwaag, Marianna van der, and Renske Cohen Tervaert. *Opstand als opdracht/The Batavian Commissions*. Amsterdam: Stichting Koninklijk Paleis te Amsterdam, 2011.

3

The Amsterdam Town Hall:
The Triumphant Statement of a Successor State

Caroline van Eck

Introduction

Traditionally, the Amsterdam Town Hall is presented in architectural history as a success story, both politically and artistically: of the Burgomasters in securing peace for the young Republic and of the entry of Palladian classicism in the Low Countries. The most important artists in the young Republic collaborated to produce a unique building, a triumph of invention, taste and daring. Yet, when one takes a closer look at the building and the circumstances of its design and construction, this success story becomes less self-evident. The Town Hall was the result of a quite drastic, if not violent, intervention into the existing medieval fabric of the Dam and its surrounding streets, which was deplored by the inhabitants.[1] Poems celebrating the new building, such as that by Jan Vos, transformed the immense engineering feat of introducing a forest of trees to carry its weight into a scene from Hell, which can be read not just as a sublime conceit, but also as a symptom of unease about the daring nature of the venture. Nor was the introduction of architecture *all'antica* entirely uncontested, replacing the Gothic with the Classical.[2] As Stijn Bussels and Lorne Darnell have recently argued, seventeenth-century architects and theorists such as Constantijn Huygens (1596–1687) considered the introduction of Renaissance architecture in the Low Countries not as a radical rupture between one style and the preceding one, but rather as a reformation of the decadence of the classical style that had occurred in medieval buildings, in a cyclical pattern of growth, flowering, decadence and reform.[3] Nevertheless, the use of colossal Composite columns in the Town Hall had clearly codified associations with Roman Imperial and Catholic architecture for any viewer acquainted with the architecture of that city. The project to build a new tower for the New Church that would display Gothic features and literally tower over the Town Hall may show that stylistic pluralism was accepted, with stylistic choice depending on the function of the building, but also suggests a concern about the hierarchy of religion and civic government which found expression in the contrast between the Gothic and the Classical.[4] Thus, the stylistic choices made in the Town Hall – the Imperial Composite Order, references to the Basilica as designed by Vitruvius and Palladio, the large sculpted pediments recalling Roman temples and Venetian villas – should be considered not just as artistic decisions, but also in the context of seventeenth-century Dutch attempts to construct a classicizing identity that is not a stylistic break, but a reaction to the vagaries of Gothic architecture, as well as an emulation of the ancients. But we can also consider these stylistic choices from a different perspective that starts from the new and unprecedented political status of the young Republic: what I propose to call successor state behaviour.

Apart from the introduction of architecture *all'antica* in Amsterdam the uniqueness of the Town Hall posed many problems, for seventeenth-century viewers as well as for twentieth-century architectural historians. There is simply nothing like it: the absence of a formal entrance with one main gate, the opening of inner space to integrate three floors into one, and the adaptation of a Roman ornamental language to local circumstances all make this building very difficult to classify both typologically and iconographically.

At the same time, the building was praised in an unparalleled series of poems by contemporaries as the eighth Wonder of the World, as the ultimate architectural embodiment of the sublime and of *magnificentia*, and an overwhelming display of the wealth of Amsterdam, the wisdom of its rulers, and the ingenuity and invention of its creators. It was nothing less than an apotheosis in stone – and subsequently in paint – of the city, in which the pedimental reliefs show all parts of the world paying tribute to Amsterdam, and its citizens were transposed into the centre of the universe when they walked on the marble maps laid in the floor of the Citizens' Hall. In this book, we try to understand the paradox that the Town Hall, despite defying all usual classifications was instantly hailed as a triumph, by investigating the constructions behind and beyond the construction: by analysing how poems, travel accounts or images together created constructions in word and image of the building, which aided in understanding this unique and stunning edifice, and in doing so, helped to construct, and perpetuate, its reputation of uniqueness.

A long tradition of architectural scholarship, inaugurated by Katharine Fremantle's still unsurpassed study of 1959, and enriched more recently by the work of Ottenheym, Vlaardingerbroek, and others, has produced many arguments for sources of parts of the design to be found in the treatises of Palladio and Scamozzi, and in reconstructions of the Temple and Palace of Solomon published in the sixteenth and seventeenth centuries. In his contribution to this book, Vlaardingerbroek argues very plausibly that the design was based on reconstructions of the Palace of Solomon by Juan Bautista Villalpando.[5] Basilicas as designed by Vitruvius and Palladio provided a typological solution for the handling of spaces.

This tradition is distinguished by what may be called a poetics of aetiology. Its main hermeneutic strategy is to find models, parallels and especially precedents for the building, thus attempting to place it in wider contexts of political, religious or artistic ideals and stylistic traditions that evolve through practices of learning, adaptation, imitation and emulation of the Vitruvian tradition as it was further developed during the Renaissance. It is highly scholarly, and supported by often circumstantial documentary evidence. But despite all its merits, and the important knowledge it has produced, it can never be conclusive, because we lack solid documentary evidence about van Campen and Quellinus's ideas, or those of their patrons.

This very inconclusiveness leaves room for different readings. Taking as its starting point the novelty and exceptional character of the building, I will consider anew two elements of its design: the triumphal arch motif; and festoons. Instead of an iconographic analysis of the sculptural ornament as a visual statement of civic and political ideals, the use of the triumphal arch motif will be considered as an architectural and sculptural manifestation of successor state behaviour; the festoons will be considered not as part of a Dutch emulation of Roman architecture, but as a vehicle for style transfer. The term 'successor state' is used to describe the states resulting from the demise of empires such as those of Alexander the Great, Rome or Charlemagne.[6] The Dutch Republic, which came into being after the disintegration of the Habsburg Empire, is clearly a case of a successor state. Although rarely employed outside political history, the concept is useful as well to understand artistic developments in which state patronage plays a major role, because it throws new light on the connections between political and artistic behaviour. In particular, it shows a recurring pattern of stylistic choice: successor states tend to revert to the style of the regime to which they claim to be the legitimate heir, or if that is lacking, to a style with a particularly relevant set of connotations or prestige. Thus, Augustus rejected Hellenism in favour of Greek Classicism of the fourth century BC, and Charlemagne tried to restore the style of the Roman Empire.[7]

Also, instead of taking the *all'antica* design to be the result of a process of learning to imitate Roman and Renaissance architecture, in which the ultimate aim is to display a perfect understanding of its principles and equally perfect judgment in adaptation to local circumstances without ever losing sight of the canonical rules of Renaissance architecture, the importation of architecture *all'antica* will be considered here as a process of stylistic transfer. In other words, the perspective is that of a movement away from the canon as developed in Greece and Italy. The Town Hall is here considered as the stone embodiment of the trajectory of classical architecture towards a new phase of transformation and appropriation, rather than as the result of an attempt to imitate oriented towards Greece and Rome. The vehicle for these new points of view will be a series of biographical vignettes of conspicuous features of the Town Hall that aim to recover their historical and cultural resonance in seventeenth-century Amsterdam.

The Dutch Republic as a successor state

With the Peace of Westphalia, the Republic of the Seven United Provinces was officially recognized as a sovereign state by Spain, France and the Vatican States. It thus became independent from the Habsburg Empire, and one of the successors to the Duchy of Burgundy, of which the Low Countries had become a part in 1428. In Pieter Corneliszoon Hooft's *Nederlandsche Historien*, an account of the Dutch Revolt that is modelled on Tacitus' *Annales*, there is a clear awareness that the Duchy of Burgundy was a successor state, originating from the fragmentation of the Roman Empire.[8] In European history, the Dutch Revolt was a unique event. It was not the first time that a group of citizens had broken away from their feudal rulers, however: Florence had done so in the thirteenth century, but to become a Grand Duchy that was officially still a liege of the Habsburg Emperors. The Republic chose its own dynasty to play the role of ceremonial and military leader, but this leader was always subject to the authority of the States-General. It had also won religious freedom.[9] This triumph posed interesting challenges. One of them was how the young Republic could claim legitimacy.

In the seventeenth century, such claims were still entirely conceived in terms of a pedigree. Thus James I, the first British king to rule over England, Scotland and part of Ireland, had his court architect Inigo Jones fabricate a Roman past, including a Roman origin for Stonehenge, to bolster his claim that in the process of *translatio imperii* Imperial Rome had migrated first from Italian Rome by way of Constantinople to Habsburg Vienna, and subsequently to Stuart London.[10] In the case of the Dutch, two possible, and equally artificial, pedigrees seemed plausible: one connecting the Calvinists to the Jews of the Old Testament, who like them, had to fight religious and political tyranny to find freedom; the other was to construct a lineage leading back to the Batavians who had first been close allies of the Romans, but subsequently revolted against them.

Considered in this light, the numerous classical allegories in poems written to celebrate the Town Hall take on a new meaning. Instead of slightly downtrodden and old-fashioned rehearsals of mythological court allegory, the tale of the gods coming down from their Olympian abodes to admire the Town Hall by Jan Vos, to name but the most sophisticated specimen, can now be read as an attempt to make the new state part of the classical tradition.[11] They all suggest that the Town Hall is just as fitting a screen on which to project Olympian mythology as the palaces of the Roman nobility who claimed their ancestry went back to Roman Republican families. Caspar Barlaeus' speech to celebrate the foundation of the Athenaeum Illustre in Amsterdam, the *Mercator Sapiens* of 1632, is perhaps the most sophisticated attempt to inscribe the Amsterdam merchant class into the classical tradition. Just as Leon Battista Alberti (1404–72) showed that painting and architecture could be fitting subjects for a humanist treatise, Barlaeus argued that commerce could be lifted from the acquisition of lucre to a more civilized activity. His peroration to the Amsterdam merchants concludes with the suggestion that Minerva will now join Mercury on the banks of the Amstel, as a result of what might be called successful successor behaviour: 'You are now treading in the footsteps of the most famous kings, emperors, and princes.'[12]

The description of the Town Hall in Danckerts' Introduction to the *Afbeelding van't Stadthuys* takes this search for a pedigree even further, because it opens with a localized version of the primitivist myth of the origin of human societies in the dispersal of tribes after the collapse of the Tower of Babel. The majority of primitivist accounts of the origin of society available to Danckerts go back to Alberti and Vitruvius and their aetiology of human society in the building of huts, that is in the collaboration and exchange needed for the development of crafts such as masonry or carpentry. They also draw on the Old Testament. But Danckerts gives a local twist to such fictional origins by stating that after the end of this first Golden Age, mankind needed town halls to have their fierce instincts and unruly behaviour curbed. Those of Venice and Rome are given as examples of this stabilizing role. The Capitoline Hill is credited with a substantial agency that manifests itself in its power to repel Barbarian invaders.[13]

The reference to both Rome and Venice is significant here, because Venice began to consider itself in the fifteenth century as the true successor to Augustan Rome. It started to use the myth of Venetian peace-making as a vehicle to propagate this image of itself, most prominently in the frescoes adorning the

Sala del Maggior Consiglio and the Sala dello Scrutinio in the Doge's Palace.[14] Macchiavelli (1469–1527) noted this in his *Discorsi*, translated into Dutch in 1615 and 1652, and a text which was widely read by European intellectual elites for its emblematic portrayal of the revolt against Rome's last king, Tarquinius Superbus.[15] But Venice also played a major role in the revival of one particularly meaningful element of Roman material culture, and used it to symbolize this variety of successor state behavior: the Roman triumphal arch. The first post-classical triumphal arch made of stone was the one the Venetians built for the *Ingresso della terra* of their city's Arsenal.[16]

Bringing the Roman Empire to the Amstel: The triumph

Triumphs are everywhere in the Town Hall. They are the first to address the visitor, in the reliefs of the Dam Square façade, which show the four parts of the world placing tributes at Amsterdam's feet and bringing homage to the city. In the Burgomasters' room, the chimney mantle has a relief showing the triumph of Fabius Maximus Cunctator, one of Rome's mayors (Figure 3.1). Although not very conspicuous, its location is highly determined, as it faces the very prominent and lavish display of Amsterdam's coat of arms in the Tribunal; next to it hangs the black marble version of Huygens' congratulatory poem for the Burgomasters.

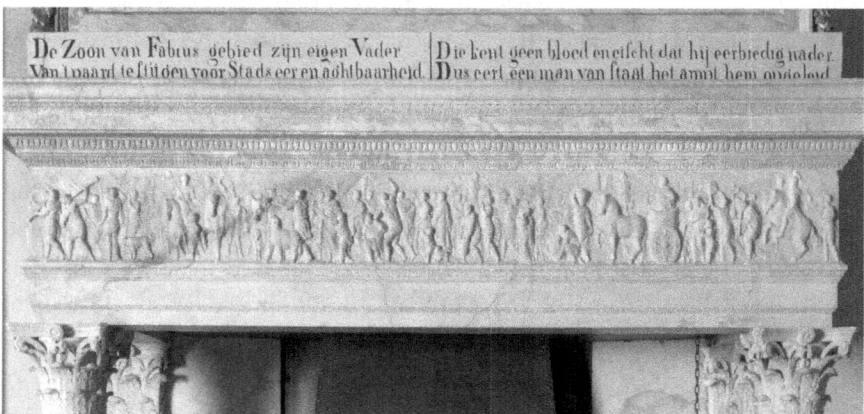

Figure 3.1 Detail of chimney overmantle relief in Burgomasters' room, showing the triumph of Fabius Maximus Cunctator attributed to Artus Quellinus. Courtesy Stichting Koninklijk Paleis Amsterdam. © The Royal Palace of Amsterdam, photograph: Tom Haartsen.

Other references are more indirect. Several doorway designs are derived from the Roman triumphal arch and its early modern descendants. They include the entrances from the north and south sides of the Citizens' Hall leading to what are now the royal appartment and Salon of the English quarter (Figure 3.2). Their massing of pilasters recall the triumphal gates erected for Maria de Medici's visit to Amsterdam in 1638. The monumental frames at both ends of the northern and southern galleries are a reprise of a Roman triumphal arch, such as that of Titus, with reliefs in the arches representing deities. The northern gallery, with Jordaens' *Peace of the Batavians and Rome*, has a monumental passage in the shape of a gate whose spandrels are decorated with allegorical figures and deities derived from Roman triumphal arches. In fact, Fremantle showed in 1961 that many of the allegorical figures and divinities in these reliefs are inspired by Rubens' designs for the Joyous Entry of Cardinal-Infante Ferdinand into Antwerp, published by Gevaerts as the *Pompa Introitus Ferdinandi* in 1642.[17] Thus, a large

Figure 3.2 Passage from the Citizens' Hall leading to what are now the royal apartment and Salon of the English quarter. Courtesy Stichting Koninklijk Paleis Amsterdam. © The Royal Palace of Amsterdam, photograph: Benning & Gladkova.

group of ceremonial transitional spaces, entries, gateways and pediments display features derived from the Roman triumph. It has often been noted that the entire decoration of the Town Hall can be read as an apotheosis of Amsterdam as the bringer of Peace and the centre of the universe – the divine, permanent counterpart to the human, ephemeral triumph lasting only a few days at most.

The meanings that the triumph carried for a cultured seventeenth-century designer or viewer have been far less studied. By its very functional and typological indeterminacy, the triumphal arch – a cross between a large sculpture and a building – lent itself very well to adaptation and transformation.[18] But it also attracted ambivalent feelings, and documented Christian tensions about the use of Roman architecture we rarely find mentioned explicitly in texts, most tellingly in Mantegna's Vienna *Saint Sebastian* (1456–9) where the ruined triumphal arch signals the collapse of pagan Antiquity.

Renaissance revivals of the Roman triumph and the artefacts associated with them are particularly telling illustrations of the agency and ambivalences surrounding the intrusive survival of Roman artefacts. From late Antiquity, the triumph became a symbol for Roman culture as a whole.[19] The ritual of the triumph was among the first elements of Roman culture to be revived in the early Renaissance, by fourteenth-century humanists such as Petrarch and Boccaccio. Petrarch's retelling of the triumph of Scipio Africanus in his epic poem *Africa* was probably the first post-classical attempt to reconstruct such an event and was largely based on Livy's description in Book XXX of *Ab urbe condita*.[20] The triumph also served as the hermeneutic device guiding one of the first attempts at a systematic antiquarian reconstruction of public and private life in ancient Rome, Flavio Biondo's *Roma Triumphans* of 1457–9. As early as 1326, the Condottiere Castruccio Castracane's entry into Lucca after his victory over the Florentines was a conscious attempt at imitating the triumphs of Caesar. This was the start of a long tradition that included a performance of the triumph of Augustus over Cleopatra under Pope Paul II in 1466, and a representation of the triumph of Aemilius Paullus for Lorenzo il Magnifico in Florence. When Pope Julius II, who was more concerned with the restoration of Imperial Rome than any other pope, celebrated his victory over Bologna in 1506, triumphal arches were scattered across Rome, combined with Christian altars to contain this invasion of pagan elements, culminating in a reconstruction of the Arch of Constantine in front of the Vatican.[21] Somewhat later in the sixteenth century, the Emperor Charles V also made a triumphant entry along the Via Sacra, which would become a major inspiration for subsequent entries north of the Alps. Across all the arts, and throughout Italy and subsequently the rest of Europe, the

Figure 3.3 Perugino, *Christ Giving the Keys to St Peter*, 1481, fresco, 330 × 550 cm. Vatican: Sistine Chapel. Photo Scala, Florence.

triumph became one of the most frequently used features of Roman culture to be reused, appropriated, and transformed in the Early Modern period.[22] Triumphal arches served as the setting for depictions of main episodes from the life of Christ and the Saints.[23] Perugino's *Christ giving the Keys to Saint Peter* (c. 1481–2) in the Sistine Chapel, for instance, is set in an imaginary Antiquity framed by two depictions of the Arch of Constantine with festoons added, to which I will return later (Figure 3.3). The triumphal arch thus served as a major vehicle for style and culture transfer, as was noted in the nineteenth century by Jacob Burckhardt, Gottfried Semper and Aby Warburg.[24] The latter even identified the ephemeral Renaissance recreations and revivals of the Roman triumph as the main channel through which the forms and rites of Greco-Roman culture were kept alive. Incidentally, the motif of transfer of Roman culture is announced in a discreet, but unmistakeable way in the title page of the *Afbeelding van 't Stadt Huys van Amsterdam*. There, the statue of Tiber displayed on the Piazza of the Capitoline Hill is transformed into a Dutch river.[25]

The reliefs depicting the triumph of Fabius Maximus Cunctator in the Amsterdam Burgomasters' Room are particularly evocative, because their composition clearly echoes scenes from Andrea Mantegna's *Triumphs of Caesar*.[26] The scene showing the triumphant general's chariot for instance clearly recalls Mantegna's depiction of Caesar's chariot, with the same massing of soldiers,

Figure 3.4 Andrea Mantegna, *Triumphs of Caesar*, Canvas VII: Julius Caesar, 1485–92, egg and glue tempera on canvas, 266 cm × 278 cm. Hampton Court. Courtesy Royal Collection Trust, Her Majesty Queen Elizabeth II 2020.

horses and standard-bearers (Figure 3.4). When the *Afbeelding* was published, these were in the collection of the Stuart kings in Hampton Court, but engravings and tapestry versions of the cycle had begun to circulate in the early sixteenth century, in Italy as well as the Low Countries. Erasmus Quellinus, the brother of Artus, who worked with him on the Town Hall, made a free copy which is now in Prague (Figure 3.5).[27] At the end of the century, the *Triumphs of Caesar* would become one of the most prized art treasures of King-Stadholder William III. He would have them cleaned and restored several times, and used them as inspiration for his own resplendent, and highly controversial, triumphal entry into The Hague in 1691, yet another major instance of a new ruler displaying a suitable, but invented pedigree.[28]

Figure 3.5 Peter Paul Rubens and Erasmus Quellinus, *Free Copy after Mantegna's Triumphs of Caesar Canvas II and IX*, canvas on oak panel, 87 × 91 cm, 1630s, Courtesy National Gallery, Prague.

Style transfer: Festoons and garlands

Both the exterior and interior of the Town Hall are covered in garlands, or '*festonnen*' as van Campen called them, but these have received little attention, despite their omnipresence. Van Campen obviously considered them very important, as he gave them such a conspicuous place, designing many of them himself. They also figure prominently in his other buildings, for instance in the designs for the gallery of Buren Castle attributed to him.[29] They were published in a separate volume, *Verscheidene Nieuwe Festonnen*, published in 1655 and 1678 (Figure 3.6).[30] They are also perhaps the clearest manifestation, together with van Campen's transformations of Corinthian and Composite capitals, of the process of style transfer at work in the Town Hall.[31] In his capitals he replaced the traditional

Figure 3.6 Title page of *Verscheidene Nieuwe Festonnen geinventeert door Iacob van Campen*, engraving by Michiel Mosyn after a drawing by François Dancx of a design by Jacob van Campen, 157 × 202 mm (Amsterdam: Frederick de Wit, 1655–78), Rijksmuseum Amsterdam, Public Domain.

elements derived from acanthus leaves, rosettes or heraldic elements, with objects signifying the sources of Amsterdam's wealth: fish, grain and fruit. The garlands are equally transformed from their Roman originals, such as those designed by Raphael for the Villa Farnesina, to display very plastic plump fruits, vegetables or sunflowers. Thus, they clearly illustrate how the Town Hall is not only an attempt at faithful imitation and emulation, on its own terms, of classical architecture. Van Campen also takes highly connoted key elements such as the festoons, and transforms them, in an act of appropriation, into an expression of local wealth and abundance. Rather than the model of flowering, decay and reformation developed by Huygens, as Bussels and Darnell have established, we can observe here at work how the transfer of style works materially: in the adaptation and transformation of classical elements into a new coherent design that speaks both of Roman origins and a new, Dutch episode in the *longue durée* of classical architecture.

But festoons have a much longer biography, once one realizes that they are the descendants of the garlands that in Greco-Roman Antiquity were used in sacrifice, or to honour gods and humans. Like festoons, garlands are part of the very large, and very old, family of honorific and protective structures made by pleating vegetal elements. They were used as symbols of consecration, and have been worn from time immemorial. In Roman sacrificial rites everything could be decorated with such garlands, but their use was also conspicuous in Roman triumphs, where the triumphant general and his army were allowed to wear them for the occasion. They may appear to modern observers as frivolous, enlivening and cheerful ornament, but their original role was much more serious: to protect the wearer, and change their status from the profane and the human into the sacred and the divine. They protected their wearer, but were themselves also protected, because they could not be thrown away after use.[32]

Even in Antiquity, garlands became the object of historical record and inquiry. In the context of this essay Flavius Josephus' *Jewish War* (c. 75 CE) is particularly relevant, since this text was an important source for the identification of the Dutch with the Jews. Here, garlands are presented as a particularly telling symbol of *Pax Romana* and the happiness which would result from it, the *Felicitas Temporum*.[33] They were also richly documented in an equally influential text, but from a rather different, Christian perspective, in Tertullianus' treatise *De Corona*. This diatribe against the Roman custom of crowning military heroes with garlands had the perhaps unintended effect of preserving much otherwise unknown material about these objects and their pagan ritual meanings. In the seventeenth century, their use was documented in the major essay in the historical anthropology of religion, Guillaume du Choul's *Discours de la religion des Romains* of 1631. Not surprisingly, they also appear in Gerardus Vossius' encyclopaedic overview of religious practice, the *De Theologia gentili et physiologia Christiana sive de origine ac progressu idololatriae ... libri ix*, first published in 1641. Since this is a history of idolatry, festoons are not integrated into a Christian tradition, but their exhaustive documentation in Roman religious practice did document their omnipresence in Roman culture for seventeenth-century Dutch readers.[34]

In the Renaissance festoons or wreaths and triumphal arches meet in an unexpected, but suggestive way: in Perugino's *Christ giving the Keys to St Peter*, the two images of the Arch of Constantine have considerable garlands made of green foliage added to their attic. This suggests some post-classical awareness of the association between the triumphal arch, the triumph, and the motif of the garland or festoon.

All this suggests that the omnipresence of garlands in the Town Hall is not simply a manifestation of van Campen's tendency to fill empty flat spaces with relief, or of a desire to decorate the building with the variety and opulence that fitted its elevated status.[35] When the origins of garlands in Greek and Roman religion are taken into account. as they were investigated in the seventeenth century by Du Choul and Vossius, to name but a few, they acquire a much richer meaning, if not agency, and function: that of protecting the building, indicating its divine status, and perhaps even suggesting God's grace, which is manifested in the abundance of harvests, and the wealth that Amsterdam derived from it.

Conclusion

This essay started with a reminder of the uncertainty and novelty of the situation of the young Republic in the 1640s, and the uniqueness of the Town Hall, which defied all usual classification, yet was instantly hailed as a Wonder of the World. By focusing on some features of the Town Hall that appear unobtrusive or rather minor, such as the references to the triumphal arch or the garlands, I have tried to show how looking at some episodes of the biographies of these elements, and the meanings they had for seventeenth-century viewers can help to think differently about what made this such a successful building. It did not exclusively impress the viewers so much because of what we now tend to see as a triumphant new chapter in the adaptation of models developed by Palladio or Scamozzi, the iconography, the stunning use of materials or its virtuoso *Raumgestaltung*. Something else is going on here as well. These features worked together to create that characteristic ideal of successor states: a new cultural memory by means of stylistic coherence while presenting this new memory as a return to ideal origins. Instead of effectuating a movement backwards in time, tracing the origins of design features, object biographies move forward, from their origins to their meaning in seventeenth-century Amsterdam. Thus, the Town Hall embodies the triumphant claim of a successor state to be the centre of the universe by incorporating objects from very old, but potent, traditions and cultural or religious practices such as the triumph or the sacrifice, in such a way that they give a solid foundation of historical precedent to this future-oriented projection of Amsterdam as the new Rome or Venice.

Notes

1 *Afbeelding van 't Stadthuys van Amsterdam, in dartigh coopere Plaaten, geordineert door Jacob van Campen en geteeckent door Jacob Vennekool* (Amsterdam: Dancker Danckerts, 1665), Introduction by Dancker Danckerts, 4.

2   See Koen Ottenheym, '"Defaecatissimis temporibus Graecorum ac Romanorum" : Constantijn Huygens' quest for the 'true' principles of architecture in 17th-century Holland', in *Reibungspunkte,* ed. Hans Hubach a.o. (Petersberg: Michael Imhof Verlag, 2008), 217–24, for the view of the introduction of Renaissance architecture as a triumphant dispersion of Gothic error created by Constantijn Huygens.
3   Lorne Darnell and Stijn Bussels, 'How to classicize Modern Architecture? Connections between Romans & Goths in the Dutch Golden Age', in *Antiquity in The Netherlands,* ed. Art di Furia (Amsterdam: Amsterdam University Press, forthcoming).
4   See Thomas von der Dunk, *Torens en traditie. De worsteling van classicistische architecten met een middeleeuws fenomeen* (Leiden: Primavera Pers, 2015); Koen Ottenheym, 'The Attractive Flavour of the Past – Combining new Concepts for Ecclesiastical Buildings with References to Tradition in Seventeenth-Century Holland', in *Protestantischer Kirchenbau der Frühen Neuzeit in Europa. Grundlagen und neue Forschungskonzepte – Protestant Church Architecture in Early Modern Europe. Fundamentals and New Research Approaches,* ed. Jan Harasimowicz (Regensburg: Schnell u. Steiner, 2015), 99–114; and Gabri van Tussenbroek, *De toren van de Gouden Eeuw. Een hollandse strijd tussen gulden en god* (Amsterdam: Prometheus, 2017). For the use of building styles to express unease and ambivalence, albeit in a later period, see Richard Wittman, *Architecture, Print Culture, and the Public Sphere in Eighteenth-Century France* (London: Routledge, 2007).
5   Cf. Pieter Vlaardingerbroek, *Het paleis van de Republiek. Geschiedenis van het stadhuis van Amsterdam* (Zwolle: WBOOKS, 2011), 72–5.
6   See for instance the essays by John F. Haldon, 'The Byzantine Successor State', and by Ian Wood, 'The Germanic Successor States', in *The Oxford Handbook of the State in the Ancient Near East,* ed. Peter Fibiger Bang and Walter Scheidel (Oxford and New York: Oxford University Press, 2018).
7   On successor state behaviour as a concept to explain stylistic choices see Tonio Hölscher, *The Language of Images in Roman Art,* trans. A. Snodgrass and A. Künzl-Snodgrass (Cambridge and New York: University of Cambridge Press, 2004) and 'Greek styles and Greek art in Augustan Rome: Issues of the Present versus Records of the Past', in *Classical Pasts: The Classical Traditions of Greece and Rome,* ed. J.I. Porter (Princeton, NJ: Princeton University Press, 2006) 237–259; C.A. van Eck and M.L. Versluys, 'The Hôtel de Beauharnais in Paris: Egypt, Rome, and the Dynamics of Cultural Transformation', in *Housing the New Romans,* ed. K. von Stackelberg and E. Macaulay-Lewis (Oxford: Oxford University Press, 2016), 54–92. *Ambitious Antiquities: Constructions of a Glorious Past in the Early Modern Netherlands and in Europe,* ed. Koen Ottenheym and Karl Enenkel (Leiden: Brill, 2019), although it does not analyse the constructions of a past in terms of successor

state behaviour, gives many instances that illustrate it. Most relevant in this context is the essay by Pieter Vlaardingerbroek: 'An Appropriated History: The Case of the Amsterdam Town Hall (1648-1667)', 455-81.

8   Pieter Corneliszoon Hooft, *Nederlandsche Historien* (Leiden: Elsevier, 1642 and 1654), see for instance the opening page.

9   See also Jonathan Israel, *The Dutch Republic. Its Rise, Greatness and Fall 1477-1806* (Oxford: Clarendon Press, 1995), 506-52.

10 See my *Inigo Jones rebuilds Stonehenge. Architectural History between Memory and Narration* (Amsterdam: Architectura & Natura Press, 2006).

11 Joost van den Vondel, *Inwydinge* (Amsterdam: Fontein, 1655), ll. 70-5, 145-55, 897, 977-80, 180-94; J. Vos, *Inwydinge* (Amsterdam: Lescaille), 338-9.

12 Casparus Barlaeus, *The Wise Merchant: Oration on Combining the Pursuit of Trade and Philosophy, Held to Inaugurate the Illustrious School of Amsterdam on 9 January 1632*, ed. and trans. Anna-Luna Post and Corinne Vermeulen (Amsterdam: Amsterdam University Press, 2019), 59.

13 *Afbeelding van 't Stadt Huys van Amsterdam* (Amsterdam: Dancker Danckerts, 1661), 1-4.

14 See Patricia Fortini Brown, 'Painting and History in Renaissance Venice', *Art History* 7, no. 3 (1984): 263-94; Filippo de Vivo, 'Historical Justifications of Venetian Power in the Adriatic', *Journal of the History of Ideas* 64, no. 2 (2003): 159-76.

15 See f.i. John Pocock, *The Machiavellian Moment* (New Jersey: Princeton University Press, 2016), Chapter Seven: Rome and Venice.

16 Heiner Borggrefe, 'Triumphal Arch', in *Brill's New Pauly*, ed. Manfred Landfester, English Edition by Francis G. Gentry. Consulted online on 20 December 2019 [http://dx.doi.org.ezp.lib.cam.ac.uk/10.1163/1574-9347_bnp_e15305350]

17 Kathrine Fremantle, 'Themes from Ripa and Rubens in the Royal Palace in Amsterdam', *Burlington Magazine* 103 (1961): 258-64. On the *Pompa* see most recently *Rubens' Pompa Introïtus Ferdinandi*, ed. Antine Knaap and Michael Putnam (Turnhout: Brepols, 2014).

18 On Roman triumphs in general see Mary Beard, *The Roman Triumph* (Cambridge, MA: Harvard University Press, 2007), and Ida Östenberg, *Staging the World: Spoils, Captives, and Representations in the Roman Triumphal Procession* (Oxford: Oxford University Press, 2009). On late Republican triumphs such as the one by Fabius Maximus see Carsten H. Lange, *Triumphs in the Age of Civil War: The Late Republic and the Adaptability of Triumphal Tradition* (London: Bloomsbury, 2016). On the triumphal arch's adaptability, see Richard Brilliant, *The Arch of Septimius Severus in the Roman Forum* (Rome: Publisher, 1967); and Antonio Pinelli, 'Feste e trionfi: continuità e metamorfosi di un tema', in *Memoria dell'antico nell'arte italiana*, ed. Salvatore Settis (Turin: Einaudi, 1985), vol. 2, 281-353. See also Bruno Klein, 'Napoleons Triumphbogen in Paris und der Wandel der offiziellen

Kunstanschauungen im Premier Empire', *Zeitschrift für Kunstgeschichte* 59 (1996): 244-69 for another, late instalment in the adaptation of the triumphal arch by yet another regime that saw itself as a successor state to the Roman Empire.
19   Antonio Pinelli, 'Feste e trionfi: continuità e metamorfosi di un tema', in *Memoria dell'antico nell'arte italiana*, ed. Salvatore Settis (Turin: Einaudi 1985), vol. 2, 281-353.
20   Werner Weisbach, *Trionfi* (Berlin: G. Grote'sche Verlagsbuchhandlung, 1919), 10-12.
21   Weisbach, *Trionfi*, 13-16, and Paul Kristeller, *Andrea Mantegna* (London: Longman's, Green and Co, 1901), 287-8.
22   Robert Baldwin, 'A Bibliography of the Literature on Triumphs', in: *"All the World's a Stage". Art and Pageantry in the Renaissance and Baroque*, ed. B. Wisch and S.S. Munshower, (University Park: Pennsylvania State University 1990), vol. 1, 359-85.
23   Borggrefe, 'Triumphal Arch' (see note 16).
24   Jacob Burckhardt, *Die Cultur der Renaissance in Italien* (Basel: Druck und Verlag der Schweigbauserischen Verlagsbuchhandlung, 1860), 355-426; Gottfried Semper, *Der Stil* (Frankfurt: Verlag für Kunst und Wissenschaft, 1860-1863), vol. 1, 'Excurs. Das Tapezierwesen der Alten', §66, 276-323; Aby Warburg, *Sandro Botticellis 'Geburt der Venus' und 'Frühling'* (1893), in: Aby Warburg: *Gesammelte Schriften (Die Erneuerung der heidnischen Antike. Kulturwissenschaftliche Beiträge zur Geschichte der europäischen Renaissance)*, ed. Horst Bredekamp & Manfred Diers (Berlin: Akademie Verlag, 1998), Bd I.1, 1-68 and 307-28, here 66.
25   'Ekstatische Nymphe . . . trauernder Flußgott', *Porträt eines Gelehrten*, ed. Robert Galitz and Brita Reimers (Hamburg: Warburg-Haus, 1995).
26   The main studies are: Charles Martindale, *The Triumphs of Caesar by Andrea Mantegna, in the Collection of Her Majesty the Queen at Hampton Court* (London: Harvey Miller, 1979); and the relevant entries in the catalogues of the exhibition on Mantegna held in the Royal Academy in London in 1992, and in the Louvre in Paris in 2008-09; see also Tony Halliday, 'The literary sources of Mantegna's "Triumphs of Caesar"', *Annali della Scuola Normale Superiore di Pisa, Classe di Lettere e Filosofia* 24 (1994): 337-96; Richard Cocke, 'The changing face of the Temple of Janus in Mantegna's "The Prisoners": politics and the patronage of the "Triumphs of Caesar"', *Zeitschrift für Kunstgeschichte* 55 (1992): 267-74.
27   Thomas Arlt, *Andrea Mantegna's Triumph Caesars: ein Meisterwerk der Renaissance in neuem Licht* (Vienna: Böhlau Verlag, 2005), 73.
28   Robin Simon, '"Roman-Cast Similitude". Cromwell and Mantegna's *Triumphs of Caesar*', *Apollo* 134 (1991): 223-7; Rudolf Dekker, *Family, Culture and Society in the Diary of Constantijn Huygens Jr, Secretary to Stadholder-King William of Orange* (Leiden: Brill, 2013); Ben Broos et al., *Paintings from England: William III and the Royal Collections* (The Hague: Mauritshuis, 1988); Alexander Dencher, 'Commemorating Conquest: The triumphal entry of William III of Orange into The Hague in 1691', unpublished PhD Thesis Leiden University 2020.

29 The drawing is reproduced in *Jacob van Campen. Het klassieke ideaal in de Gouden Eeuw*, ed. Jacobine Huisken, Koen Ottenheym and Gary Schwartz (Amsterdam: Architectura & natura Pers/Stichting Koninklijk Paleis, 1995), 128.

30 *Verscheidene Nieuwe Festonnen geinventeert door Iacob van Campen*, title page, engraving by Michiel Mosyn after a drawing by François Dancx of a design by Jacob van Campen (Amsterdam: Frederick de Wit, 1655-78). See Peter Führing, *Ornament Prints in the Rijksmuseum II: the Seventeenth Century* (Amsterdam and Rotterdam: Rijksmuseum Sound and Vision, 2004), 62.

31 Joost van den Vondel's *Inwydinge van 't Stadthuis t' Amsterdam* (Amsterdam: Fontein, 1655), lines 680-9 describes the columns as the bearers of Greek and Roman culture to Amsterdam.

32 See Rolf Hurschmann, 'Wreath, Garland', in *Brill's New Pauly*. Consulted online on 20 December 2019 [http://dx.doi.org.ezp.lib.cam.ac.uk/10.1163/1574-9347_bnp_e622060]; Charles Daremberg and Victor Saglio, 'Corona', in *Dictionnaire des antiquités grecques et romaines* (Paris: Hachette, 1877-1919), I.2, 1520-37 has a wealth of classical references and varieties of garlands; Richard Turcan, 'Les guirlandes dans l'art classique', *Jahrbuch für Antike und* Christentum 14 (1971): 92-139; Germaine Guillaume-Corier, 'L'ars coronaria dans la Rome antique', *Revue archéologique* N.S. 2 (1999): 331-70.

33 Flavius Josephus, *The Jewish War*, translated by Henry St John Thackeray (London: William Heinemann Ltd and New York: G.P. Putnam's Sons, 1928), VII.71-72, 526-7.

34 *De Theologia gentili et physiologia Christiana sive de origine ac progressu idololatriae ... libri ix* (Amsterdam: Pieter and Iohannes Blaeu, 1700), 51, 76, 106 and passim.

35 Festoons are also frequently mentioned in poems about the Town Hall, for instance in Everard Meyster's *Hemelsch Land-Spel of Godenkout* (Amsterdam: Gedruckt voor de Lief-Hebbers, 1655), 22; or Joost van den Vondel's *Inwydinge van 't Stadthuis t' Amsterdam* (Amsterdam: Fontein, 1655), lines 240 ff.

Bibliography

Baldwin, Robert. 'A Bibliography of the Literature on Triumphs.' In *'All the World's a Stage': Art and Pageantry in the Renaissance and Baroque*, edited by Barbara Wisch and Susan Scott Munshower, 359-82. University Park: Pennsylvania State University, 1990.

Barlaeus, Casparus. *The Wise Merchant: Oration on Combining the Pursuit of Trade and Philosophy, Held to Inaugurate the Illustrious School of Amsterdam on 9 January 1632*. Edited and translated by Anna-Luna Post and Corinne Vermeulen. Amsterdam: Amsterdam University Press, 2019.

Beard, Mary. *The Roman Triumph*. Cambridge, MA: Harvard University Press, 2007.

Borggrefe, Heiner. 'Triumphal Arch.' In *Brill's New Pauly*, edited Manfred Landfester. English Edition by Francis G. Gentry. Consulted online on 20 December 2019 [http://dx.doi.org.ezp.lib.cam.ac.uk/10.1163/1574-9347_bnp_e15305350].

Brilliant, Richard. *The Arch of Septimius Severus in the Roman Forum*. Rome: American Academy in Rome, 1967.

Broos, Ben a.o. *Paintings from England: William III and the Royal Collections*. The Hague: Mauritshuis, 1988.

Brown, Patricia Fortini. 'Painting and History in Renaissance Venice.' *Art History* 7, no. 3 (1984): 263–94.

Burckhardt, Jacob. *Die Cultur der Renaissance in Italien*. Basel: Druck und Verlag der Schweigbauserischen Verlagsbuchhandlung, 1860.

Cocke, Richard. 'The changing face of the Temple of Janus in Mantegna's "The Prisoners": politics and the patronage of the "Triumphs of Caesar".' *Zeitschrift für Kunstgeschichte* 55 (1992), 267–74.

Daremberg, Charles and Victor Saglio. 'Corona.' In *Dictionnaire des antiquités grecques et romaines*, vol. I.2, 1520–37. Paris: Hachette, 1877–1919.

Darnell, Lorne and Stijn Bussels. 'How to classicize Modern Architecture? Connections between Romans & Goths in the Dutch Golden Age.' In *Antiquity in The Netherlands*, edited by Art di Furia. Amsterdam: Amsterdam University Press, in press.

De Vivo, Filippo. 'Historical Justifications of Venetian Power in the Adriatic.' *Journal of the History of Ideas* 64, no. 2 (2003): 159–76.

Dekker, Rudolf. *Family, Culture and Society in the Diary of Constantijn Huygens Jr, Secretary to Stadholder-King William of Orange*. Leiden and Boston: Brill, 2013.

Dencher, Alexander. 'Commemorating Conquest: The triumphal entry of William III of Orange into The Hague in 1691.' Unpublished PhD thesis, Leiden University, 2020.

Fremantle, Katharine. 'Themes from Ripa and Rubens in the Royal Palace in Amsterdam.' *Burlington Magazine* 103 (1961): 258–64.

Führing, Peter. *Ornament Prints in the Rijksmuseum II: the Seventeenth Century*. Amsterdam and Rotterdam: Rijksmuseum Sound and Vision, 2004.

Galitz, Robert and Brita Reimers (eds.). '*Ekstatische Nymphe . . . trauernder Flußgott*', *Porträt eines Gelehrten*. Hamburg: Warburg-Haus, 1995.

Guillaume-Corier, Germaine. 'L'*ars coronaria* dans la Rome antique.' *Revue archéologique* N.S. 2 (1999): 331–70.

Haldon, John F. 'The Byzantine Successor State.' In *The Oxford Handbook of the State in the Ancient Near East*, edited by Peter Fibiger Bang and Walter Scheidel. Oxford and New York: Oxford University Press, 2018.

Halliday, Tony. 'The literary sources of Mantegna's "Triumphs of Caesar".' *Annali della Scuola Normale Superiore di Pisa, Classe di Lettere e Filosofia* 24 (1994): 337–96.

Hölscher, Tonio. 'Greek styles and Greek art in Augustan Rome: issues of the present versus records of the past.' In *Classical pasts. The classical traditions of Greece and Rome*, edited by James I. Porter, 237–59. Princeton, NJ: Princeton University Press, 2006.

Hölscher, Tonio. *The Language of Images in Roman Art*. Translated by A. Snodgrass and A. Künzl-Snodgrass. Cambridge and New York: University of Cambridge Press, 2004.

Hooft, Pieter Corneliszoon. *Nederlandsche Historien*. Leiden: Elsevier, 1642 and 1654.

Hurschmann, Rolf. 'Wreath, Garland.' In *Brill's New Pauly*, edited Manfred Landfester. English edition by Francis G. Gentry. Consulted online on 20 December 2019 http://dx.doi.org.ezp.lib.cam.ac.uk/10.1163/1574-9347_bnp_e15305350.

Israel, Jonathan. *The Dutch Republic. Its Rise, Greatness and Fall 1477–1806*. Oxford: Clarendon Press, 1995.

Jacobine Huisken, Koen Ottenheym and Gary Schwartz (eds.). *Jacob van Campen. Het klassieke ideaal in de Gouden Eeuw*. Amsterdam: Architectura & Natura Pers/Stichting Koninklijk Paleis, 1995.

Josephus, Flavius. *The Jewish War*. Translated by Henry St John Thackeray. London: William Heinemann Ltd and New York: G.P. Putnam's Sons, 1928.

Klein, Bruno. 'Napoleons Triumphbogen in Paris und der Wandel der offiziellen Kunstanschauungen im Premier Empire.' *Zeitschrift für Kunstgeschichte* 59 (1996): 244–69.

Lange, Carsten H., *Triumphs in the Age of Civil War: The Late Republic and the Adaptability of Triumphal Tradition*. London: Bloomsbury, 2016.

Martindale, Charles. *The Triumphs of Caesar by Andrea Mantegna, in the Collection of Her Majesty the Queen at Hampton Court*. London: Harvey Miller, 1979.

Meyster, Everard. *Hemelsch Land-Spel of Godenkout*. Amsterdam: Gedruckt voor de Lief-Hebbers, 1655.

Östenberg, Ida. *Staging the World: Spoils, Captives, and Representations in the Roman Triumphal Procession*. Oxford: Oxford University Press, 2009.

Ottenheym, Koen. '"Defaecatissimis temporibus Graecorum ac Romanorum": Constantijn Huygens' quest for the "true" principles of architecture in 17th century Holland.' In *Reibungspunkte*, edited by Hans Hubach a.o., 207–24. Petersberg: Michael Imhof Verlag, 2008.

Ottenheym, Koen. 'The Attractive Flavour of the Past – Combining new Concepts for Ecclesiastical Buildings with References to Tradition in Seventeenth-Century Holland.' In *Protestantischer Kirchenbau der Frühen Neuzeit in Europa. Grundlagen und neue Forschungskonzepte – Protestant Church Architecture in Early Modern Europe. Fundamentals and New Research Approaches*, edited by Jan Harasimowicz, 99–114. Regensburg: Schnell und Steiner, 2015.

Ottenheym, Koen and Karl Enenkel (eds.). *Ambitious Antiquities. Constructions of a Glorious Past in the Early Modern Netherlands and in Europe*. Leiden: Brill, 2019.

Pinelli, Antonio. 'Feste e trionfi: continuità e metamorfosi di un tema.' In *Memoria dell'antico nell'arte italiana*, edited by Salvatore Settis, vol. 2, 281–353. Turin: Einaudi, 1985.

Pocock, John. *The Machiavellian Moment*. New Jersey: Princeton University Press, 2016.

Semper, Gottfried. *Der Stil*. Frankfurt: Verlag für Kunst und Wissenschaft, 1860–1863.

Simon, Robin. '"Roman-Cast Similitude". Cromwell and Mantegna's *Triumphs of Caesar*.' *Apollo* 134 (1991): 223-7.

Turcan, Richard. 'Les guirlandes dans l'art classique.' *Jahrbuch für Antike und Christentum* 14 (1971): 92-139.

Van Campen, Jacob and François Dancx. *Verscheidene Nieuwe Festonnen geinventeert door Iacob van Campen*. Amsterdam: Frederick de Wit, 1655-78.

Van Campen, Jacob. *Afbeelding van 't Stadthuys van Amsterdam, in dartigh coopere Plaaten, geordineert door Jacob van Campen en geteeckent door Jacob Vennekool*. Amsterdam: Dancker Danckerts.

Van Eck, Caroline. *Inigo Jones rebuilds Stonehenge. Architectural History between Memory and Narration*. Amsterdam: Architectura & Natura Press, 2006.

Van Eck, Caroline and Miguel John Versluys. 'The Hôtel de Beauharnais in Paris: Egypt, Rome, and the dynamics of cultural transformation.' In *Housing the New Romans*, edited by Katherine von Stackelberg and Elizabeth Macaulay-Lewis, 54-92. Oxford: Oxford University Press, 2016.

Van Tussenbroek, Gabri. *De toren van de Gouden Eeuw. Een hollandse strijd tussen gulden en god*. Amsterdam: Prometheus, 2017.

Vlaardingerbroek, Pieter. 'An Appropriated History: The Case of the Amsterdam Town Hall (1648-1667).' In *Ambitious Antiquities. Constructions of a Glorious Past in the Early Modern Netherlands and in Europe*, edited by Koen Ottenheym and Karl Enenkel, 455-81. Leiden: Brill, 2019.

Vlaardingerbroek, Pieter. *Het paleis van de Republiek. Geschiedenis van het stadhuis van Amsterdam*. Zwolle: WBOOKS, 2011.

Von der Dunk, Thomas. *Torens en traditie. De worsteling van classicistische architecten met een middeleeuws fenomeen*. Leiden: Primavera Pers, 2015.

Vondel, Joost van den. *Inwydinge van 't Stadthuis t'Amsterdam*. Amsterdam: Fontein, 1655.

Vos, Jan. 'Inwydinge.' In *Alle de Gedichten van Jan Vos*, 338-339. Amsterdam: Lescaille, 1662.

Vossius, Gerardus. *De Theologia gentili et physiologia Christiana sive de origine ac progressu idololatriae . . . libri ix*. Amsterdam: Pieter and Iohannes Blaeu, 1700.

Warburg, Aby. 'Sandro Botticellis "Geburt der Venus" und "Frühling".' 1893. In Aby Warburg, *Gesammelte Schriften (Die Erneuerung der heidnischen Antike. Kulturwissenschaftliche Beiträge zur Geschichte der europäischen Renaissance)*, edited by Horst Bredekamp and Manfred Diers, 1-64. Berlin: Akademie Verlag, 1998.

Weisbach, Werner. *Trionfi*. Berlin: G. Grote'sche Verlagsbuchhandlung, 1919.

Wittman, Richard. *Architecture, Print Culture, and the Public Sphere in Eighteenth-Century France*. London: Routledge, 2007.

Wood, Ian. 'The Germanic Successor States.' In *The Oxford Handbook of the State in the Ancient Near East*, edited by Peter Fibiger Bang and Walter Scheidel, n.p. . Oxford and New York: Oxford University Press, 2018.

4

'Far More to Wonder, than to Fathom Completely': One Hundred Poems Devoted to the Town Hall

Stijn Bussels, Caroline van Eck and Laura Plezier

In seventeenth-century Europe, the laudatory poem was one of the most prominent literary genres.[1] Countless poems were written in praise of a person or object that played a major role in constructing social identities. Every memorable event in the political life of a nation or city and in the individual lives of the elite needed poets writing appropriate praise. Ascending the throne or taking important public offices, as well as the birth, wedding and funeral of preeminent persons were as a rule accompanied with verses that celebrated the virtues of these men and women. They were often intimately connected with art and architecture. Innumerable panegyrics were written to celebrate portraits and sing the praises of the sitter and the artist. In poems praising royal palaces or the houses and mansions of the rich, the qualities of the architecture were merged with the virtues of the owner or inhabitant.

This essay will relate the popularity of laudatory poems to the Amsterdam Town Hall. Panegyrics of paintings and buildings enjoyed a Golden Age in the young Dutch Republic.[2] Nevertheless, the poems are heavily neglected by Dutch literary historians, who dismiss them as cheap verses full of clichés purely written for money's sake. Art and architectural historians studying the seventeenth-century Republic disregard them because the poems lack a straightforward analysis of artworks or buildings; there would be too much poetic licence. The neglect is undeserved. This essay will clarify how the corpus of poems praising the Town Hall offer a unique insight into social and political perceptions of a major building. No other important public building of the seventeenth century in Europe, perhaps with the exception of Versailles, generated such a rich and varied poetical response.[3]

The poems document the perception of the Town Hall, by contemporaries who often directly witnessed its construction. They rehearse traditional themes in such poems, such as harmonious proportions and the use of rich materials. But they also speak of extreme reactions to the building and its art works. Creating amazement in the viewer or visitor was the ultimate objective. Third, poets often focus on the relation between the building and its founders. They suggest political contexts, connect artworks and the building itself with the politics of the Burgomasters and the city at large, and present the Town Hall as visible evidence of the excellence of those in charge. The poems frequently present the structure or its works of art as clear evidence of the prosperous future emulating previous Golden Ages, mostly taken from the Greco-Roman, Biblical or their own national history. Often, the logic of a *translatio imperii* is followed in which similar objects from a prosperous past are presented as evidence of an unbroken pedigree connecting the present to that past and paradoxically of a bright future as well.[4] Some poems went even further, creating an entirely artificial pedigree for the Town Hall, and by implication Amsterdam, as the rightful successor to the Jewish Kingdom of Solomon or the Roman Republic.

Starting from the political context shared by the Town Hall, its artworks and the poems, enables us to revisit this literary genre and more particularly the exceptional number of poems written to celebrate the Town Hall. Our research has brought to light more than 100 poems on the building, written from the early 1640s, when the first plans for the building were made, until the end of the century, with a surge around the laying of the first stone in 1648 and the inauguration of the building in 1655.[5] Even in seventeenth-century Europe, this was unique. Moreover, they display considerable diversity in length, genre, style and intended audience. The very first poem is a couplet by Mattheus Gansneb Tengnagel (1613–52) written in 1641. In 1655, Joost van den Vondel (1587–1679) wrote an ode of 1,378 lines on the inauguration of the Town Hall and Everard Meyster (1617–79) merged allegory and pastoral play, staging Vitruvius, Michelangelo and other famous architects. The corpus is also highly intertextual. Meyster explicitly mentions previous poets in his own poem as the ones who truly comprehend the amazing building. When the personage of Michelangelo is not able to fully comprehend the Tribunal by himself, he calls three Dutch poets for help. The literary topos of speaking with the dead is reversed, since a dead architect calls for living writers.[6] It must have had a surprising, if not humoristic, effect to hear the following verses come out of Michelangelo's mouth:

Ha van de Vondel, komt gy Asseling, gy Bos,
Gy schrand're geesten komt, maeck uwe tongen los,
En helpt ons met u Geest die geestigheên beschrijven,
Daer wy, en elck voorstil, en stom staen moeten blijven.[7]

Oh, come [Joost] van den Vondel, you [Thomas] Asselijn, you [Jan] Vos,
You shrewd spirits come, loosen your tongues,
And help us with your Intellect to describe these ingenuities,
Since we can only stand in front of it totally dumbfounded.

The close connections between the many panegyrics of the Town Hall – both implicit and explicit – also reveal a solid political embedding. Most of the poems present a similar discourse on the Burgomasters, presenting the grand building as a *pars pro toto* for their rule. Poets praise the Town Hall for its overwhelming impact on the visitors and see this as clear evidence that Amsterdam is the rightful heir to the Roman Republic governed by excellent Senators, or to the Jewish Kingdom of Solomon. Direct praise of an individual Burgomaster was not entirely out of the question, but could easily be considered inappropriate, or could lead to rivalry. Conspicuous spending, for instance in the deployment of rich materials such as Carrara marble, required a delicate balancing act in the Republic, as associations with royal public display had to be avoided. Poets also had to deal with the fact that Burgomasters were only appointed for one year. All these circumstances favoured a displacement of praise away from the persons of the Burgomasters towards their Town Hall.

Old traditions

Whereas the laudatory poems on the Town Hall are exceptional in number and in their close interaction with each other, they can be connected with rhetorical traditions going back to Antiquity.[8] The description of the palace of Alcinous (Homer's *Odyssey*, 7.81f) or the Sun Palace (Ovid's *Metamorphoses* 2.1f) shaped the genre of architectural description. In the Middle Ages, buildings were described in chivalric romance, such as Von Scharfenberg's *Jüngere Titurel*, which contains a description of the Temple of the Grail. This tradition feeds into later descriptions of buildings such as Chaucer's House of Fame, Marot's Temple of Cupid and Tasso's Palace of Armida. All these texts are about buildings that did not really exist. Nevertheless, they influenced the panegyrics of the Town Hall, by their expression of the amazement the buildings caused, and by contrasting this to everyday life. Humans are overwhelmed, stupefied and made ecstatic by the exceptional splendour brought before their eyes. These descriptions of wondrous architecture often have moral aspects, and thematize our relation to what is extremely high above us, which Ovid calls *sublimis*. The Roman poet discusses human reactions to the sublime Sun Palace by contrasting the morally negative *hubris* with the positive virtue *humilis*. Phaeton's ecstasy, caused by the Sun Palace, makes him haughty, which ultimately leads to his death.[9]

Another important rhetorical tradition is that of the *laus urbium*, the praise of a city.[10] Ever since Herodotus's description of Babylon in *The Persian Wars* (1.178.2), cities have been praised for their excellence. Following the revival of the genre by the Byzantine scholar Manuel Chrysoloras in his *Comparison of Old and New Rome* (a comparison of Rome and Constantinople), Italian and German humanists expanded the genre to include cities to the North of the Alps. Hans Sachs praised German cities, and Lodovico Guicciardini applied his rhetorical skill to cities in the Low Countries.[11] These *laudes urbium* do not give a neutral account of what can be seen in a city, but rather evoke its marvellous character and relate this to the great merit of the city's leaders and the dynamism of its citizens. There are many examples of leaders paying poets to write a *laus urbium*. This makes it difficult to see where wonder as an actual experience elicited by visiting a city stops, and where wonder as a propagandistic device to enforce the position of a founder begins, just as is the case with the laudatory poems on the Town Hall.

The rhetorical exercise of the description, or *ekphrasis* of an actual building, was another major tradition that shaped Amsterdam panegyric. These include classical authors' descriptions of the Seven Wonders of the World.[12] Originally meant to point ancient travellers to actual destinations and what would be the highlights of their journeys around the world, by the early modern period the Wonders of the World had been lost or destroyed. But the recollection of them still served as a fixed and authoritative reference for extreme possibilities in the display of power in periods of political, economic, and cultural greatness.[13] The idea of the successor state – which Caroline van Eck has discussed in the previous essay – is important here, as relating new buildings to the ancient wonders implied that the present would be a new period of flowering. Next to the Greco-Roman tradition there are also biblical descriptions of buildings, the most influential being the description of the Temple of Solomon, which in the medieval and early modern periods shaped the design of many churches. Solomon's Palace was an important model for the Town Hall as well, as Pieter Vlaardingerbroek has argued in his essay for this book.[14]

These three related rhetorical traditions – descriptions of fictitious architecture, the *laus urbium* and descriptions of real buildings – not only influenced the poems on the Town Hall, but were also extremely popular across all of seventeenth-century Europe. This can be seen in John Milton's fantastic Pandemonium, Thomas Greill's praise of Munich, Pedro Calderón de la Barca's glorification of the Retiro Palace and Madame de Sévigné's tribute to Versailles.[15] The country house poem is also part of this tradition. Influenced by Pliny the Younger's description of his villa, it blossomed in England in the work of Ben Jonson and Andrew Marvell and in France with Jean de La Fontaine and, as already mentioned, in the Republic in the work of Constantijn Huygens (1596–1687).[16] Finally the medieval tradition of the *descriptio templi* – the description of Christian churches with its strong theological overtones and tendency to present the building as a material manifestation of the divine – which goes back to Eusebius' description of the inauguration of an early-Christian church, and was continued by Paulus Silentiarius, and Suger of Saint Denis, enriched the rhetorical genres outlined here with theological elements. It continued to develop fully as a literary tradition in the seventeenth century, particularly in Germany and Britain.[17]

Praise put to political purpose

Due to a lack of interest in laudatory poems on architecture, a thorough understanding of their use in the seventeenth-century Republic, as well as in the rest of Europe, is lacking as yet. On the basis of our study of the poems devoted to the Town Hall, however, we can present some initial insights. Those written by the most celebrated poets were eventually published in collections and collected works, even during the seventeenth century. To begin with, however, most of the poems celebrating the new building were usually disseminated individually, as they were printed on loose sheets, and the more substantial ones on leaves bundled in simple quires without a cover. They were not unlike pamphlets, sold cheaply and easily distributed. Since most of the poems are closely related to the founders and present the Town Hall time and again as a thing of pure wonder, they disseminated the intended effect widely, especially at the ceremonial events of the laying of the first stone and the inauguration which brought together a mass of people.

For the inauguration ceremony, the Burgomasters paid Vondel (among other poets) for his *Consecration (Inwydinge)* (Figure 4.1).[18] Here, the poet gives us an indication of what must have taken place during the ceremony, although this

Figure 4.1 Frontispiece of Joost van den Vondel, *Inwydinge van 't Stadthuis t' Amsterdam* (Amsterdam: Fontein, 1655), photo by author.

of course is seen through the lens of praise. Vondel describes how thousands of men and women are standing at the gates eager to enter the city and to participate in the ceremony of the Burgomasters and the Magistrates entering the building in parade. To describe the role of the bystanders, Vondel uses the word 'inzingen' which is a contraction of 'zingen' (to sing) and 'inzegenen' ('to consecrate').[19] This harmonious union in song echoes the Burgomasters' desire for a perfect *communitas*. The *Wilhelmus*, commemorating William the Silent, the founding father of the Dutch Republic (which centuries later became the national anthem) and other popular songs dating from the Dutch Revolt were sung together. Besides, as many panegyrics celebrating the ceremony were written in Dutch in simple rhyme and rhythm, we can assume that the short poems could have served as songs for this special occasion as well.[20]

Anthology

In what follows, we give the first English translations of some of the most significant laudatory poems on the Town Hall. We follow a chronological order. Starting with the very first poem published in 1641, and then continuing with odes devoted to the laying of the first stone in 1648, we pay special attention to the poems written in 1655, the crucial year for the Town Hall when it was officially put to use. In that year, many remarkable verses where devoted to the building, often with an explicit reference to the festive occasion and the founders. Poets constantly emphasize the connection between the founders and the building in the years after the inauguration. We end our anthology in the 1660s, when the largest sums to finance the huge building project had already been spent. Poets could now explicitly connect a specific Burgomaster or another prominent figure from the Amsterdam elite individually to the Town Hall, often in poems written for births, weddings and funerals. Whereas the huge cost was still an issue in the 1650s, a decade later this was felt less urgently and therefore individual connections with the building could far more easily be made without making the person of praise too vulnerable for critique.

The first poem

Mattheus Gansneb Tengnagel, notorious for his invectives and scabrous verses, wrote his *Amsterdam Linden Leaves* (*Aemsterdamsche Lindebladen*) in 1641 in an attempt to strengthen his reputation as a poet.[21] This volume of laudatory poems on his beloved birthplace contains a couplet which offers the very first praise of the future Town Hall. It was probably written shortly after the city council had decided to build it (see Pieter Vlaardingerbroek's essay in this book). Thus, the work that would shortly lead to innumerable verses, had very humble origins. Moreover, it is uncertain how the poem was received, what the Burgomasters thought of it, let alone if they commissioned it, and whether it improved the poet's bad reputation. Nevertheless, Tengnagel's two verses already address some important elements of praise which would often return in subsequent poems. Whereas it was still unclear what the building would look like, the poet already builds in his two verses a solid basis to defend its construction by presenting it as a consolidation of the city's prosperity and the resulting flowering of the arts. His clever play on the double meaning of the Dutch '*toekomend*', which can mean both 'future' and 'arriving', conveys the sense that, even though the appearance of the Town Hall was still unknown, it was close to being realized. By mentioning a temple to administer justice, he invokes the Temple of Jerusalem and reminds his readers that the Amsterdam citizens are the new Chosen People, a frequent argument in later laudatory poems. Tengnagel's reference to divine jurisdiction corresponds to the importance the Burgomasters gave to the Tribunal from the first plans for the building.[22]

Op het toekomende Raedhuis
De rijckdom en de konst, die meester, deese knecht,
Zijn uyt op Tempelbouw voor 't Goddelijcke recht.[23]

On the future Town Hall
Riches and art, one master, the other servant,
Aim at edifying a Temple for Divine jurisdiction.

Ceremonial odes

Although Joost van den Vondel wrote his most famous poem on the Town Hall for the occasion of its inauguration in 1655, the poet dedicated an elaborate poem to the laying of the first stone in 1648 as well. In the latter, he dramatizes the ceremony by using the format of a tragic chorus with its strophe, anti-strophe and epistrophe. Through this experiment in dramatization, the poet tried to emulate Greco-Roman literary models, just as he was doing in his tragedies of the same period.[24] Appropriating the ancient literary model was one way of placing Amsterdam's recent success in the classical tradition. But his emulation went beyond such formal aspects by introducing the cities of Athens, Rome and Amsterdam as if they were living persons. Athens is personified as an architectural connoisseur and Rome as a successful conqueror, but Amsterdam is the person combining these two qualities. Thanks to her colonial expansion, the city conquered much larger territories than Rome had ever done. Moreover, the city also started to construct the Town Hall. Although the building was not yet visible, Vondel already describes it as such an impressive building that it even amazes Athens. The description of the four young sons or nephews of the Burgomasters who ceremonially laid the first stone connects the past, present and future, as it predicts dynastic longevity for the city's political elite. This insistence on the building as an embodiment of the connections between past, present and future is another frequent theme in the poems.

Zang.
Athene en Rome dragen by
Een zonderlinge lievery

Van kunsten, elck in zijn gewest.
De Bouwkunst voegt Athene best,
En andre wetenschappen meer;
Het strijdbre Rome voeght een speer
En schilt, gelijck een krijghsheldin,
Op datze 't aerdrijck overwinn',
En met den Burgemeestersrock,
Dan alles wat zij overtrock
Met vliegende Arenden, haer Goôn,
Berechte, en onder haar geboôn
Doe zwichten d'overheerde liên,
Die 't aertsgebiet naer d'oogen zien.
Dus zijnze beide in lof zoo rijck,
Elckandre in zegen ongelijck,
Het zy bij nootlot, of geval;
Want een bezit het zelden al.[25]

Tegenzang.
Maer AMSTERDAM, zoo zwaer met gout
Gekroont, en uit Godts schoot bedouwt
Met zegen, voert haer oorloghsvlagh
Tot in den ondergaenden dagh,
Van 't blozende Oosten, en beklimt,
Van daer de steile Noortbeergrimt,
De Zuidas met haer stoute kiel.
Zymint den Vrydom als haer ziel,
En na dien dierbevochten schat
Zoo kroontze 't merktvelt van de stadt,
Den Visschersdam, met een gebouw
Waer voor d'Athener strijken zou,
En stom staen met zijn open mondt;
Hoewel hy zich den bouw verstont;
Hij zou gerief en majesteit
En tijtverdurende eeuwigheit
Verknocht zien in een Hoofdgesticht,
De glori van mijn bouwgedicht.

Toezang.
Geen droevig voorspook kan men ramen
Uit uwen grontbouw; PANKRAS, GRAEF,
En VALCONIER, en SCHAEP, uw Namen,

In witten marmer, net en braef
Gehouwen, houden hunnen luister,
   En flonckren in den zwarten nacht,
Als klare starren, die by duister
   Ontfangen grooter glans, en kracht.
Bezwalcktze, in 't bloejen van uw jaren,
   Met geen gebreken: volght uw bloet,
Die 't Burgemeesters-ampt bewaren,
   En houdt dien burgerlijcken voet,
Als rechte Neven, rechte Zoonen;
Zoo zal de Deught uw jaaren kroonen.

Strophe

Athens and Rome contribute
An extraordinary love
For the arts, each in its own domain.
Athens applies Architecture best,
As well as many other sciences;
Soldierly Rome adds a spear
And a shield, like a war heroine,
To make Amsterdam conquer the world,
And judge, wearing the burgomasters' tabard
All [regions] that she commands
With flying Eagles, her Gods,
And subjugate under her laws
Those she dominates
Who want to comprehend her wishes.
Thus they are both to be praised fully,
Incomparable to each other in victory,
Through fate, or coincidence;
As one can only seldom possess it all.

Antistrophe.

But AMSTERDAM, so heavily crowned
With Gold, and covered with dew from God's bosom,
Leads her battle flag to victory
Until the setting day ,
Of the blushing East, and climbs,
From there to the steep Arctic Circle,
[Sails till] the South Pole Circle with her brave keel.
She loves Freedom as her soul,
And after this hard-fought treasure

She crowns the market of the city,
The Fishers' Dam [Dam Square], with a building
To which the citizen of Athens would yield,
And stand dumbfounded with open mouth;
Although he did comprehend architecture;
He would have seen comfort and majesty
And eternity that endures eternity
Knit together in a Principal Edifice,
The glory of my building poem.

Epistrophe
No sad phantom will emerge
From these foundations; PANKRAS, GRAEFF,
And VALCONIER, and SCHAEP, your Names,
   Carved clearly and assiduously in white marble,
Will keep their splendour
   And will radiate in the dark night,
As bright stars, that by darkness
   Receive even more radiance, and power.
Do not sully them, in the flowering of your years,
   With any failing: follow your blood,
That preserves the Burgomasters' Office,
   And keep this civil way of life
As straight Cousins, straight Sons;
Thus Virtue will crown your years.

The most famous poem

To celebrate the inauguration of the Town Hall in 1655, Vondel wrote what would become the most famous laudatory poem devoted to the building, a poem of no less than 1,378 lines, paid for by the Burgomasters.[26] Many other poets tried to emulate this. Vondel's main aim was to defend the huge building costs by presenting Amsterdam as the centre of the world and therefore evidently in need of a magnificent building. The poet follows a proto-capitalist logic in which the costs are legitimised as an investment in the future.

  1   Gelijck nu d'ackerman de zeissen slaet in d'airen,
          En heenstreeft, door een zee van gout en goude baren,
          Zoo weckt ons Amsterdam, door overvloet van stof,
          Om in den vruchtbren oeghst van zijnen rycken lof
  5   Te weiden met de penne, en vrolijck in te wyen
          De hoogtijdt van 't Stadthuis en burgerheerschappyen,

        Met een de jaermerckt, die, met haeren open schoot,
        Alle omgelege steên en bontgenooten noodt
        Op 't heerelijck bancket van allerhande gading,
10   Die 't nimmer zat gezicht genoegen en verzading
        Belooft, door zoo veel schat, gerief, verscheidenheên,
        Als kunst en hantwerck hier nu stapelen op een.
        Dat zoo veel duizenden, als sterck ter poorte indringen,
        Zich spoeden naer den Dam, om 't wyfeest in te zingen,
15   In 't midden van ons vloên, den Amstel en het Y,
        Met al de burgerjeught van d' oude en nieuwe Zy,
        Op 't heldere geklanck der zilvere trompetten,
        Het dondren van kortouwe, en maetklanck van musketten,
        Het vliegen van de vaene, en luid triomfgeschal;
20   Terwijl elck element van blyschap juichen zal,
        De hemel huppelen, en alle starretranssen
        In 't ronde, als hant aen hant, rontom ons Raethuis danssen,
        De Bruit, daer 't al om danst, en die, zo fier en ryck,
        Op haeren schoonsten dagh en 't kussen, zit te pryck.
25   De Leeuw des hemels schynt de hoofstadt van de landen
        Wiens schilt gehanthaeft wort van leeuwen, onder 't branden
        Te zeegnen, met een lucht, uit zyne keel gestort,
        Te maetigen zyn vier, om frisch en onverdort,
        De graftlaen en het loof der boomen te bewaeren.
30   De straelen van zyne maene en glinsterende hairen
        En oogen steecken niet zoo vinnigh op ons hooft;
        Als had hy dezen dagh en zyn triomf belooft
        Een koele lentezon: want dit gestarnt, by vlaegen,
        Den geest verstickende, door 't gloên der heetste dagen
35   En weecken, koestert nu den zanglust, en de Min,
        En Oegstmaent gaet met lust, gelijck de Maymaent, in.
           Ghy Heeren, die de Stadt, gelyck vier hooftpylaeren,
        Met raet en wysheit stut, in 't rypste van uw jaeren,
        Grootachbre Vryheer GRAEF, en Ridder MAERSEVEEN,
40   Oprechte telgh van POL, en SPIEGEL, die 't Gemeen
        Ten burgerspiegel streckt, gewaerdight ons gezangen
        Te hooren, daer 't muzyck uw' intre zal ontfangen
        Met blyschap op den stoel, en 't eerlyck wapenkruis;
        Uw burgermeesterschap het ingewyt Stehuis
45   Vercieren, meer dan kunst, besteet aen witte marmers;
        En d'oude burgery haer hoofden en beschermers

Begroeten, uit den drang, van overal vergaêrt.
De burgervaders zyn met recht alle eere waert.[27]

1   *Just like a farmer cuts the ears with his scythe,*
    And glides through a sea of gold and golden waves,
    Similarly, Amsterdam exhorts us by its abundance of subject matter
    To pasture with our pen in the fertile harvest of its rich praise
5   *And to inaugurate full of joy the great moment*
    Of the Town Hall and the rule of burghers,
    At the moment of the annual market which, with open arms,
    Invites all surrounding cities and allies
    For a delicious banquet to everyone's taste
10 *And which promises joy and satisfaction to faces that never tire,*
    Thanks to so many treasures, commodities, varieties,
    As art and artisanry have accumulated here.
    So many thousands, eagerly entering the gates,
    Hurry towards Dam Square, to start the inauguration ceremony with their song,
15 *With, in the middle of our throng, the rivers Amstel and Y*
    Bringing all youth of the old and the new part of town,
    On the clear sounds of silver trumpets,
    The thunder of artillery, and the rhythmical sound of muskets,
    The flying of flags, and loud triumphal horn blowing;
20 *While every element will rejoice in happiness,*
    Heaven will skip, and all stars of the galaxies
    Dance in the round, hand in hand, around the Town Hall,
    The Bride, the centre of the dancing universe, and who, so proud and rich,
    sits triumphant in her most beautiful day and seat.
25 *The Lion of heaven [the sun] shines over the capital of countries,*
    Whose shield is supported by lions, and blesses
    While burning with a breeze coming from his throat.
    He tempers his fire in order to preserve
    Fresh and unwithered the canals and the foliage.
30 *The rays of his manes and glittering hair*
    And of his eyes do not viciously pierce our head;
    As if he had promised for this triumphal day
    A fresh sun of spring: as this constellation, at moments,
    Suffocating our mind with the glow of the hottest days
35 *And weeks, now fosters the lust for songs and love*
    In the Harvest Month, just as he does in the Month of May.

> *You Lords, who support the City like four central pillars*
> *With advice and wisdom, in the most mature of your years,*
> *Most venerable nobleman GRAEF, and Knight MAERSEVEEN*
> 40 *Honest scion of POL, and SPIEGEL, who offers*
> *To the common people a burgher-mirror, deign to hear*
> *Our songs, since the music will grace your joyful entry*
> *on the seat and the honest cross [of Amsterdam's coat of arms];*
> *Your Burgomastership adorns the inaugurated Town Hall*
> 45 *Even more than the art lavished on white marble;*
> *And the throng of old citizenry, gathered from everywhere,*
> *Who wants to greet its leaders and protectors.*
> *The fathers of burghers deserve all honour.*

Jacob van Campen and Daniel Stalpaert surpassed Orpheus and Amphion, as the former did not use magic to move forests for the foundations and stones for the building of the Town Hall. However, Vondel was unable to pass by the struggle between van Campen and Stalpaert which ultimately led to van Campen leaving the building project, and being absent at the inauguration. The conflict was probably caused by a difference of opinion about the construction of the vaults of the galleries and the large rooms adjacent to the Citizens' Hall, in which the Burgomasters followed Stalpaert's view.[28]

> (...) heeft Orfeus eertijts bossen
> 555 Verplant met zijne lier, Amfion met zijn snaer
> De steenen oit verzaemt, om Thebe wonderbaer
> Te stichten tot een stadt; 't is t'Amsterdam gebleecken
> In waerheit, onverbloemt, en zonder dichters streekcen.
> Het Noortsche mastbosch neemt het Raethuis op den rugh.
> 560 De rots van Benthem danst, de Wezerstroom wordt vlugh.
> De Wester marmerklip den maetzang volght van Kampen
> En Stalpaert, die bezweet noch arbeit vliên, noch rampen,
> Noch opspraeck, nu en dan gesprongen van hun scheen,
> Te vrede datze zich verbouwen voor 't Gemeen.

> *Where Orpheus once transplanted*
> 555 *Forests with his lyre, and with his strings Amphion*
> *brought together stones, to found Thebes*
> *Miraculously as a city; this became manifest in Amsterdam*
> *In truth, without any poets' tricks.*
> *The Northern forest of poles takes the Town Hall on its back.*
> 560 *The rock of Bentheim dances, the stream of the river Weser quickens.*

*The Western marble cliff follows the harmony of Campen
And Stalpaert, who in sweat do not avoid hard work, nor disasters,
Nor discredit, which sometimes snaps at their ankles,
But happy that they can serve the Common cause.*

The builders of the Town Hall not only surpassed the mythological heroes, but the architects Vitruvius and Apollodorus of Damascus as well. The latter was famous for constructing Trajan's Column.

>   Vitruvius trede aen,
> En zelf Apollodoor, bouwmeester van Trajaen,
> Wiens naelt noch heden praelt te Rome, voor onze oogen;
> 650 Zy vinden dit gebouw door al zyn leên voltogen,
> Van boven tot beneën. geene outheit dit verdooft.
> Het heeft zyn middenlijf, zijne armen, voeten, hooft,
> En schouders, elck om 't netst. het heeft zyn ingewanden,
> Elck lidt, elck ingewant zyn ampt, gebruick, en standen.
> 655 Hier leeft en zweeft de ziel van ons Wethoudery,
> Gelyck een Godtheit, in, en ziet het zeilryck Y
> Met 's weerelts oeghsten en Oostindiën geladen.

>   *Enter Vitruvius,
> And even Apollodorus, the architect of Trajan,
> Whose needle [column] this very day adorns Rome before our eyes;
> 650 They find this building perfect in all its members,
> From up till down. No antiquity can mute this.
> It has its torso, its arms, feet, head,
> And shoulders, all at their best. It has its intestines,
> Every member, every bowel its task, use and hierarchy.
> 655 Here lives the soul of our City Council,
> Like a Deity, and sees the river Y full of sailing ships
> Loaded with the world's harvests and East-Indian cargo.*

Vondel starts his praise of the decorations of the Town Hall by pointing at the use of the Composite and the Corinthian order, presented here as the bringers of Greek culture to Amsterdam.

>   Men ziet, van buiten en van binnen, drie kolommen,
> Gekoren uit de vyf aeloude, konstigh brommen,
> In bey de stadiën, voor 't opgetogen oogh.
> De laegste uit twee gemengt, en d'ongemengde om hoogh.
> 685 D'Ionische, en Korintsche, als in een huwlijck, onder,
> Gesmolten ondereen, wort, tot een weereltsch wonder,

Gedraegen van den voet, en draeght Korinthen weêr
Uit Griecken t' Amsterdam om hoogh, tot Aemstels eer.

One sees, outside and inside, three columns,
Chosen from the five ancient, artfully on display,
On both floors, for the elated eye.
The lowest is mixed of two, the unmixed the highest.
685 *Below, the Ionic and Corinthian, as in a marriage*
Fused together, are elevated by a pedestal
Into one of the world's wonders, and carry in their turn Corinth
From Greece to Amsterdam to the honour of the Amstel.

By the end of the poem, it has become evident that every architect or artist in Europe will have to study the building and its artworks closely to become truly accomplished. The chain of *emulatio* is extended in time backwards from Greece and Rome to the Chaldeans, and now culminates in Amsterdam.

Wie nu bouwmeester, of een schildergeest wil worden,
Of Fidias in kunst en beeldehouwery,
1180 Die zal, uit gansch Euroop, zich spoeden naer het Y,
En onzen trotzen Dam, met penne, en verwe, en koole,
Om in dit nieuw Stadthuis, als in de hooghste schoole
Van Pallas, uit het brein van Jupiter geteelt,
Te tekenen al wat de leerlust hem beveelt
1185 t' Ontworpen op papier, en perckement, en doecken.
Zoo ging de Grieck van outs de kunst te Memfis zoecken,
De Roomsche jeught t'Athene, en elck by dien Romain.
Nu toont u Amsterdam, beknopt by een, in 't klein,
Wat Memfis wat Athene en Rome t' zamenhaelden;
1190 Toen deze, als eigenaers, met al hun leengoet praelden,
En zwoeren, elck om 't zwartst, met onbeschaemden mont,
Dat dit geen leenkunst was, maer ieders eigen vont,
Inzonderheit de Grieck, al kan hy niet ontschreeuwen
Dat d'eerste kunstbron vloeide uit d'ader der Chaldeeuwen.

Who now wants to become an architect or painter,
Or Phidias in art and sculpture,
1180 *Will have to hasten from all over Europe to the river Y,*
And to our proud Dam, with pencil, paint, or charcoal,
To draw in the new Town Hall, since it was created in the highest school
Of Pallas, born from the head of Jupiter,
All what the passion for learning orders him

1185 To design on paper, parchment and canvas.
Thus, the Greek of yore went to search the art in Memphis,
The Roman youth in Athens, and everyone with this Roman.
Now Amsterdam shows you, closely knit together, in a small space,
What Memphis, what Athens and Rome have brought together;
1190 When these, as owners, showed off all their borrowings,
And swore, in contest with each other, that they were their own invention,
Especially the Greek, but even though he cried loudest, he could not deny
That the first source of art sprang from the veins of the Chaldeans.

Vos emulates Vondel

With a laudatory poem of 1,000 lines written for the inauguration, playwright and glazier Jan Vos (1612–67) clearly wanted to charm the Burgomasters who had given him the commission for the windows of the Town Hall.[29] By doing so, he also competed with Vondel. At the time Vos felt confident, as his play *Aran and Titus*, premiered in 1641, was enjoying an unprecedented success on the Amsterdam stage, and was kept in repertoire for decades. Much of the play's acclaim was due primarily to its extensive staging of bloodshed, often inspired by Seneca's tragedies.[30] In the preface of a later play, Vos would admit that he emulated Vondel through the straightforward rendering of cruelties.[31] His poem on the Town Hall is also distinguished by a dwelling on the horrific aspects of the construction and its boundless engineering ambition.

> Men valt met macht aan 't werk. de schup gaat naar de gront.
> Men ziet ter hoolen in, als in de hel zijn mondt.
> Men graaft de graaven wech, op 't kerkhof vet van lijken.
> De dooden moeten voor de levendige wijken.[32]

> *The work is attacked with all might. The spade enters the soil.*
> *There they see holes, as in the mouth of hell.*
> *They dig away the graves, on the graveyard saturated with corpses.*
> *The dead have to give way to the living.*

> Noorweegen heeft voor 't Y haar bosschen afgehouwen:
> Men slaatze, door getal van handen, met metaal
> En yzre blokken, door de grondt, naar Plutoos zaal.
> Het hof van d'afgrondt dreunt door d'overzwaare slaagen.
> De Vorst van 't helsche ryk, omheint van zieleplaagen,
> Verschrikte voor 't geschal dat hem het hart doorboort.

For the river Y, Norway has cut off its forests:
They drive them, through number of hands, with metal
And iron blocks, through the soil, down to Pluto's hall.
The overheavy blows make the court of the abyss resound.
The Prince of the hellish empire, surrounded by infestations of souls,
Is terrified by the shattering noise that penetrates his heart.

Men ryt de boezem van het aardtryk gants in twee,
Om 't ingewant van steen, door beitels scharp van sneê,
En mookers hardt van staal, voor eeuwigh uit te scheuren.
De Berggoôn, die 't geweldt in 't hardt gebergt bespeuren,
Verbergen zich van angst in d'allerdiepste kolk.
D'alteelend' Aarde riep: wat naadert ons voor volk?
Wie durft myn steene troon met wapentuig belaagen?
Gy zult, o dartelen! uw stout bestaan beklaagen.
(...) neen, riep de Stadt der steeden:
Nu dat ik aan het Y, het lusthof van de vreede,
Een heiligh Raadthuis bouw, kom ik by u om stof.
De vruchtbaar' Aarde zweegh, en opende haar hof,
Op dat'er Amsterdam de steenen uit zou kappen.

They tear open the bosom of the earth, right in two,
To pull out for ever the intestines of stone,
With sharp chisels and sledges of strong steel,
The mountain gods, who feel the violence in the strong mount,
Hide in fear in the deepest gully.
The all-breeding Earth cried: What kind of people is approaching us?
Who dares to put siege to my throne of stone with weaponry?
Oh fools, you shall pity your bold existence.
(...) no, shouted the City of cities:
Now that I am building along the river Y, a place for peace,
A holy Town Hall, I come to you for materials.
The pregnant Earth was silenced, and opened her court,
So that Amsterdam could cut the stones there.

Support for van Campen

In honour of his neighbour, Jacob van Campen, the eccentric country gentleman Everard Meyster wrote his *Heavenly Pastoral Play* (*Hemelsch Land-Spel*).[33] It is arguably the strangest laudatory poem of all 100, combining praise of the rural setting around Amersfoort, a town close to Utrecht, in which both men had their estates, with praise for the Amsterdam Town Hall.[34] Also, the panegyric has the format of a pastoral allegorical play in which Jupiter orders Vitruvius, Apelles, Scamozzi, Raphael, Michelangelo, Holbein and Van Heemskerck to come to Meyster's mansion. The famous artists and architects explain to the Olympians assembled the wonders of the new building. This is not easy, as they have to acknowledge often that the wondrous construction leads 'far more to wonder, than to fathom completely'.[35] The play ends in total confusion with Michelangelo, the master of the *terribilità*, describing the heads of Medusa and the Fury Erynnis of the Tribunal (Figure 4.2).

Figure 4.2 Artus Quellinus and workshop, Medusa head in the Tribunal of the Town Hall, 1651–2, marble. Courtesy Stichting Koninklijk Paleis Amsterdam. © The Royal Palace of Amsterdam, photograph: E&P Hesmerg.

MICHELANGELO – Was 's rechters oogh, was 't Swaerd, en kroon in marmor steen
Opt aerdigst' uytgewrogt: verselschapt met twee hoofden
Vol slangh-hair opgepronkt, dien ons 't gesicht beroofden
Van voorts daer all's te zien; zoo warens' uytgeworcht,
Zoo zagens' op ons aen, of self het helsch gedroght
Erynnis, en Medus', ons levend' hadden willen
Verscheuren en vertreen; wy staen schier noch en trillen,
Als wy'r gedenken aen, my dunkt, sy volgen noch.[36]

JUPITER – Maer stil, sijns' ons hier niet dicht by? Ey luystert toch,
My dunck, uyt 't donderen, dat sy de reusen stuuwen
Ten leegen Hemel in, en teegen ons op-ruuwen
Al 't Goddeloost' gespuys, of yetwes diergelijck
Van berg' en wapen-klanck (vermetel aengedreeven)
Wil op ons Hemel aen; 't sa laetw'ons derwaerts geeven;
Licht houd' haer Pallas staen tot wy'r gekomen zijn;
Waer hulp in tijds by quam, daer weeck vaeck het fenijn.

MICHELANGELO – The judge's eye, his sword and crown were wrought
In a most artful way in marble: Accompanied by two heads
with dazzling display full of snake-hair, which blinds our eyes
to everything that would be visible there; They were wrought
In such a way that they stared at us as if even the hellish creatures
Erynnis and Medusa wanted to tear us apart alive,
and to trample on us; we are still trembling,
When we remember them, I think they still follow us.

JUPITER – But quiet, are they [Medusa and Erynnis] not nearby us? Oh listen,
Me thinks, listening to the thunder, that they push the giants
Towards the empty skies, and goad against us
All the godless brood of the subterranean realm.
Or similar clangour of mountains and arms (driven boldly)
Wants to storm our Heaven; let us go there;
Possibly Pallas can keep them away until we arrive;
Where help came in time, there venom often retreated.

Pure wonder

In 1657 Constantijn Huygens, the secretary of the Princes of Orange, wrote his *Congratulations to the Noble Lords Rulers of Amsterdam, in its new Town Hall* (Geluck aen de ee. heeren regeerders van amsterdam in haer niewe stadthuijs) to have it recited at an official dinner in honour of the powerful Amsterdam merchant Johan Huydecoper van Maarsseveen (1599–1661).[37] This may have been in support of Huydecoper's ambitions to become Burgomaster for the fifth time. Directly after the event, the poem was printed on loose leaves and widely distributed. Very shortly after the merchant was successful in his re-election bid, the poem was reproduced in calligraphy, commissioned by the Burgomasters. Framed in ebony, the calligraphed version of Huygens' poem adorned their room (Figure 4.3). Today, we can still see the poem displayed prominently in that room. Not the paper version, however, but one engraved in black stone made in the early 1660s. According to Huygens, Amsterdam is so strong that the new building will easily be replaced by a subsequent one that will be even better, just as the van Campen's Town Hall surpasses its medieval predecessor.

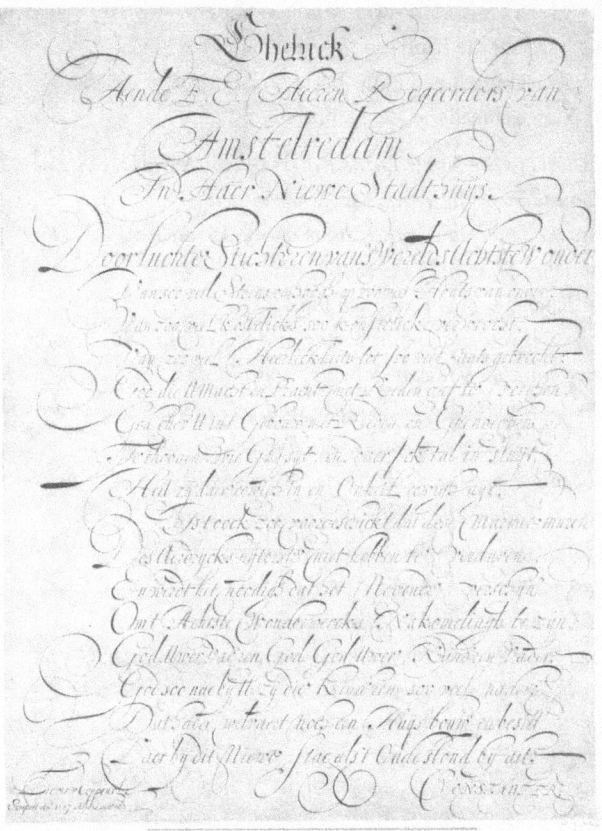

Figure 4.3 Lieven Willemsz. Coppenol, calligraphic writing with Constantijn Huygens' *Congratulations to the Noble Lords Rulers of Amsterdam, in its new Town Hall*, 1657, pen, 706 × 504 mm. Rijksmuseum Amsterdam, Public Domain.

Geluck aen de ee. heeren regeerders van amsterdam in haer niewe stadthuijs
Doorluchte Stichteren van 's Werelds Achtste wonder,
Van soo veel Steens om hoogh op soo veel Houts van onder,
Van soo veel kostelicks soo konstelick verwrocht,
Van soo veel heerlickheits tot soo veel nuts gebrocht;
God, die U Macht en Pracht met Reden gaf te voeghen,
God gev' u in 't Gebouw met Reden en Genoeghen
Te thoonen wie ghij zijt, en, daerick 't al in sluijt,
Heil zij daer eewigh in en Onheil eewigh uijt.
Is 't oock soo voorgeschickt, dat deze Marmer-muren
Des Aerdrijcks uyterste niet hebben te verduren,
En, werdt het noodigh dat het Negende verschijn'
Om 't Achtste Wonderwercks nakomelingh te zijn,
God, uwer Vad'ren God, God uwer Kind'ren Vader,
God soo naeby U, zij die Kind'ren soo veel nader,
Dat haere Welvaert noch een Huijs bouw' en besitt'
Daer bij dit Niewe stae als 't Oude stond bij dit.[38]

Congratulations to the Noble Lords Rulers of Amsterdam, in its new Town Hall
Illustrious Founders of the World's Eighth Wonder,
Miraculously made out of so much stone above, so much Wood below,
Of as many riches so artfully created,
Of as many delights brought so much to use;
God, who ordered you to combine Power and Splendour with Reason,
God may give you that you can show in the Building
Who you are with Reason and Pleasure, and, as I include the universe,
May Salvation dwell there eternally, and Evil be eternally absent.
It has also been pre-ordained that these Marble walls
Will not have to endure the final moments of the Earth,
And, would it be necessary that the Ninth appears,
To be the descendant of the Eight Wonder Work,
God, your Father's God, God, the Father of your Children,
God so close to you, even if those Children are so much closer,
May her Prosperity build and own a House
To which the New will stand as the Old to this.

Truly sublime

Huygens devotes a poem to the floor of the Citizens' Hall as well, which was at the time the largest interior secular space open to the public in Europe. On its

Figure 4.4 The Citizens' Hall of the Amsterdam Town Hall, courtesy Stichting Koninklijk Paleis Amsterdam. © The Royal Palace of Amsterdam, photograph: Wim Ruigrok.

floor visitors could admire two maps of the world and one of the heavens, after a design by the celebrated cartographer Willem Blaeu (Figure 4.4). With every map having a diameter of 624 centimetres (246 inches), they are the largest ever made and illustrated Amsterdam's position as the centre of cartography.

Op de aerdtcloot inden vloer van 't stadhuijs tot Amstelredam
Die op dit vloeren lett,
En op dit heerlijck welven,
moet seggen by syn selven,
Voorseker dese Wet
Bestaet in all' haer leden
Uijt hoogh vernufte lien;

Sij leeren ons met reden
De werelt te vertreden
En opwaert aen te sien.³⁹

Op den hemelcloot aldaer
Leert onder het gewemel
Van 'twoelighe Stadthuijs
Gedencken aen den Hemel,
En treedt vrij in 'tgedruijs,
Als vander aerd' geresen
Op Sterr en Son en Maen;
Hier werdt u in bewesen
Hoe dat het eens naer desen
Den saligen sal gaen.

On the globe in the floor of the Town Hall of Amsterdam
Who pays attention to these floors,
And to the delightful curve,
Has to say to himself,
For sure this Law
Consists in all its members
Of highly ingenious men;
They teach us with reason
To walk across the world
And to gaze upwards.

On the heavenly vault in the same place
Learn in the jostle
Of the crowded Town Hall
To bear in mind Heaven
And enter freely into the bustle,
As if you rise from earth
Towards the Stars and Sun and Moon;
Here it is proven to you
How it once after this [life]
Will turn out for the blessed.

A magnificent capitol

In his poem *Triumphant Amsterdam* (*Het triomfeerende Amsteldam*), Jan Zoet (1609–74), a proud citizen of Amsterdam, as well as a fierce defender of the Oranges, focusses on the stately reception of Prince William, the future

King-Stadholder William III, in 1666 in the Town Hall.[40] The poet celebrates the event as a reconciliation of the city with the Oranges. Their relation was seriously troubled, certainly after the so-called 'Attack on Amsterdam', a failed attempt by William's father, William II, in July 1650, to occupy the city and break the power of the Burgomasters.[41] At the start of the poem, Zoet puts the building in an international perspective of the most important governmental sites in European history.

> Myn praalrijk Kapitool verstrekte, in het byzonder,
> Aan 't allerkeurigste oog, meer dan een achtste Wonder;
> >   Want, waar 't gezigt zig keerd, daar staat het harte ontsteld.
> >   Wat, binnen Roome, eertyds, in 't pronktal wierd geteld.
> Dat moest, voor dit Gebouw, terstond de vlagge strijken.
> Het Keizerlikke Hof moet, voor de waarde wijken
> >   Van Amsteldams Stadhuis. De Louvre van Parijs
> >   Geeft, aan mijn meesterstuk, zeer gaaren d'opper prijs,
> Veel min kan Withal daar in 't allerminst by haalen:
> Maar 't geen mijn Keizerin, in volle praal, doet praalen,
> >   Niet in Albastersteen, in Kooper, Zilver, Goud,
> >   In Zinnebeelden, of in Schildery, daar 't Zout
> Des Staats op word verbeeld, op veelerhande wijzen,
> In 't allerminst bestaat. Men ziet mijn Hoofdzon rijzen,
> >   Door d'Agtbaarheeden van mijn Burgemeesterschap:
> >   Mijn *Valkenier*, mijn *Tulp*, die, met zijn geurig zap,
> De dooden haast verwekt, en wederom doet leeven.
> Mijn *Vlooswijk*, en mijn *Graaf*, op 't roer des Staats bedreeven.[42]

My magnificent Capitol gave, in particular
To the most discerning eye, more than an eighth Wonder of the World;
> *Because, wherever the eye looks, the heart is moved.*
> *Buildings in Rome previously flaunted*
Must before this Building immediately lower their flags.
The Imperial Court must bow to the value
> *Of the Town Hall of Amsterdam. The Louvre in Paris*
> *Gladly accords to my masterpiece the highest prize,*
Even less has Whitehall to compare:
But what makes my Empress triumph in full splendour, does not exist
> *In Alabaster stone, in Copper, Silver, Gold,*
> *In Emblems, nor in a Painting, where the Worth*
Of the State is depicted, in diverse ways,
My primary Sun can be seen ascending,

> Through the respectability of the office of the Burgomasters:
> *My* Valkenier, *my* Tulp, *who with his fragrant elixir,*
> *Almost rouses the dead, and brings them back to life.*
> *My* Vlooswijk, *and my* Graaf, *skilled in steering the State.*

A funeral

From the 1660s onwards, we see that poets increasingly describe the Town Hall as the particular achievement of one Burgomaster, often in verses written for the occasion of a birth or marriage of one of his descendants or his own funeral. For the funeral of the powerful Burgomaster Johan Huydecoper van Maarsseveen (1599–1661), for example, the family commissioned the respected classicist poet Lucas Rotgans (1653–1710) to write an elegy that would connect his rich political career with the Town Hall that he advocated so fervently.

> 't Was Maarsseveen, die voor een reeks van jaaren
> In d'Amsterstadt, uit Pallas heiligdom
> En Themis school, ten dienst der burgerschaaren,
> Langs vaders spoor op 't hooge Raadhuis klom.[43]
>
> Daar is zijn zorg vernuft en deugt gebleeken.
> Daar vond zijn geest, zo werkzaam, ruime stof.
> Indien ik zweeg, de beelden zouden spreeken.
> De vierschaar gaat nog zwanger van zijn lof.
>
> *It was Maarsseveen, who after a series of years*
> *In Amsterdam, from Pallas' shrine*
> *And Themis' school, at the service of the burghers,*
> *Climbed the high Town Hall following his father's trail.*
>
> *There his care, intelligence and virtue became apparent.*
> *There his spirit, so active, found much work.*
> *If I would keep quiet, the sculptures would speak.*
> *The tribunal is still pregnant with his praise.*

Notes

1 For a general study, see J.A. Burrow, *The Poetry of Praise* (Cambridge: Cambridge University Press, 2008). Additionally, there are many specialized studies, often from a political point of view, e.g. Terence Allott, 'Serious Games: Panegyrics of Louis XIV,

1686', *Seventeenth-Century French Studies* 14, no. 1 (1992): 65–8; Joanne Altieri, *The Theatre of Praise: The Panegyric Tradition in Seventeenth-Century English Drama* (Newark: University of Delaware Press, 1986); Mark Bannister, 'Heroic Hierarchies: Classical Models for Panegyrics in Seventeenth-Century France', *International Journal of the Classical Tradition* 8 (2001): 38–59; Stefano Colombo, 'The rhetoric of celebration in seventeenth-century Venetian funerary monuments' (PhD diss., University of Warwick, 2016), esp. Chapter 2; Jean-Jacques Gabas, 'La Fontaine et la louange de Louis XIV', *Seventeenth-Century French Studies* 6, no. 1 (1984): 111–19; James Garrison, *Dryden and the Tradition of Panegyric* (Berkeley: University of California Press, 1975); Stéphane Macé, 'Grandeur standing the test of death: Massillon's eulogy for Louis XIV', *XVIIe siècle* 269 (2015): 623–32; John McManamon, *Funeral Oratory and the Cultural Ideals of Italian Humanism* (Chapel Hill: The University of North Caroline Press, 1989); Victoria Moul, 'England's Stilicho: Claudian's Political Poetry in Early Modern England', *International Journal of the Classical Tradition* (May 2019), online: https://link.springer.com/article/10.1007%2Fs12138-019-00529-z (Consulted 2 March 2019); David Norbrook, 'Panegyric of the Monarch and its Social Context under Elizabeth I and James I' (D.Phil. thesis, Oxford University, 1978); Milan Pelc, 'Panegyric Emblem Books. Jesuits and the Habsburg Emperors: Some Examples Related to 17th-Century Croatia', *Primljen* 43 (2019): 59–74; Claude Summers and Ted-Larry Pebworth (eds), *The Muses Common-Weale. Poetry and Politics in the Seventeenth Century* (Columbia: University of Missouri Press, 1988).
2   See primarily Gregor Weber, *Der Lobtopos des 'lebenden' Bildes* (Hildesheim: Olms, 1991) starting from a long laudatory poem on painting by Jan Vos from 1654; Eddy Verbaan, *De woonplaats van de faam* (Hilversum: Verloren, 2011) concentrates on the *laudes urbium* in the seventeenth-century Republic (cf. infra).
3   E. Delerot, *Ce que les poètes ont dit de Versailles* (Versailles: Bernard, 1870).
4   See Karl Enenkel and Konrad Ottenheym (eds), *The Quest for an Appropriate Past in Literature, Art and Architecture* (Leiden: Brill, 2018) and Karl Enenkel and Konrad Ottenheym (eds), *Ambitious Antiquities, Famous Forebears. Constructions of a Glorious Past in the Early Modern Netherlands and in Europe* (Leiden: Brill, 2019).
5   This research is primarily done in the PhD project of Laura Plezier as part of the ERC starting grant 'Elevated Minds: The Sublime in the Public Arts in Seventeenth-Century Paris and Amsterdam'. She has studied poems entirely devoted to the Town Hall, as well as praising the building in a poem concentrating on another subject. Most of the poems that we can date come from the inauguration and the decade after this ceremony. Cf. Stijn Bussels, 'Meer te verwonderen, als immer te doorgronden. Het Amsterdamse stadhuis, een overweldigende burgerspiegel', *Tijdschrift voor Geschiedenis* 126, no. 2 (2013): 234–48 and Marijke Spies, 'Minerva's commentaar: Gedichten rond het Amsterdamse stadhuis', *De zeventiende eeuw*, 9, no. 1 (1993): 15–33.

6   Jürgen Pieters, *Speaking with the Dead: Explorations in Literature and History* (Edinburgh: Edinburgh University Press, 2005).
7   Everard Meyster, *Hemelsch Land-Spel of Goden Kout, Der Amersfoortsche Landdouwen. Bevattende den buytensten Opstal van't Nieuwe Stad-Huys* (Amsterdam: s.n., 1655), 75.
8   Paul Friedländer, *Kunstbeschreibungen justinianischer Zeit* (Hildesheim: Georg Olms Verlag, 1969); Gisbert Kranz, *Das Architekturgedicht* (Köln: Böhlau Verlag, 1988); Carole Newlands, 'Architectural Ecphrasis in Roman Poetry', in *Generic Interfaces in Latin Literature: Encounters, Interactions and Transformations*, ed. Theodore D. Papanghelis, Stephen J. Harrison and Stavros Frangoulidis (Berlin: De Gruyter, 2013), 55–78; Frans Slits, *Het Latijnse stededicht. Oorsprong en ontwikkeling tot in de zeventiende eeuw* (Amsterdam: Thesis Publishers, 1990); Christine Smith, *Architecture in the Culture of Early Humanism: Ethics, Aesthetics and Eloquence 1400–1470* (Oxford: Oxford University Press, 1992); Ruth Webb, 'The Aesthetics of Sacred Space: Narrative, Metaphor and Motion in *Ekphraseis* of Church Buildings', *Dumbarton Oaks Papers* 53 (1999): 59–74.
9   For Ovid's use of the concepts *sublimis, hubris*, and *humilis* and their reception in the seventeenth-century Dutch Republic, see Stijn Bussels, 'Theories of the Sublime in the Dutch Golden Age. Franciscus Junius, Joost van den Vondel and Petrus Wittewrongel', *History of European Ideas* 42, no. 7 (2016): 882–92.
10 Laurent Pernot, *La rhétorique de l'éloge dans le monde gréco-romain* (Paris: Institut d'Etudes Augustiennes, 1993), I, 178–214.
11 For more examples, see Kranz, *Das Architekturgedicht*.
12 Peter A. Clayton and Martin J. Price (eds), *The Seven Wonders of the World* (London and New York: Routledge, 1988).
13 John and Elizabeth Romer (eds), *The Seven Wonders of the World: A History of the Modern Imagination* (New York: Henry Holt & Co, 1995).
14 William James Hamblin and David Rolph Seely, *Solomon's Temple: Myth and History* (London: Thames & Hudson, 2007) and Anne-Françoise Morel, *Glorious Temples or Babylonic Whores. The Culture of Church Building in Stuart England Through the Lens of Consecration Sermons* (Leiden: Brill, 2019), esp. 66–72.
15 For more examples, see Kranz, *Das Architekturgedicht*.
16 G.R. Hibbart, 'The Country House Poem of the Seventeenth Century', *Journal of the Warburg and Courtauld Institutes* 19, no. 1/2 (1956): 159–74. Recent bibliography in Anne M. Myers, *Literature and Architecture in Early Modern England* (Baltimore: The Johns Hopkins University Press, 2013), Ch. 2; Eleanor Titcomb, 'Introduction', in Jean de la Fontaine, *Le songe de vaux* (Geneva: Droz, 1967): 1–47; Willemien de Vries, *The Country Estate Immortalized: Constantijn Huygens' Hofwijck* (Washington: Dumbarton Oaks, 1990).
17 Ulrich Schlegelmilch, *Descriptio templi: Architektur und Fest in der lateinischen Dichtung des konfessionellen Zeitalters* (Regensburg: Schnell & Steiner, 2003).

18 Geeraardt Brandt, *Het leven van Joost van den Vondel* ('s-Gravenhage: Frijhoff, 1932), 68. Cf. Marijke Spies, 'Minerva's commentaar': 15.
19 Joost van den Vondel, *Inwydinge van 't Stadthuis t' Amsterdam* (Amsterdam: Fontein, 1655), v. 14. See the lemma 'inzingen' in: http://gtb.inl.nl/iWDB/search?actie=article&wdb=WNT&id=M028425&lemma=inzingen&domein=0&conc=true (consulted March 2, 2020).
20 Jan Zoet explicitly mentions the singing of the popular song *Wilhelmus* in his 'Het triomfeerende Amsteldam', in Jan Zoet, *d' Uitsteekenste digtkunstige werken* (Amsterdam: Phlip Verbeek, 1714), 125 (v. 46).
21 G.J. van Bork and P.J. Verkruijsse (eds), *De Nederlandse en Vlaamse auteurs van middeleeuwen tot heden met inbegrip van de Friese auteurs* (Weesp: De Haan, 1985), 562.
22 Pieter Vlaardingerbroek, *Het paleis van de Republiek. Geschiedenis van het stadhuis van Amsterdam* (Zwolle: WBOOKS, 2011), 14 and 29.
23 Mattheus Gansneb Tengnagel, 'Op het toekomende Raedhuis', in Mattheus Gansneb Tengnagel, *Aemsterdamsche Lindebladen* (Amsterdam: Nicolaes van Ravesteyn, 1641), 21.
24 E.g. Stijn Bussels, 'Vondel's *Brothers* and the Power of Imagination', *Comparative Drama* 49, no. 1 (2015): 49-68.
25 Joost van den Vondel, 'Bouwzang', in *Olyf-krans der Vreede,* ed. Reyer Anslo (Amsterdam: Houthaak, 1649), 393-4.
26 For a Dutch edition, as well as a thorough explanation of Vondel's extensive poem, see Joost van den Vondel, *Vondels Inwydinge van 't Stadthuis van Amsterdam,* ed. and ann. by Saskia Albrecht et al. (Muiderberg: Coutinho, 1982).
27 Joost van den Vondel, *Inwydinge van 't Stadthuis t' Amsterdam* (Amsterdam: Fontein, 1655), vv. 1-48.
28 Koen Ottenheym, 'Architectuur', in *Jacob van Campen. Het klassieke ideaal in de Gouden Eeuw,* ed. Jacobine Huisken, Koen Ottenheym and Gary Schwartz (Amsterdam: Architectura & Natura Pers, 1995), 198.
29 Nina Geerdink, 'Een glazenmaker op de Parnas. Twee carrières van Jan Vos (1610-1667)', *De Zeventiende Eeuw* 27, no. 2 (2012): 180-93.
30 The most elaborate introduction to the drama is still W.J.C. Buitendijk, 'Inleiding', in Jan Vos, *Toneelwerken,* ed. W. J. C. Buitendijk (Assen: Van Gorcum, 1975), 47-97. For the latest bibliography on the play, see Nina Geerdink, 'Het vraagstuk van een wraakstuk. Jan Vos' "Aran en Titus"', in Schokkende boeken!, ed. Rick Honings, Lotte Jensen and Olga van Marion (Hilversum: Verloren, 2014), 39-46.
31 Marijke Meijer Drees, 'Toneelopvattingen in beweging. Rivaliteit tussen Vos en Vondel in 1641', *De Nieuwe Taalgids* 79 (1986): 453-60.
32 Jan Vos, 'Inwyding van het Stadthuis t' Amsterdam', in Jan Vos, *Alle de gedichten* (Amsterdam: Lescaille, 1662), 337-9.

33 For a comprehensive discussion of the poem, see Stijn Bussels, 'Medusa's Terror in the Amsterdam Town Hall, Or How to Look at Sculptures in the Dutch Golden Age', in *Idols to Museum Pieces. The Nature of Sculpture, its Historiography and Exhibition History, 1640–1880*, ed. Caroline van Eck (Berlin: De Gruyter, 2017), 85–102.
34 Dianne Hamer and Wim Meulenkamp, *De dolle jonker: Leven en werk van Everard Meyster (c. 1617–1679)* (Amsterdam: Bekking, 1987).
35 'Meer te verwonderen, als immer te doorgronden'. Meyster, *Hemelsch Land-Spel*, 22.
36 Meyster, *Hemelsch Land-Spel*, 78.
37 Stijn Bussels, Laura Plezier and Marc Van Vaeck, 'Amsterdam sierlijk verbonden met God. Het lofdicht op het Amsterdamse stadhuis van Constantijn Huygens', *Spiegel der Letteren* 59, no. 2/3 (2017): 261–90.
38 Constantijn Huygens, 'Geluck aen de EE. Heeren Regeerders van Amsterdam, in haer niewe Stadthuijs', in Constantijn Huygens, *Gedichten*, ed. by J.A. Worp (Groningen: Wolters, 1899), VI, 108.
39 Constantijn Huygens, 'Op de aerdtcloot' and 'Op den Hemelcloot', in Huygens, *Gedichten*, VI, 82–3.
40 Rudolf Cordes, *Jan Zoet, Amsterdammer (1609–1674). Leven en werk van een kleurrijk schrijver* (Hilversum: Verloren: 2008).
41 Maarten Prak and Diane Webb, *The Dutch Republic in the Seventeenth Century: The Golden Age* (Cambridge: Cambridge University Press, 2005), 193.
42 Jan Zoet, 'Het triomfeerende Amsteldam', in Jan Zoet, *d' Uitsteekenste digtkunstige werken* (Amsterdam: Phlip Verbeek, 1714), 124–6.
43 Lucas Rotgans, *Elegy on Joan Huydecoper van Maarsseveen*, unpublished, Utrecht Archives, Entry 67, Archive of the Family Huydecoper, n. 80.

Bibliography

Allott, Terence. 'Serious Games: Panegyrics of Louis XIV, 1686.' *Seventeenth-Century French Studies* 14, no. 1 (1992): 65–8.
Altieri, Joanne. *The Theatre of Praise: The Panegyric Tradition in Seventeenth-Century English Drama*. Newark: University of Delaware Press, 1986.
Bannister, Mark. 'Heroic Hierarchies: Classical Models for Panegyrics in Seventeenth-Century France.' *International Journal of the Classical Tradition* 8 (2001): 38–59.
Bork, G.J. van, and P.J. Verkruijsse (eds). *De Nederlandse en Vlaamse auteurs van middeleeuwen tot heden met inbegrip van de Friese auteurs*. Weesp: De Haan, 1985.
Brandt, Geeraardt. *Het leven van Joost van den Vondel*. 's-Gravenhage: Frijhoff, 1932.
Buitendijk, W.J.C. 'Inleiding.' In Jan Vos, *Toneelwerken*, ed. W. J. C. Buitendijk, 47–97. Assen: Van Gorcum, 1975.

Burrow, J.A. *The Poetry of Praise*. Cambridge: Cambridge University Press, 2008.
Bussels, Stijn. 'Meer te verwonderen, als immer te doorgronden. Het Amsterdamse stadhuis, een overweldigende burgerspiegel.' *Tijdschrift voor Geschiedenis* 126, no. 2 (2013): 234–48.
Bussels, Stijn. 'Vondel's *Brothers* and the Power of Imagination.' *Comparative Drama* 49, no. 1 (2015): 49–68.
Bussels, Stijn. 'Theories of the Sublime in the Dutch Golden Age. Franciscus Junius, Joost van den Vondel and Petrus Wittewrongel.' *History of European Ideas* 42, no. 7 (2016): 882–92.
Bussels, Stijn, Laura Plezier and Marc Van Vaeck. 'Amsterdam sierlijk verbonden met God. Het lofdicht op het Amsterdamse stadhuis van Constantijn Huygens.' *Spiegel der Letteren* 59, no. 2/3 (2017): 261–90.
Bussels, Stijn. 'Medusa's Terror in the Amsterdam Town Hall, Or How to Look at Sculptures in the Dutch Golden Age.' In *Idols to Museum Pieces. The Nature of Sculpture, its Historiography and Exhibition History, 1640–1880*, edited by Caroline van Eck, 85–102. Berlin: De Gruyter, 2017.
Clayton, Peter A., and Martin J. Price (eds). *The Seven Wonders of the World*. London and New York: Routledge, 1988.
Colombo, Stefano. 'The rhetoric of celebration in seventeenth-century Venetian funerary monuments.' PhD diss., University of Warwick, 2016.
Cordes, Rudolf. *Jan Zoet, Amsterdammer (1609–1674). Leven en werk van een kleurrijk schrijver*. Hilversum: Verloren: 2008.
Delerot, E. *Ce que les poètes ont dit de Versailles*. Versailles: Bernard, 1870.
Enenkel, Karl, and Konrad Ottenheym (eds). *The Quest for an Appropriate Past in Literature, Art and Architecture*. Leiden: Brill, 2018.
Enenkel, Karl, and Konrad Ottenheym (eds). *Ambitious Antiquities, Famous Forebears. Constructions of a Glorious Past in the Early Modern Netherlands and in Europe*. Leiden: Brill, 2019.
Friedländer, Paul. *Kunstbeschreibungen justinianischer Zeit*. Hildesheim: Georg Olms Verlag, 1969.
Gabas, Jean-Jacques. 'La Fontaine et la louange de Louis XIV.' *Seventeenth-Century French Studies* 6, no. 1 (1984): 111–19.
Garrison, James. *Dryden and the Tradition of Panegyric*. Berkeley: University of California Press, 1975.
Geerdink, Nina. 'Een glazenmaker op de Parnas. Twee carrières van Jan Vos (1610–1667).' *De Zeventiende Eeuw* 27, no. 2 (2012): 180–93.
Geerdink, Nina. 'Het vraagstuk van een wraakstuk. Jan Vos' "Aran en Titus".' In *Schokkende boeken!*, ed. Rick Honings, Lotte Jensen and Olga van Marion, 39–46. Hilversum: Verloren, 2014.
Hamblin, William James, and David Rolph Seely. *Solomon's Temple: Myth and History*. London: Thames & Hudson, 2007.

Hamer, Dianne, and Wim Meulenkamp. *De dolle jonker: Leven en werk van Everard Meyster (c. 1617–1679)*. Amsterdam: Bekking, 1987.

Hibbart, G.R. 'The Country House Poem of the Seventeenth Century.' *Journal of the Warburg and Courtauld Institutes* 19, no. 1/2 (1956): 159–74.

Huygens, Constantijn. 'Op de aerdtcloot' and 'Op den Hemelcloot.' In Constantijn Huygens, *Gedichten*, ed. by J.A. Worp, VI, 82–3. Groningen: Wolters, 1899.

Huygens, Constantijn. 'Geluck aen de EE. Heeren Regeerders van Amsterdam, in haer niewe Stadthuijs.' In Constantijn Huygens, *Gedichten*, ed. by J.A. Worp, VI, 108. Groningen: Wolters, 1899.

Kranz, Gisbert. *Das Architekturgedicht*. Köln: Böhlau Verlag, 1988.

Macé, Stéphane. 'Grandeur standing the test of death: Massillon's eulogy for Louis XIV.' *XVIIe siècle* 269 (2015): 623–32.

McManamon, John. *Funeral Oratory and the Cultural Ideals of Italian Humanism*. Chapel Hill: The University of North Caroline Press, 1989.

Meijer Drees, Marijke. 'Toneelopvattingen in beweging. Rivaliteit tussen Vos en Vondel in 1641.' *De Nieuwe Taalgids* 79 (1986): 453–60.

Meyster, Everard. *Hemelsch Land-Spel of Goden Kout, Der Amersfoortsche Landdouwen. Bevattende den buytensten Opstal van't Nieuwe Stad-Huys*. Amsterdam: s.n., 1655.

Morel, Anne-Françoise. *Glorious Temples or Babylonic Whores. The Culture of Church Building in Stuart England Through the Lens of Consecration Sermons*. Leiden: Brill, 2019.

Moul, Victoria. 'England's Stilicho. Claudian's Political Poetry in Early Modern England.' *International Journal of the Classical Tradition* (May 2019), online: https://link.springer.com/article/10.1007%2Fs12138-019-00529-z (Consulted 2 March 2019).

Myers, Anne M. *Literature and Architecture in Early Modern England*. Baltimore: The Johns Hopkins University Press, 2013.

Newlands, Carole. 'Architectural Ecphrasis in Roman Poetry.' In *Generic Interfaces in Latin Literature: Encounters, Interactions and Transformations*, edited by Theodore D. Papanghelis, Stephen J. Harrison and Stavros Frangoulidis, 55–78. Berlin: De Gruyter, 2013.

Norbrook, David. 'Panegyric of the Monarch and its Social Context under Elizabeth I and James I.' D.Phil. thesis, Oxford University, 1978.

Pelc, Milan. 'Panegyric Emblem Books. Jesuits and the Habsburg Emperors: Some Examples Related to 17th-Century Croatia.' *Primljen* 43 (2019): 59–74.

Pernot, Laurent. *La rhétorique de l'éloge dans le monde gréco-romain*. Paris: Institut d'Etudes Augustiennes, 1993.

Pieters, Jürgen. *Speaking with the Dead. Explorations in Literature and History*. Edinburgh: Edinburgh University Press, 2005.

Prak, Maarten, and Diane Webb. *The Dutch Republic in the Seventeenth Century: The Golden Age*. Cambridge: Cambridge University Press, 2005.

Romer, John and Elizabeth (eds). *The Seven Wonders of the World: A History of the Modern Imagination*. New York: Henry Holt & Co, 1995.

Schlegelmilch, Ulrich. *Descriptio templi: Architektur und Fest in der lateinischen Dichtung des konfessionellen Zeitalters*. Regensburg: Schnell & Steiner, 2003.

Slits, Frans. *Het Latijnse stededicht. Oorsprong en ontwikkeling tot in de zeventiende eeuw*. Amsterdam: Thesis Publishers, 1990.

Smith, Christine. *Architecture in the Culture of Early Humanism: Ethics, Aesthetics and Eloquence 1400–1470*. Oxford: Oxford University Press, 1992.

Spies, Marijke. 'Minerva's commentaar: Gedichten rond het Amsterdamse stadhuis.' *De zeventiende eeuw*, 9, no. 1 (1993): 15–33.

Summers, Claude, and Ted-Larry Pebworth (eds). *The Muses Common-Weale: Poetry and Politics in the Seventeenth Century* (Columbia: University of Missouri Press, 1988).

Tengnagel, Mattheus Gansneb. 'Op het toekomende Raedhuis.' In Mattheus Gansneb Tengnagel, *Aemsterdamsche Lindebladen*, 21. Amsterdam: Nicolaes van Ravesteyn, 1641.

Titcomb, Eleanor. 'Introduction.' In Jean de la Fontaine, *Le songe de vaux*, 1–47. Geneva: Droz, 1967).

Verbaan, Eddy. *De woonplaats van de faam*. Hilversum: Verloren, 2011.

Vlaardingerbroek, Pieter. *Het paleis van de Republiek. Geschiedenis van het stadhuis van Amsterdam*. Zwolle: WBOOKS, 2011.

Vondel, Joost van den. 'Bouwzang.' In *Olyf-krans der Vreede*, ed. Reyer Anslo, 393–4. Amsterdam: Houthaak, 1649.

Vondel, Joost van den. *Inwydinge van 't Stadthuis t' Amsterdam*. Amsterdam: Fontein, 1655.

Vondel, Joost van den. *Vondels Inwydinge van 't Stadthuis van Amsterdam*, ed. and ann. by Saskia Albrecht et al. Muiderberg: Coutinho, 1982.

Vos, Jan. 'Inwyding van het Stadthuis t' Amsterdam.' In Jan Vos, *Alle de gedichten*, 333–52. Amsterdam: Lescaille, 1662.

Vries, Willemien de. *The Country Estate Immortalized: Constantijn Huygens' Hofwijck*. Washington: Dumbarton Oaks, 1990.

Webb, Ruth. 'The Aesthetics of Sacred Space: Narrative, Metaphor and Motion in Ekphraseis of Church Buildings.' *Dumbarton Oaks Papers* 53 (1999): 59–74.

Weber, Gregor. *Der Lobtopos des 'lebenden' Bildes*. Hildesheim: Olms, 1991.

Zoet, Jan. 'Het triomfeerende Amsteldam.' In Jan Zoet, *d' Uitsteekenste digtkunstige werken*, 124–6. Amsterdam: Phlip Verbeek, 1714.

5

The Portrait of a Building

Stijn Bussels

Many buildings have a face. They look, they even speak, but buildings do not speak alone, nor do they speak by themselves. Buildings speak with and through texts and images. Together they perform conversations for a large audience. Sometimes that conversation is delicate and elegant, sometimes powerful and overwhelming, sometimes pompous and excessive. These conversations can deal with the building itself, with the place where it stands, with its founders and architects, with a higher reality, with desires and even with our deepest fears. We find telling examples in the Amsterdam Town Hall. The speech of the Town Hall is performative. It gives the city and her rulers dignity and esteem. That has pointed out already in the only English monograph on the subject, Katharine Fremantle's *The Baroque Town Hall of Amsterdam*, now sixty years old.[1] In what follows, I will not look at the impact of the building itself, as Fremantle and several other authors have done, but I will focus on how seventeenth-century artists represent the building and even strengthen its impact in their work.[2] The seventeenth-century paintings of the Town Hall, as well as the drawings and prints (separate or included in books, such as travel guides) are almost impossible to count and were quickly distributed throughout the whole of Europe.

Previous research has related visual representations of the Town Hall to the popularity of maps, panoramas and bird's-eye-view perspectives of Amsterdam.[3] Equally popular were the literary counterparts, the genre of the poem praising a city, the so-called *laus urbium*.[4] The preceding chapter has discussed the very substantial number of poems written in praise of Amsterdam and its Town Hall. All these visual and textual representations of Amsterdam are not surprising, as in the mid-seventeenth century the city was a commercial and financial hub. The citizens of Amsterdam, led by their four Burgomasters, strove for strong autonomy to protect this prosperity as well as possible. This desire fed into the large stream of images and descriptions of the city as a coherent whole. The

Amsterdam success attracted a rich set of seekers after riches and fortune.[5] Visual and textual imagery of the city was equally used to make sure that the identity of the city would not become blurred in the growing diversity and quick transformations of the city that this immigration brought along. The construction of the Town Hall can be related to this centripetal ambition, as well as the poems praising the building, but certainly the hundreds of paintings and drawings and the thousands of prints representing the building as well.

In this essay I focus on how in the context of the Town Hall a new genre comes to full fruition, a genre that I would like to call the 'portrait of a building'.[6] This genre is defined by the feature that an artist visualizes a real building in such a way that that building is endowed with character. Therefore, the use of a portrait to depict either a human or a building is equally valid: just like an artist has to depict a person as recognizably as possible, but in the same time has to emphasize his or her particular characteristics, the portraitist of a building has to represent that building. It has to be clearly identifiable, but the artist can also draw attention to certain features and represent them as humanlike characteristics.[7] Thus, these portraits are different from previous representations where buildings play a prominent role, but are subordinated to particular narratives. Even centuries before, buildings appeared in works of art to place an historical event or an ideal situation in a particular setting. In the celebrated *The Allegory of Good and Bad Government* (1339), Ambrogio Lorenzetti provides the very first accurate panoramic view of a city, Siena, since Antiquity.[8] Only two centuries later, however, painterly strategies are used to the full to animate buildings – to give them a face.

A direct precursor of such a portrait can be found in a 1628 etching of Haarlem's Grand Square after a design of Pieter Saenredam (1597–1665) (Figure 5.1).[9] This etching shows an urban space from three sides. The viewpoint is chosen in such a way that the viewer seems to be looking out from a window on the first floor of an imaginary house located at the fourth side of the square. This view point contrasts sharply with sixteenth-century architectural perspectives, with the etchings of Hans Vredeman de Vries (1527–1607) as prominent examples (Figure 5.2), where the viewer stands on a far higher point and thus looks *over* the buildings to the city walls. The perspective that Saenredam uses, by contrast, creates the illusion that the viewer of the painting is standing a bit higher than the people on the Grand Square and thus can look directly at the central building, Haarlem Town Hall.

To show how the Amsterdam Town Hall brings this tradition to full growth, we can start with a painting by the Haarlem painter Gerrit Berckheyde (1638–

The Portrait of a Building 119

Figure 5.1 Jan van de Velde after Pieter Jansz. Saenredam, 'View on the Grand Square with Town Hall of Haarlem', as published in Samuel Ampzing, *Beschryvinge ende lof der stad Haerlem* (Haarlem: Adriaen Roman, 1628). Rijksmuseum Amsterdam, Public Domain.

Figure 5.2 Johannes or Lucas van Doetechum after Hans Vredeman de Vries, 'View on a city with palaces and canal from a bird's eye perspective', as published in *Variae Architecturae formae* (Antwerp: Theodoor Galle, 1601). Rijksmuseum Amsterdam, Public Domain.

98), one of the most famous and innovative artists to depict the building. No fewer than thirty-six works by him depicting the Town Hall are preserved.[10] One of the earliest of these, now in the Royal Museum of Fine Arts in Antwerp, dates from 1668 (Figure 5.3).[11] Like Saenredam, the painter shows the vivacity of groups of people immersed in conversation and trade on the square. Here, the viewer sees a city that is full of life where the whole world comes to trade and whose international dignity is affirmed by means of the new, impressive building. Berckheyde goes further than Saenredam, however, in juxtaposing these daily activities with the monumentality of the Town Hall.

Berckheyde uses painterly techniques to the full in order to visualize this monumentality. Next to this central building, there are two other buildings that define the view on Dam Square, the Weigh House and the New Church. The painter places the Weigh House in a deep shadow while he throws full light and a varied shadow on the façade of the Town Hall. He makes the most of the whiteness of the latter's façade by contrasting it with the dark stone of the former. The painter enhances the prominence of the corner and middle bays by bringing them further forward than they are in the actual building. He also carefully represents the colossal Composite columns running over two floors, as well as the grand festoons in between the floors. This all results in a rich play of

Figure 5.3 Gerrit Adriaensz. Berckheyde, *The Town Hall on Dam Square*, 1668, oil on canvas, 70 × 110 cm. KMSKA, photo: Hugo Maertens, Public Domain.

chiaroscuro. Besides, he pays attention to the fact that the pediment is sculpted in a whiter stone than the rest of the façade. Thus, we get a façade that is monumental and spirited at the same time.

Moreover, the viewpoint is chosen in such a way that the Weigh House blocks most of the view of the New Church, but obstructs only a very small part of the view of the Town Hall. Thus, with his choice of viewpoint, Berckheyde gives prominence to the Town Hall and shows the building in its full splendour without failing to show the actual situation on Dam Square. Further, Berckheyde uses a strikingly large space – one-third of the canvas – to show the grounds in front of the Town Hall. By representing Dam Square as a space that gradually runs up towards the Town Hall, he stresses the monumentality of the central building even more. As a result, none of the figures on the square stands higher than the steps of the entrance. Moreover, the cobblestones – with their patterning following the vanishing line of the perspective – makes the upward effect even more prominent. They increase the sense of space and direct the viewer's gaze inescapably to the Town Hall.

Besides the emphasis on the building's monumentality, Berckheyde also 'portrays' it, as the building seems to have characteristics similar to humans. Thanks to the perspective used, the Town Hall appears to recline a little. Thus the central bay and the carillon suggest a human head that is proudly held high. It is also remarkable that the vanishing point of the perspective is not in the middle, but has moved slightly to the left. Due to this shift away from the centre, the building seems to turn a little in order to look in a certain direction.

Rixtel's praise

The idea of the Town Hall being portrayed as a person is certainly not new; it was suggested by contemporaries of Berckheyde. Of special interest is the laudatory poem *On the Town Hall of Amsterdam painted by the illustrious Painter Gerrit Berckheyden of Haarlem* (*Op het Stadthuys van Amsterdam, Geschildert door den vermaerden Schilder Gerrit Berckheyden van Haerlem*). It was written by Pieter Rixtel (1643–73), a fellow townsman of the painter, and published in 1669, so just a year after the painting was done.[12] Only a few modern art and literary historians have read the poem, and if they have done so, they have labelled it as 'a long verse full of clichés' ('een lang en clichématig vers').[13] However, in my opinion Rixtel's laudatory poem is totally the opposite: it is a clever play in which architecture, painting and literature are closely connected.

As the title indicates, it is not a poem about the Town Hall, but a poem about *Berckheyde's painting of the Town Hall*. Moreover, as we shall see, the poet not only focusses on the building itself and its pictorial representation, he also involves famous laudatory poems on the Town Hall. In this way we can read the poem as a complex reflection on the relation between different means to present Amsterdam, as a *paragone* where diverse mediums are tested in their effectivity.

At the very start of the poem, Rixtel observes that in Berckheyde's painting the building is painted from the 'shoulders' and writes that this is done precisely in the same way as a person might lift up their head proudly, since in the painting the Town Hall raises 'bravely the Marble Crown of Its/His Head, on Shoulders of White Freestone' ('moediger zijn Marm're Kruyn, op Schouderen van Witte Arduyn').[14] After a few introductory verses, Rixtel uses a prominent means of his own medium, personification, to do exactly the same. The poet transforms the Town Hall into a living being that addresses the reader. The talking building praises Berckheyde for – among other qualities – showing how 'the Sun caresses my Brow' ('de Zon my 't Voorhooft streelt'). However, it is far from easy to get a grip on what kind of living being is actually speaking here. Due to the fact that in seventeenth-century Dutch the possessive noun 'zijn' can be both 'its' and 'his', Rixtel can suggest the building is animated by using grammatical ambiguity.[15] To put it more precisely, it is not clear if the reader is confronted with a living human or an animated object.

Besides, the reader cannot immediately define how the personification has to be interpreted. Does it merely stand for the new building? In what follows, Rixtel plays with the idea that something more is going on. He makes the Town Hall say that it/he owns its/his animation first and foremost to Berckheyde. The topos of praising works of art for creating life has a rich history.[16] Homer praised the divine Shield of Achilles by describing actions represented on it as if they took place before his eyes.[17] In early modern Europe, the topos is used time and again to acclaim a portrait for keeping a person alive, even if that person has passed away.[18] Rixtel gives a new twist to this popular topos: his portrait of the building not only keeps it alive, but brings it to life in the first place. Thanks to the animation, the painter further constructs the Town Hall, if not in brick, but in paint. The role of the architect and the painter, and the status of the architectural prototype and its painted representation, become intermingled. Rixtel tried to create an inextricable knot confronting his readers with the complexities of medial intersections.

Directly after this intermingling, the poet refers to his own medium. Poetry brings the Town Hall to life, too. In order to make this clear, he refers to one of the most famous poems dedicated to the Town Hall, namely Joost van den Vondel's poem written for the Town Hall's ceremonial inauguration in 1655.[19] The talking building proclaims that it/he is 'carried by Maro [Virgil], Vondel, the honour of the Poets, as far as his Songs can please the Ear, yet flies my Fame no further than where one can find Dutch Ears' ('Gevoert van Maro, Vondel, d'eer/ Der Dighteren, werd' om gedragen,/ Soo ver zyn Zangen 't Oor behagen,/ Nogh vlieght myn roem niet verder, dan/ Men Neerduytse Ooren vinden kan').[20] So, following the words of the building, the Vondel's poem carries it/him, but only in the places where Dutch is read. The portrait of Berckheyde surpasses poetry as it reconstructs the Town Hall with paint and thus transcends national language barriers, even at the expense of his own medium. In doing so, the poet introduces a surprising hierarchy. Since painting reaches further than Vondel's poetry and much further than van Campen's building, the newly made artwork of the relatively young Berckheyde – the painter did not yet enjoy the excellent reputation he would have at the end of his career – surpasses the praise of the celebrated poet, even when Vondel is seen as on a par with Virgil. Even more surprisingly, the painting outperforms the grand building designed by the most famous architect of that time, the building on which all poems and images actually relied.

Besides using the metaphor of 'carrying', Rixtel also writes that the poem and portrait of the building can 'climb' higher than the building itself. His metaphors separate his personification from the architectural construction. In the animation of word and image, the personification seems to take on a life of its own apart outside of the prototype. This choice further illustrates that the relation between the building, the portrait and the poem is far from evident. The portrait and the poem are not entirely subordinated to their duty of representing the Town Hall. The poet presents all three as mediums to spread the prosperity of Amsterdam. The three mediums convey the name and fame of the city; they let that name and fame 'climb', be that in different ways. Therefore, Rixtel does not start from the building and then look at the portrait and poem. Instead he presents the Town Hall, as well as its portrait and laudation as *partes pro toto* of the city's prosperity. So, they do not merely show the prosperity but also form an important part of it. Rixtel suggests that architecture, the visual arts and literature play full parts of the city's success, with the visual arts as the most successful. Therefore, the poet's play with animation essentially falls back on Amsterdam's vibrancy and connects the liveliness of the people in front of Berckheyde's painting with the Town Hall, its laudatory poems and its portraits. Thus he does not fully acknowledge the primacy of architecture.

Once Rixtel has established this nuance, he further reflects on his own medium and on painting to use a popular point of reference as a way of praising the Town Hall. Time and again, Dutch seventeenth-century poets repeated each other by writing that the building emulated the seven ancient Wonders of the World and therefore could rightfully be named the eighth Wonder, Rixtel surprises by going one step further to praise Berckheyde. To conclude his poem, the poet takes over from the talking building again and says that 'the Eighth Wonder, constructed in Stone, stands near the river Y, but the Ninth, is the Eighth, in this Painting' ('Het Aghtste Wonder staat, van Steen gebout, aen't Y,/ Maer 't Negenste, is dat Aghtste, in deze Schildery').[21] Right up to the end, the poet deconstructs the uniqueness of the wondrous building so as to create the suggestion that Amsterdam performs a chain reaction of wonders in diverse mediums, but most prominently in painting, where the building is portrayed with international approval.

God's grace

Rixtel does not go into detail about how Amsterdam brings about that wondrous chain reaction. By contrast, other poets focus less on the medial reflection, but on the hidden causes behind the construction of the wondrous Town Hall and more generally the exceptional flowering of the city of commerce. That cause is a miracle which is entirely God's doing. Several poets present the impressive building as proof of divine grace. One of the most famous authors making the connection between the building and the latter is the politician and art lover Constantijn Huygens (1596–1687). He does this in his congratulations addressed to the four Burgomasters, written in 1657. A few years later the laudatory poem was engraved in black marble and even today it is displayed prominently in the Burgomasters' chamber in the Town Hall, now Royal Palace (Figure 5.4).[22] After a reference to the ancient tradition of the seven Wonders of the World, Huygens addresses God. He writes: 'God, who ordered you to combine Power and Splendour with Reason,/ God may give you that you can show in the Building/ Who you are with Reason and Pleasure' ('God, die U Macht en Pracht met Reden gaf te voeghen,/ God gev' u in 't Gebouw met Reden en Genoeghen/ Te thoonen wie ghij zijt').[23] As impressive as it might be, in the eyes of the poet a building is in the end merely a sign of God's grace.

Now we can return to the portraits of the building where artists also tried to show God's grace. We can start with a direct predecessor of Berckheyde's portrait,

Figure 5.4 Elias Noski, stone engraved with Huygens' poem, 1660, ebony, gilding and black marble, 100 × 90 cm, Amsterdam Museum, Courtesy Stichting Koninklijk Paleis Amsterdam. © The Royal Palace of Amsterdam, photograph: Tom Haartsen.

a drawing by Jacob van der Ulft (1621–89) from 1653 (Figure 5.5). While the similarities are remarkable, on the drawing the tower of the New Church is much higher than in Berckheyde's portrait. The artist visualizes the plans of the so-called 'religious faction' within the Amsterdam municipality headed by Burgomaster Willem Cornelis Backer (1595–1652). He wanted to crown the New Church with the highest tower in the Dutch Republic to increase God's

Figure 5.5 Jacob van der Ulft, *Market on Dam Square*, 1653, drawing, 276 × 472 mm. Collectie Atlas Splitgerber, Courtesy of Stadsarchief Amsterdam, Public Domain.

benevolence over the city. Recent studies by Thomas von der Dunk and Gabri van Tussenbroek have reconstructed the tensions between the plans for a tower and the Town Hall.[24] On the surface they were about how to spend limited financial means, but the real conflict was about whether the Calvinist faction or the merchants should rule the city. Eventually, after the death of Backer in 1652, the plans for the tower became less and less dominant.

However, van der Ulft made the drawing a year after Backer's death. Therefore, it could be an ultimate attempt to promote the plans for the tower. The artist presents the tower shoulder to shoulder with the Town Hall, as he depicts a view on Dam Square with both the Town Hall and the church tower completed (whereas in fact the building was still unfinished at the time, and the tower merely planned). The style of the two buildings is different, which reflects the difference in their functions.[25] However, whereas Berckheyde highlighted these differences by his use of colours and shadows, van der Ulft uses the same colours for both buildings.

Figure 5.6 Hendrick Mommers, *Market Scene before the Dam*, c. 1665, oil on canvas, 84.5 × 120.7 cm. Dyrham Park, Gloucestershire, courtesy of the National Trust.

Another Haarlem painter, Hendrick Mommers (1619–93), was inspired by the drawing of van der Ulft as well. His view on Dam Square dating from *c.* 1665 is now in Dyrham Park; three variants are still preserved (Figure 5.6).[26] Once again the similarities with the drawing are striking, although Mommers has left out the projected tower of the New Church, just like Berckheyde did. This is a painting that requires careful attention, as it is not merely a visual document of how Dam Square must have looked like in the mid-seventeenth century. In comparison with van der Ulft, Mommers plays in a different way with the rendering of light. With the exception of a ray of sunshine on some figures in the foreground, only the Town Hall receives full light, much more than the New Church behind the Weigh House. The new building seems to radiate a sharp white light, strangely illuminating a rectangular space right in front of the building. The artist may have wanted to emphasize the use of white stone for the façade or to suggest that the space in front of the building was paved with white stones. However, there is also another interpretation for this bright white light, an interpretation that can be connected with Huygens' congratulation poem in which the supernatural rendering of light can be seen as an attempt to present the building as an instrument of God, a medium through which He expresses His extraordinary relation with Amsterdam.

Resurrection

To further argue that Mommers' extraordinary bright light can be linked with divine providence, we can look at depictions of the burning of the old Town Hall. The medieval building entirely burned down in 1652. Viewed with architectural parameters the building did not amount to much, and was only a conglomerate of different buildings and styles constructed throughout the ages. Nevertheless, the fire was engraved on the collective memory, although not presented as a disaster, but as a token of God's foresight.

The fire was depicted time and again in countless images, such as a painting by Jan Beerstraaten (1622–66) (Figure 5.7).[27] It is an accurate topographical document that can be localized within inches, thus memorializing a ruin that had to be demolished to make way for the new Town Hall. Only thanks to the burning and demolition could Amsterdam show herself in renewed glory. Beerstraten visually preserves the old splendour of the city, as the painting can be placed within the widely spread aesthetic appreciation of ruins of that time.[28] The frontal view and the emphasis on the horizontal and vertical lines, the sober colours with

Figure 5.7 Jan Beerstraaten, *Ruins of the old Town Hall*, c. 1660, oil on canvas, 110 × 145 cm. Courtesy of Rijksmuseum Amsterdam, Public Domain.

striking light and dark effects and the close framing, make the ruin grand and monumental, almost heroic.[29] In a similar way, Maarten van Heemskerck (1498–1574) had depicted the ancient ruins of Rome. So, by presenting the ruins of the old Town Hall as a monument, once again, the respectable history of Amsterdam under God's protection is compared with the history of the Eternal City.

Many laudatory poems mention this fire as well, linking it to God's foresight. The poets present the new Town Hall as evidence that the fire of the old Town Hall fits perfectly within the good intentions of God for Amsterdam. Although the construction of the new Town Hall started long before the fire, the poets suggest that the fire was actually the crucial event that led to the new Town Hall. Rixtel, for instance. makes this connection. As we just saw, the poet animates the Town Hall to let it/him praise the portrait Berckheyde made of it/him. However, the poet refers not only to the new Town Hall, but also to the old one, as the animated Town Hall speaks about its/his old embodiment as well, the medieval building.

This can be compared with the theory of the two bodies of the king (or queen), famously discussed by Ernst Kantorowicz.[30] In medieval and early modern political theory, the ruler has a body natural, a personal and mortal body, as well as a body politic that coincides with the political position he/she holds and is handed down from parents to children. In the political context of the Dutch Republic and the city of Amsterdam, this political theory could not be easily adopted, but was still a too dominant way of thinking to neglect.[31] Although only a small number of families held the important political positions, a clear dynastic succession was out of the question. So, after the Dutch had dismissed the Habsburg rulers, they could no longer clearly present a body natural. Most certainly not in Amsterdam, a city that time and again had opposed attempts by the princes of Orange to claim the body politic of the highest rulers in the Republic.[32] The four Burgomasters could not claim the body politic of the ultimate power in the city either. Every year they had to be replaced. Moreover, as there were four of them, that body politic would have suffered from a dissociative identity disorder. The idea that the body politic became related to a building instead of a person is not farfetched. As we already saw, Rixtel and other poets animate the Town Hall as a living entity. The rhetoric concerning the fire of the old Town Hall shows us how the building is a concrete, mortal body, as well as a body politic that is resistant against death. Just as the king never dies, so the Town Hall of Amsterdam will never disappear.

Rixtel uses the phoenix as a symbol of the eternal existence of the Town Hall. The very first words of the speaking Town Hall are: 'I am, from the smoking ashes of my ancestor, / risen as a Phoenix' ('Ik ben, uyt Voorzaets rokende

Asschen, / Gelyk een Phaenix, op-gewasschen'). This bird is often linked with Christ, who sacrificed Himself for the wellbeing of humankind. The recurring reference to the fire opens up associations with the resurrection of Christ, but it also makes the animation of the building more complex. We have already indicated how hard it is to fully assess the precise functioning of Rixtel's personification due to the intermingling of the Town Hall and its portrait. The personification is all the more multifaceted, as there is not so much one particular building at stake, but a succession of town halls.

One portrait of the old Town Hall plays an important role in the idea of resurrection under God's protection. The painting was done by Pieter Saenredam, who actually painted it years after the actual fire (Figure 5.8). Recently, Lorne Darnell has argued that the Burgomasters had the painting put in their room, right in front of Huygens' poem engraved in marble. Because of this position we can see Saenredam's painting as a pendant of the poem, as if both were in conversation.[33] In his poem Huygens speaks about the eighth and ninth Wonder of the World; or the new Town Hall and the Town Hall that eventually would replace the latter if destructed. In his painting, Saenredam portrays the old Town

Figure 5.8 Pieter Saenredam, *The Old Town Hall of Amsterdam*, 1657, oil on panel, 65.5 × 84.5 cm. Courtesy of Rijksmuseum, Public Domain.

Hall in a scene of sobriety and rest. So, in this diptych, past, present and future are taken into account in word and image.

Once again, it is Rixtel that creates more clarity in how the portrait of the old Town Hall functions in the heart of the new Town Hall, since the poet praises not only Berckheyde's portrait of the new Town Hall, but Saenredam's portrait of the old Town Hall as well.

> Dat oudt Gebouw, gesloopt aen Vonken,
> Lagh langh in Assche, en Puyn, versonken,
> En wiert niet meer genoemt, indien
> Het sigh niet op 't Paneel liet zien,
> Door *Saenredams* Pençeel en Verven:
> Die *Spaer-Geest,* heeft het, voor zyn sterven,
> Herbooren, en, eer 't lagh gebukt,
> De Doodt, die 't al vernielt, ontrukt;[34]

> *That old Building, demolished by Fire,*
> *Laid for a long time in Ashes and Debris,*
> *And was no longer mentioned, if*
> *Its view would not have been visible on Panel*
> *With* Saenredam's *brush and Paint:*
> *This* Saving-Spirit, *let it/him, before it/he died,*
> *Reborn, and before it/he was subjected,*
> *He took it/him from the Death, who destroys it all;*

Just as a deceased person is kept alive thanks to his or her portrait, the talking Town Hall holds that Saenredam has succeeded to keep the old Town Hall alive. Thanks to the painting hanging in the room of the Burgomasters, the respectability of the old Town Hall is literally incorporated in the new body of the Town Hall. The old phoenix had to die for a resurrection to be possible, but thanks to the painting the honour attached to the old building is transferred to its new iteration. The portrait of the old Town Hall makes sure that the room of the Burgomasters can 'still shine, thanks to the old splendour' ('nogh glans trekt, uyt dien ouden prael').

Across the borders

Until now I have focused on the connections between the visual arts and poetry in their imagining of the Town Hall. However, next to transmedial connections, we can also consider the international connections that were sparked off by the construction of the Amsterdam building. The genre of the portrait of a building is a significant example of the fact that we cannot consider the Dutch seventeenth century in splendid isolation. The portraits of the Town Hall enjoyed international acclaim. In his laudatory poem on Berckheyde's portrait, Rixtel already hoped that the painting would be viewed by the whole world. This was not a hyperbole. For example, when Cosimo III de' Medici visited the Town Hall in 1668, he purchased the very same day a portrait of the building by Jan van der Heyden. The fact that four years later Cosimo asked his agent in the Republic to visit Van der Heyden to inquire whether other paintings of the Town Hall were for sale proves that his purchase was not a mere whim.[35]

Moreover, visual artists across the whole of Europe were inspired by the portraits of the Amsterdam Town Hall to paint other grand buildings. The influence on Italian *vedute* painters has already been studied. The so-called 'father of *vedute*' is a painter from Amersfoort, Caspar van Wittel, who at the end of the seventeenth century under the name of Gaspare Vanvitelli acquired name and fame with his cityscapes, as well as his portraits of buildings in Rome and Venice.[36] Van Wittel was influenced by the portraitists of the Town Hall.

Whereas the influence of Dutch painters such as Berckheyde through van Wittel on famous *vedutisti* such as Canaletto is already well established, the international context of the rise of the building portrait as a genre is understudied. Here, too, the Dutch played an important role. At the start of the seventeenth century ancient buildings and ruins, as well as imaginary cityscapes or *capricci* are represented in many prints, drawings and paintings of Dutch artists in Rome, such as Pieter van Laer and Willem van Nieulandt.[37] Their role in initiating this genre can be seen for instance in the latter's 1609 depiction of the Arch of Septimius Severus. The architecture is given centre stage, represented neither from the front nor laterally, but from one of the corners (Figure 5.9). As a result, its setting at the foot of the Capitoline Hill is clearly shown and the grandness of the arch is contrasted with the Tabularium directly behind it which actual appearance is toned down. Moreover, thanks to this viewpoint, the three richly coffered semi-circular vaults, so much admired and copied in the early modern period, are maximally brought to the fore.

Alongside these Italian contexts there is also a French connection. In the seventeenth century, many Dutch artists were active in the French capital and their images of the most important buildings would be influential for decades, if not centuries. One of the earliest Dutch artists to paint Parisian buildings was the Haarlem painter, Abraham de Verwer (1585–1650).[38] Seven of

Figure 5.9 Willem van Nieulandt (II), *The Arch of Septimus Severus*, 1609, drawing, pen and brown ink over black chalk, 20.2 × 27 cm. Kupferstichkabinett Staatliche Museen zu Berlin. © 2020, Photo Scala, Florence/bpk, Bildagentur für Kunst, Kultur und Geschichte, Berlin.

his cityscapes of the Louvre are still preserved. I consciously call them 'cityscapes' and not 'portraits', since these paintings can be situated in the 'prehistory' of the portraits of buildings. They are an early step in the direction, but not yet a portrait, as they do not yet depict the Louvre as if it is a person or as if it has human characteristics.

With his paintings of the Louvre, de Verwer experiments with light and light reflection. In a series of paintings of the Grande Galerie seen from the Pont-Royal, of which three are preserved in the Musée Carnavalet (Figures 5.10–12), he tries to capture how the sun and the clouds chequer the ambience of the building in a subtle way. The three paintings are almost identical – but not entirely: the number of figures standing on the quaysides is different, as is the number of boats, and the laundry is displayed differently. So here time plays its role. There is a time-lapse: the pink morning sun gives the Louvre a rosy glow, the midday sun sharpens the façade and makes it white, while the evening sun caresses the building with golden tones. Subsequently in the seventeenth and throughout the eighteenth centuries, the interest in the influence of sunlight will

Figure 5.10 Abraham de Verwer, *The Louvre Grande Galerie, view of Paris from the Barbier bridge*, c. 1640, oil on wood, Musée Carnavalet. Credit: Bridgeman Images.

Figure 5.11 Abraham de Verwer, *Galerie du Louvre and the Porte Neuf*, c. 1640, Oil on panel, Musée du Louvre. Credit: Bridgeman Images.

Figure 5.12 Abraham de Verwer, *The Louvre Grande Galerie, view of Paris from the Barbier bridge (upstream)*, c. 1640, oil on wood, Musée Carnavalet. Credit: Bridgeman Images.

be a major element in the development of the portrait of a building by *vedute* painters among others, but these experiments would culminate in the portraits of Rouen Cathedral painted by Claude Monet at the end of the nineteenth century.

De Verwer's paintings also gives more insight into the political context of the origins and early development of this genre. More specifically, these paintings make clear that European rulers were very interested in each other's buildings. The focus that de Verwer put on the Grande Galerie was not defined by artistic motives alone. The Grande Galerie was begun in 1594 under Henri IV, and was finished in 1610, in the period when Prince Frederick Hendrick of Orange lived in Paris. Two decades later, when he had become Stadholder, he asked de Verwer to paint it.[39] Frederick Hendrick was also interested in the broader urbanistic interventions by Henri IV and Louis XIII on the right bank of the river Seine. The so-called *Plein* (a square adjacent to the *Binnenhof* in The Hague), constructed in the 1630s, was an answer to these Parisian interventions. Later in the century the Oranges and the Bourbons would continue looking attentively at each other's buildings, with the competition between William III and Louis XIV the climax of this rivalry that was fought out with stones, as well as words and paint.[40]

Notes

1 Katharine Fremantle, *The Baroque Town Hall of Amsterdam* (Utrecht: Haentjens Dekker & Gumbert, 1959).
2 Fleurbaay and Goossens already discussed the images of the Town Hall but from a less transmedial and international perspective: Ellen Fleurbaay, *The Building of Amsterdam Town Hall, now the Royal Palace Amsterdam. The Eighth Wonder of the World* (Amsterdam: Stichting Koninklijk Paleis, 1982) and Eymert-Jan Goossens, *Het Paleis in de schilderkunst van de Gouden Eeuw* (Zwolle: Waanders, 1997).
3 B. Bakker and E. Schmitz (eds), *Het aanzien van Amsterdam. Panorama's, plattegronden en profielen uit de Gouden Eeuw* (Bussum: Toth, 2007). Cfr. Christopher Brown, *Dutch Townscape Painting* (London: National Gallery London, 1972); Giuliano Briganti, *The View Painters of Europe* (London: Phaidon, 1970); Rolf Fritz, *Das Stadt- und Strassenbild in der holländischen Malerei des 17. Jahrhunderts* (Inaug. diss., Berlin, Stuttgart, 1932); Jeroen Giltaij and Guido Jansen (eds), *Perspectieven. Saenredam en de architectuurschilders van de 17^e eeuw* (Rotterdam: Museum Boijmans-van Beuningen, 1991); Maria Elisabeth Houtzager (ed.), *Nederlandse architectuurschilders, 1600–1900* (Utrecht: Catalogus Centraal Museum, 1953); Carry van Lakerveld (ed.), *The Dutch Cityscape in the 17th Century and its Sources* (Bentveld-Aerdenhout: Landshoff, 1977); A. van Suchtelen and A.K. Wheelock Jr. (eds), *Hollandse stadsgezichten uit de Gouden Eeuw* (Den Haag: Mauritshuis, 2008), 82–5.
4 Eddy Verbaan, *De woonplaats van de faam. Grondslagen van de stadsbeschrijving in de zeventiende-eeuwse Republiek* (Hilversum: Verloren, 2011).
5 Erika Kuijpers, *Migrantenstad. Immigratie en sociale verhoudingen in 17^e-eeuws Amsterdam* (Hilversum: Verloren, 2005).
6 As Boudewijn Bakker already pointed out, in the seventeenth century this genre of the city scape was named with the term 'conterfeitsel', a term that in seventeenth-century Dutch comes close to our modern word 'portrait'. Boudewijn Bakker, '"Conterfeitsels" en "perspectieven". Het stadsgezicht in de Hollandse schilderkunst van de zeventiende eeuw', in Van Suchtelen and Wheelock, *Hollandse stadsgezichten*, 34–59, esp. 34.
7 For a general discussion of the portrait, see Richard Brilliant, *Portraiture* (London: Reaktion Books, 2013). For the portrait in the Dutch seventeenth century, see Mariët Westermann, *The Art of the Dutch Republic, 1585–1717* (London: Weidenfeld & Nicolson, 1996), 131–56 and Joanna Woodall, 'Sovereign Bodies: The Reality of Status in Seventeenth-century Dutch Portraiture', in Joanna Woodall (ed.), *Portraiture: Facing the Subject* (Manchester: Manchester University Press, 1997), 75–100.
8 Jack Greenstein, 'The Vision of Peace: Meaning and Representation in Ambrogio Lorenzetti's Sala Della Pace Cityscapes', *Art History* 11, no. 4 (1988): 492–510. Cf.

Quentin Skinner, 'Ambrodgio Lorenzetti's Buon Governo Frescoes: Two Old Questions, Two New Answers', *Journal of the Warburg and Courtauld Institutes* 62 (1999): 1–28.
9   Stapel, *Perspectieven van de stad*, 24.
10 Giltaij and Jansen, *Perspectieven*, cat. nr. 61, 287–9 and Van Suchtelen and Wheelock, *Hollandse stadsgezichten*, 82–5.
11 Leonore Stapel, *Perspectieven van de stad. Over bronnen, populariteit en functie van het zeventiende-eeuwse stadsgezicht* (Hilversum: Uitgeverij Verloren, 2000), 58–9.
12 Pieter Rixtel, 'Op het Stadthuys van Amsterdam, Geschildert door den vermaerden Schilder Gerrit Berckheyden van Haerlem', in his *Mengel-rymen* (Amsterdam: Van de Gaete, 1717 (Haarlem, 1669)), 36–40. Digital version on Google Books: https://books.google.com/books?id=rxJeAAAAcAAJ (consulted 19 September 2018). Cf. van Suchtelen and Wheelock, *Hollandse stadsgezichten*, cat. nr. 9 for a discussion in how far Rixtel actually praised this painting.
13 Giltaij and Jansen, *Perspectieven*, 287. Only in the context of Saenredam some attention is given to the poem. Gary Schwartz and Marten Jan Bok, *Pieter Saenredam: The Painter and His Time* (London: Thames and Hudson, 1990), 242.
14 Rixtel, 'Op het Stadthuys van Amsterdam', 36.
15 Thanks to Olga van Marion for advising me on this subject.
16 See among many other literature, Stijn Bussels, *The Animated Image. Roman Theory on Naturalism, Vividness and Divine Power* (Berlin: Akademie Verlag, 2012) and Caroline van Eck, *Art, Agency and Living Presence: From the Animated Image to the Excessive Object* (Boston: De Gruyter, 2015).
17 Fritz Graf, 'Ekphrasis. Die Entstehung der Gattung in der Antike', in Gottfried Boehm and Helmut Pfotenhauer (eds), *Beschreibungskunst/Kunstbeschreibung. Ekphrasis von der Antike bis zur Gegenwart* (München: Fink, 1995), 143–55.
18 Besides Westermann and Woodall mentioned in previous notes, see the exhibiton catalogue: Quentin Buvelot, et al., *Dutch Portraits: The Age of Rembrandt and Frans Hals* (Den Haag: Mauritshuis, 2007).
19 For an annotated edition, see Joost van den Vondel, *Inwydinge van 't Stadthuis t' Amsterdam,* ed. Saska Albrecht, et al. (Muiderberg: Couthinho, 1982).
20 Rixtel, 'Op het Stadthuys van Amsterdam', 39.
21 Rixtel, 'Op het Stadthuys van Amsterdam', 40.
22 See Stijn Bussels, Laura Plezier and Marc Van Vaeck, 'Amsterdam sierlijk verbonden met God. Het lofdicht op het Amsterdamse Stadhuis van Constantijn Huygens', *Spiegel der Letteren*, 59, no. 2–3 (2017): 261–90.
23 The poem can be found in Worp's edition of Huygens' manuscripts: *De gedichten van Constantijn Huygens naar zijn handschrift uitgegeven* (Groningen: Wolters, 1895) VI, 108. My translation.
24 Thomas von der Dunk, *Toren versus traditie. De worsteling van classicistische architecten met een middeleeuws fenomeen* (Leiden: Primavera Pers, 2015) and Gabri

van Tussenbroek, *De toren van de Gouden Eeuw. Een Hollandse strijd tussen gulden en God* (Amsterdam: Prometheus, 2017).

25 Koen Ottenheym, 'The Attractive Flavour of the Past. Combining new Concepts for Ecclesiastical Buildings with References to Tradition in Seventeenth-Century Holland', in Jan Harasimowicz (ed.), *Protestant Church Architecture in Early Modern Europe. Fundamentals and New Research Approaches* (Regensburg: Schnell und Steiner, 2015), 99–114.

26 One of them was offered in 1995 at the Auction Philips, Son & Neal, a second in 1999 at Christie's Amsterdam and a third in 2005 at Finarte-Semenzato Milaan. See https://rkd.nl/nl/explore/images#filters[kunstenaar]—ommersy%2C+Hendrick (consulted 19 September 2018).

27 Many thanks to Boudewijn Bakker for sharing his analysis of this painting.

28 Boudewijn Bakker, 'Oud maar niet lelijk', in *Oud en lelijk. Ouderdom in de cultuur van de Renaissance*, ed. Harald Hendrix and M.A. Schenkeveld-van der Dussen (Amsterdam: Amsterdam University Press, 1996), 37–56.

29 See Susan Kuretsky and Walter Gibson, *Time and Transformation in Seventeenth-Century Dutch Art* (Poughkeepsie: Frances Lehman Loeb Art Center, 2005), 111–39.

30 Ernst H. Kantorowicz, *The King's Two Bodies. A Study in Medieval Political Theology* (Princeton: Princeton University Press, 1957).

31 Kantorowicz, *The King's Two Bodies,* Chapter VII, and Isaac Ariail Reed, *Power in Modernity: Agency Relations and the Creative Destruction of the King's Two Bodies* (Chicago: The University of Chicago Press, 2020).

32 Geert H. Janssen, 'Political Ambiguity and Confessional Diversity in the Funeral Processions of Stadholders in the Dutch Republic', *Sixteenth Century Journal* 40 (2): 283–301 and Angela Vanhaelen, 'Recomposing the Body Politic in Seventeenth-century Delft', *Oxford Art Journal* 31, no. 3 (2008): 361–81.

33 Lorne Darnell, 'A Voice from the Past: Pieter Saenredam's *The Old Town Hall of Amsterdam*, Historical Continuity, and the Moral Sublime', *Journal of Historians of Netherlandish Art* 8, no. 2 (2016): http://www.jhna.org/index.php/vol-8-2-2016/341-darnell-lorne (consulted 19 September 2018).

34 Rixtel, 'Op het Stadthuys van Amsterdam', 37.

35 For further discussion and an elaborate bibliography, see Peter C. Sutton (ed.), *Jan van der Heyden (1637–1712)* (New Haven and London: Yale University Press, 2006), cat. nr. 9, 122–5.

36 Fabio Benzi, *Gaspare Vanvitelli e le origini del vedutismo* (Rome: Vivani Arte, 2002), 33 and Laura Laureati, *Vanvitelli. Gaspar van Wittel* (London: Robilant and Voena, 2008), 10.

37 Many thanks to Eric Jan Sluijter for pointing me at this influence.

38 Georges Pascal, 'Les premiers peintres du paysages Parisien, Abraham de Verwer', *Gazette des Beaux-Arts* 68, no. 2 (1926): 288–92; Madeline Charageat, 'Une vue du

Louvre et de l'Hotel de Nevers par Abraham de Verwer', *Bulletin du Musée Carnavalet* 2 (1949): 3–6; Jeroen Giltaij and J. Kelch, *Lof der zeevaart. De Hollandse zeeschilders van de 17e eeuw* (Rotterdam and Berlin: Museum Boijmans van Beuningen and Staatliche Museen zu Berlin, Gemäldegalerie im Bodemuseum, 1996), 133–36; Stijn Alsteens, Hans Buijs and Véronique Mathot (eds), *Paysages de France dessinés par Lambert Doomer et les artistes hollandais et flamands des XVIe et XVIIe siècles* (Paris: Fondation Custodia, 2008), 247–56.

39 On ordinance from 1639 presents that the painter received 400 *Carolusgulden* from Frederick Hendrick frot wo paintings of the building. Ariane van Suchtelen and Arthur K. Wheelock jr. (eds), *Hollandse stadsgezichten uit de Gouden Eeuw* (Zwolle: Waanders, 2008), Cat. No. 127.

40 Mark A. Thomson, 'Louis XIV and William III, 1689–1697', *The English Historical Review* 6 (1961): 37–58 and Luc Panhuysen, *Oranje tegen de Zonnekoning. De strijd van Willem III en Lodewijk XIV om Europa* (Amsterdam: Atlas, 2016).

Bibliography

Alsteens, Stijn, Hans Buijs, and Véronique Mathot. *Paysages de France dessinés par Lambert Doomer et les artistes hollandais et flamands des XVIe et XVIIe siècles*. Paris: Fondation Custodia, 2008.

Bakker, Boudewijn. 'Oud maar niet lelijk.' In *Oud en lelijk. Ouderdom in de cultuur van de Renaissance,* edited by Harald Hendrix and M.A. Schenkeveld-van der Dussen, 37–56. Amsterdam: Amsterdam University Press, 1996.

Bakker, Boudewijn, and Erik Schmitz (eds). *Het aanzien van Amsterdam. Panorama's, plattegronden en profielen uit de Gouden Eeuw*. Bussum: Toth, 2007.

Bakker, Boudewijn. '"Conterfeitsels" en "perspectieven". Het stadsgezicht in de Hollandse schilderkunst van de zeventiende eeuw.' In *Hollandse stadsgezichten uit de Gouden Eeuw,* edited by A. van Suchtelen and A.K. Wheelock jr., 34–59. Den Haag: Mauritshuis, 2008.

Benzi, Fabio. *Gaspare Vanvitelli e le origini del vedutismo*. Rome: Vivani Arte, 2002.

Brilliant, Richard. *Portraiture*. London: Reaktion Books, 2013.

Brown, Christopher. *Dutch Townscape Painting*. London: National Gallery London, 1972.

Briganti, Giuliano. *The View Painters of Europe*. London: Phaidon, 1970.

Bussels, Stijn. *The Animated Image. Roman Theory on Naturalism, Vividness and Divine Power*. Berlin: Akademie Verlag, 2012.

Bussels, Stijn, Laura Plezier, and Marc Van Vaeck. 'Amsterdam sierlijk verbonden met God. Het lofdicht op het Amsterdamse Stadhuis van Constantijn Huygens'. *Spiegel der Letteren* 59, no. 2–3 (2017): 261–90.

Buvelot, Quentin, and Rudi Ekkart. *Dutch Portraits: The Age of Rembrandt and Frans Hals*. Den Haag: Mauritshuis, 2007.

Charageat, Madeleine. 'Une vue du Louvre et de l'Hotel de Nevers par Abraham de Verwer.' *Bulletin du Musée Carnavalet* 2 (1949): 3-6.

Darnell, Lorne. 'A Voice from the Past: Pieter Saenredam's *The Old Town Hall of Amsterdam*, Historical Continuity, and the Moral Sublime.' *Journal of Historians of Netherlandish Art* 8, no. 2 (2016), http://www.jhna.org/index.php/vol-8-2-2016/341-darnell-lorne (consulted 19 September 2018).

Dunk, Thomas von der. *Toren versus traditie. De worsteling van classicistische architecten met een middeleeuws fenomeen.* Leiden: Primavera Pers, 2015.

Eck, Caroline van. *Art, Agency and Living Presence. From the Animated Image to the Excessive Object.* Boston: De Gruyter, 2015.

Fleurbaay, Ellen. *The Building of Amsterdam Town Hall, now the Royal Palace Amsterdam. The Eighth Wonder of the World.* Amsterdam: Stichting Koninklijk Paleis, 1982.

Fremantle, Katharine. *The Baroque Town Hall of Amsterdam.* Utrecht: Haentjens Dekker & Gumbert, 1959.

Fritz, Rolf. 'Das Stadt- und Strassenbild in der holländischen Malerei des 17. Jahrhunderts.' Inaug. diss., Berlin, Stuttgart, 1932.

Giltaij, Jeroen, and Guido Jansen (eds). *Perspectieven. Saenredam en de architectuurschilders van de 17^e eeuw.* Rotterdam: Museum Boijmans-van Beuningen, 1991.

Giltaij, Jeroen, and Jan Kelch. *Lof der zeevaart. De Hollandse zeeschilders van de 17e eeuw.* Rotterdam and Berlin: Museum Boijmans van Beuningen and Staatliche Museen zu Berlin, Gemäldegalerie im Bodemuseum, 1996.

Goossens, Eymert-Jan. *Het Paleis in de schilderkunst van de Gouden Eeuw.* Zwolle: Waanders, 1997.

Graf, Fritz. 'Ekphrasis. Die Entstehung der Gattung in der Antike.' In *Beschreibungskunst/Kunstbeschreibung. Ekphrasis von der Antike bis zur Gegenwart*, edited by Gottfried Boehm and Helmut Pfotenhauer, 143-55. München: Fink, 1995.

Greenstein, Jack. 'The Vision of Peace: Meaning and Representation in Ambrogio Lorenzetti's Sala Della Pace Cityscapes.' *Art History* 11, no. 4 (1988): 492-510.

Houtzager, Maria Elisabeth (ed.). *Nederlandse architectuurschilders, 1600-1900.* Utrecht: Catalogus Centraal Museum, 1953.

Huygens, Constantijn. *De gedichten van Constantijn Huygens naar zijn handschrift uitgegeven.* Groningen: Wolters, 1895.

Janssen, Geert H. 'Political Ambiguity and Confessional Diversity in the Funeral Processions of Stadholders in the Dutch Republic.' *Sixteenth Century Journal* 40 (2): 283-301.

Kantorowicz, Ernst H. *The King's Two Bodies. A Study in Medieval Political Theology.* Princeton: Princeton University Press, 1957.

Kuijpers, Erika. *Migrantenstad. Immigratie en sociale verhoudingen in 17^e-eeuws Amsterdam.* Hilversum: Verloren, 2005.

Kuretsky, Susan, and Walter Gibson. *Time and Transformation in Seventeenth-Century Dutch Art*. Poughkeepsie: Frances Lehman Loeb Art Center, 2005.

Lakervald, Carry van (ed.). *The Dutch Cityscape in the 17th Century and its Sources*. Bentveld-Aerdenhout: Landshoff, 1977.

Laureati, Laura. *Vanvitelli. Gaspar van Wittel*. London: Robilant and Voena, 2008.

Ottenheym, Konrad. 'The Attractive Flavour of the Past. Combining new Concepts for Ecclesiastical Buildings with References to Tradition in Seventeenth-Century Holland.' In *Protestant Church Architecture in Early Modern Europe. Fundamentals and New Research Approaches,* edited by Jan Harasimowicz, 99–114. Regensburg: Schnell und Steiner, 2015.

Panhuysen, Luc. *Oranje tegen de Zonnekoning. De strijd van Willem III en Lodewijk XIV om Europa*. Amsterdam: Atlas, 2016.

Pascal, Georges. 'Les premiers peintres du paysages Parisien, Abraham de Verwer.' *Gazette des Beaux-Arts* 68, no. 2 (1926): 288–92.

Reed, Isaac Ariail. *Power in Modernity: Agency Relations and the Creative Destruction of the King's Two Bodies*. Chicago: The University of Chicago Press, 2020.

Rixtel, Pieter. 'Op het Stadthuys van Amsterdam, Geschildert door den vermaerden Schilder Gerrit Berckheyden van Haerlem.' In Rixtel, Pieter. *Mengel-rymen,* 36–40. Amsterdam: Van de Gaete, 1717 (Haarlem, 1669). Digital version on Google Books: https://books.google.com/books?id=rxJeAAAAcAAJ (consulted 19 September 2018).

Schwartz, Gary, and Marten Jan Bok. *Pieter Saenredam: The Painter and His Time*. London: Thames and Hudson, 1990.

Skinner, Quentin. 'Ambrodgio Lorenzetti's Buon Governo Frescoes: Two Old Questions, Two New Answers.' *Journal of the Warburg and Courtauld Institutes* 62 (1999): 1–28.

Stapel, Leonore. *Perspectieven van de stad. Over bronnen, populariteit en functie van het zeventiende-eeuwse stadsgezicht*. Hilversum: Uitgeverij Verloren, 2000.

Suchtelen, Ariane van, and Arthur K. Wheelock, Jr. (eds). *Hollandse stadsgezichten uit de Gouden Eeuw*. Den Haag: Mauritshuis, 2008.

Sutton, Peter C. (ed.). *Jan van der Heyden (1637–1712)*. New Haven and London: Yale University Press, 2006.

Thomson, Mark A. 'Louis XIV and William III, 1689–1697.' *The English Historical Review* 6 (1961): 37–58.

Tussenbroek, Gabri van. *De toren van de Gouden Eeuw. Een Hollandse strijd tussen gulden en God*. Amsterdam: Prometheus, 2017.

Uitert, Evert van. 'Ruuwe of vervallene gebouwen.' *Kunstschrift* 2 (1992): 17–19.

Vanhaelen, Angela. 'Recomposing the Body Politic in Seventeenth-century Delft.' *Oxford Art Journal* 31, no. 3 (2008): 361–81.

Verbaan, Eddy. *De woonplaats van de faam. Grondslagen van de stadsbeschrijving in de zeventiende-eeuwse Republiek*. Hilversum: Verloren, 2011.

Vondel, Joost van den. *Inwydinge van 't Stadthuis t' Amsterdam,* edited by Saska Albrecht et al. Muiderberg: Couthinho, 1982.

Westermann, Mariët. *The Art of the Dutch Republic, 1585–1717*. London: Weidenfeld & Nicolson, 1996.

Woodall, Joanna. 'Sovereign Bodies: The Reality of Status in Seventeenth-century Dutch Portraiture.' In *Portraiture: Facing the Subject,* edited by Joanna Woodall, 75–100. Manchester: Manchester University Press, 1997.

6

The Exercise of Power: The Caryatids of the Town Hall's Tribunal

Frederik Knegtel

No other space in the Amsterdam Town Hall exhibited a closer relationship between the sculpted decoration and function of a room than the Tribunal. Its sculptural programme, directed by Artus Quellinus (1609–68), emphatically manifests the idea of overpowering and being overpowered. The grand scale of its sculptural ambition claimed attention both inside and outside the building, and for an important reason. The Tribunal was built solely for the pronouncement of death sentences, and the entirety of the room's sculptures responds to this grim function.[1] Located at the front of the building, and clearly visible to those peering through its barred windows, the Tribunal evoked the virtues of good governance and righteousness, and the vice of disobedience.

Contemporary accounts demonstrate that, in addition to providing a decorative frame to the exercise of power, the sculptures appear to be participants in this exercise. Artworks – just like people – are able to affect and shape their environment.[2] Four of the Tribunal's sculptures in particular support this interpretation. Dominating the western wall are four caryatids, which are the largest figures that Quellinus and his assistants executed for this space (Figure 6.1). Accounts and poems written by seventeenth-century Dutch writers reveal a fascination with the appearance of these caryatids, as well as the effect of these figures on their beholders. In their emphasis on shame, sadness and punishment, these contemporary responses rely strongly on Vitruvius's writings on caryatids – and such are those similarities, that these sculptures beg the question as to what extent Quellinus exploited the ideas of the Roman writer for the sake of the rituals performed in that space. In order to answer that question, this chapter will not only focus on the interest in the caryatid type and its function within and beyond the borders of the Dutch Republic, but will also demonstrate why the powerfully expressive quality of Quellinus's

Figure 6.1 The Citizens' Hall seen from the West. Courtesy Stichting Koninklijk Paleis Amsterdam. © The Royal Palace of Amsterdam, photograph: Benning & Gladkova.

figures, when placed in this international context, made them such extraordinary examples.

Punished and penitent: The Vitruvian caryatid

The design and effect of Quellinus's four marble caryatids can be truly grasped only when considering the Tribunal's public sentencing ritual, which was described in detail by the Amsterdam historiographer Olfert Dapper (1636–89) in his 1663 work *Historische Beschryving der Stadt Amsterdam*.[3] One or two days after a death sentence was passed by the Amsterdam Magistrates, the sentence itself was then pronounced in the Tribunal, which was solely built for this purpose. Upon entering the Tribunal, and before the pronouncement of the death warrant started, the condemned would already have experienced the severity of the place. For instance, the opening of its metal entrance gate – which is still preserved – made a dreadful noise; in 1663, Dapper wrote that when these doors opened, they screeched with a terrible sound ('ijselijk' meaning 'terrible' or 'dreadful' and literally 'freezing' or 'icy').[4] He adds that the upper part of this gate was richly decorated with spikes. Quellinus ensured that these sharp ornaments were echoed in the marble decorations of the room itself; the lower Ionic entablature featured one large frieze packed with snakes and skulls placed between thistles, thorns and holly. Playwright Melchior Fokkens (born c. 1620) described the prickly foliage as follows:

> Alle de cieraden in deze Vierschaar aan Lijsten, kronementen, en over al daar Loof-werk is zijn van Distelen, Doornen, Hulst, en alle scherpe vruchten en stekerige bladeren behangen, uytbeeldende de groote strengigheyt en pijnlijkheydt dezer gerechtigheydts rechtvaardige straffe.[5]

> *All of the ornaments in this Tribunal – mouldings, cornices and all of the foliage – are decorated with thistles, thorns and holly, representing the great austerity and painfulness of the righteous punishment of justice here.*

As we can read in Dapper's description, the condemned was brought to the centre of this space and made to stand before the Sheriff, who was accompanied by nine Magistrates acting as judges. They would take their place on the marble steps in front of the heavily decorated western wall of the room, while the town secretary would sit on the marble lectern against the north wall. The Sheriff pronounced the crimes of the condemned, as well as the way the sentence would be executed. After the town secretary read the verdict, the Magistrates would walk upstairs to discuss the verdict with the Burgomasters in their chamber, which was linked to the Tribunal by a large window. Having returned to the Tribunal to answer to the Sheriff, the Magistrates would again visit the Burgomasters upstairs to discuss the manner of execution. After this complex ceremony, the condemned was brought to the Chamber of Justice on the first floor, which was connected to a wooden scaffold attached to the exterior of the building. Once on this scaffold, the condemned was publicly flagellated and executed. Hence, the thorny plants in the marble frieze make another appearance, but this time are all too real: the prisoner was lashed with sharp twigs, before being decapitated or hanged. Inside, the condemned would thus already have been confronted with the instruments and sensations of pain he or she would have to endure in front of the building.

The grim purpose of the Tribunal resonates in the presence of its four caryatids. They are sculpted larger than life and are each placed on a pedestal. The two caryatids closer to the centre of the room have their hands tied behind their backs. The two outer figures fold their hands uneasily in front of their eyes, as if to prevent people from seeing their faces, or perhaps preventing themselves from seeing the spectacle unfolding in front of them. Although standing in a seemingly relaxed *contrapposto* pose, the position of their heads reveals that they all suffer greatly from the heavy load they are carrying. Quellinus conveys the impression of the immense pressure exerted by the entablature above the caryatids, which causes the back of their heads to be weighed down, bending them forward and forcing their faces downwards at a sharp angle. The viewers inside the Tribunal were able to investigate these faces expressing feelings of sadness, pain and shame. And, although their long hair seems neatly braided and tied on the top of their heads, a closer examination reveals that the hair is stuck in and around the Ionic capitals the caryatids are carrying. While two braids are tightly coiled in the spiralling volutes above them, the other locks end up twisting around the capital towards the back. This tight grip holds their heads firmly in place, preventing them from escaping their load. It is difficult to tell whether Quellinus has sculpted carved female figures or whether he has sculpted real female figures carrying capitals where once columns had been.[6]

For the Amsterdam caryatids, van Campen and Quellinus must have closely studied Vitruvian ideas. The caryatid, as a term, was first recorded by Vitruvius in an origin story included in his *De Architectura libri decem* (*Ten Books on Architecture*), written *c.* 30 BCE. The artists and architect of the Town Hall relied on a variety of early modern treatises dedicated to architecture and iconography, most notably Scamozzi's *L'idea della Architettura Universale* from 1615 – but at the basis of these sources were the ideas of Vitruvius, whose text was the only substantial antique treatise on architecture to survive.[7] Vitruvian ideas had already reached the Low Countries through Pieter Coecke van Aelst's *Die inventie der colommen met haren coronementen ende maten* (Antwerp, 1539), Hans Vredeman de Vries' *Architectura* (Antwerp, 1577), and through a complete Dutch translation by the Leiden merchant Johannes de Laet in 1649.[8] We actually know that van Campen read the Italian translation of Vitruvius by Daniele Barbaro (*I dieci libri dell'architettura di M. Vitruvio*, Venice 1556).[9] A letter written by the botanist Johan Brosterhuisen in 1642, moreover, tells us that Brosterhuisen collaborated with the poet and diplomat Constantijn Huygens and van Campen to compile an extensive architectural manual, combining a Vitruvius translation with texts by Andrea Palladio and Sir Henry Wotton.[10] It is within this milieu that Quellinus and van Campen designed the Tribunal.

The great extent to which Quellinus embraced Vitruvian ideas for the execution of his caryatids can be seen in the parallels between Vitruvius's caryatid story, on the one hand, and the design and use of the Amsterdam caryatids, on the other. Vitruvius's aetiology features prominently in the first chapter of his first book, which is dedicated to the education of the architect. The Roman writer underscores several key skills and specialized knowledge every architect has to master, and one of these is an excellent understanding of *historia*, since an architect ought to be able to provide anyone who inquires after the use of ornaments with an explanation why these motifs were introduced. As an example, Vitruvius discusses the use of caryatids, instead of columns, and adds the origin story:

> Consider, for example, if anyone has decided, in place of columns, to insert statues of women clad in *stolae* – the so-called caryatids – into his work, and above them to set cornices and mutules. For those who inquire he will give the following rationale: the Peloponnesian city of Caryae had sided with the enemy, Persia, against Greece. Subsequently, the Greeks, gloriously delivered from war by their victory, by common agreement declared war on the Caryates. And so, when they had captured the town, slaughtered the men, and laid a curse on the inhabitants, they led its noble matrons off into captivity. Nor would they allow these women to put away their *stolae* and matronly dress; this was done so that they should not simply be exhibited in a single triumphal procession, but should instead be weighted down forever by a burden of shame, forced to pay the price for such grave disloyalty on behalf of their whole city. To this end, the architects active at the time incorporated images of these women in public buildings as weight-bearing structures; thus, in addition, the notorious punishment of the Caryate women would be recalled to future generations.[11]

When the women of the town became enslaved, Vitruvius writes, they were not allowed to get rid of their gowns and ornaments, so that they became eternally recognizable as examples of captivity and shame. In other words, their clothing would remind onlookers of their past privileged life, which had ended so abruptly and violently. These tokens emphasized the gravity of the wrong choices attributed to them and stressed their new role as examples of submission. These events, Vitruvius states, led 'the architects active at the time' to design female support-figures representing the overpowered matrons. Not only does Vitruvius's legend provide an interpretation of the *origin* of the caryatid, it also describes its first use, and the reason it became used.

Of great importance here, is that Quellinus's execution of the caryatids in the Tribunal strongly conveys the dual conception of suppression that is crucial for the Vitruvian origin story; Quellinus's marble interpretations of the caryatids in the legend are 'weighted down' both figuratively, as a result of oppression and humiliation, and literally. Moreover, Quellinus places them in a space that enables them to perform this oppression, making their role like the fear-inducing and warning role of the caryatids in the Vitruvian story. And like the captured maidens, Quellinus's figures still wear their matronly clothing, albeit brutally pulled down above the waist. The associated Vitruvian message – the price of disloyalty – was addressed to all of Amsterdam's citizens, and was further reinforced by the flanking marble reliefs of Seleucus and Brutus, in which sons of high-ranking individuals are sentenced regardless of their status or high birth. The degree to which Quellinus exploits Vitruvian ideas of suffering and shame in his marble caryatids – in order to maximize their political effect – is unique, and his approach to these figures and their function appears to deviate from conventions that existed beyond the borders of the Dutch Republic. In fact, Quellinus's approach breaks free from an iconographical mode that originated in early sixteenth-century Italy and grew more dominant with every decade. To better grasp the extraordinary appearance and effect of the Amsterdam caryatids in seventeenth-century Europe, we first need to look at these earlier developments in Italian and French circles.

The caryatid in early modern Europe: Between ornament and actor

In order to design a caryatid in early modern Europe, artists were largely dependent on illustrations of editions of Vitruvius. The first illustrated edition of Vitruvius was published in 1511, by the Italian friar Giovanni Giocondo (1433–1515). Moreover, Giocondo's disciple Raphael, as well as contemporaries such as Marcantonio Raimondi, combined the study of Vitruvius's text with an interest in archaeological research and reconstruction in Rome (Figure 6.2).[12] Even though the appearance of the now popular caryatids of the Erechtheion on the Athenian Acropolis was not yet well known among Renaissance antiquarians – for the knowledge of authentic Greek art was underdeveloped in the early modern period – artists and writers in Italian and French workshops were familiar with Roman copies of the Erechtheion caryatids at the Forum of Augustus in Rome (Figure 6.3).[13] This Erechtheion model – the head upright, a slightly bended knee and flowing draperies falling in even folds – soon became an important source of influence for new illustrated editions of Vitruvius that were published in the sixteenth and seventeenth century, such as Jean Martin's French translation of 1547 with illustrations by Jean Goujon (c. 1510–c. 1565) and Walter Hermann Ryff's *Vitruvius Teutsch* from 1545–50 – both editions featuring images of caryatids indebted to Raimondi.[14]

This Erechtheion model soon became a dominant type, both in the illustration of Vitruvius and in designs by draughtsmen and sculptors. However, there were important exceptions. Some artists stayed closer to the words of Vitruvius's text, emphasizing the sense of shame and punishment of the story by means of the

Figure 6.2 Marcantonio Raimondi, *Façade with caryatids*, 1502–34. Courtesy Rijksmuseum Amsterdam, Public Domain.

posture and emotion of their figures. One early example is the Italian translation of Vitruvius from 1521 by Cesare Cesariano (1475–1543). The illustrator depicts four caryatids with bent heads and distressed faces, all supporting the entablature with both head and arms (Figure 6.4).[15] This emphasis on the affective qualities of the burden in the *historia* is quite evident: since the illustration aims to represent and thus reconstruct the original caryatid, the image follows Vitruvius's source text as accurately as possible. Quellinus's caryatids belong to the same category. We know that van Campen studied Daniele Barbaro's 1556 annotated Italian edition of Vitruvius. This means that the book entered into the artistic network of Quellinus, who worked in close collaboration with van Campen.[16] In Barbaro's edition, the Vitruvian origin story is accompanied by Andrea Palladio's illustration of three caryatids with Corinthian capitals, one of the most faithful

Figure 6.3 A caryatid from the Forum of Augustus, first-century CE copies of fifth-century BCE originals. Museo dei Fori Imperiali Roma, Public Domain.

renderings of the Erechtheion type produced during the sixteenth century. If Quellinus has studied and gained inspiration from this edition, he would have been more likely influenced by the pair of female terms on the book's title page however, both of which are shown with a bare upper body. The caryatid term, which is often depicted in this manner, might have made a stronger impression on Quellinus than their regular caryatid counterparts. In fact, Quellinus's caryatids do betray several similarities with some semi-nude caryatid terms from Vredeman de Vries' *Caryatidum (vulgus termas vocat) sive Athlantidum multiformium* from 1565 (Figure 6.5). Not only are many of the terms in the book bare-chested, some of them are also depicted with inclined heads and torsos, weighted down by the entablature above them.[17]

Figure 6.4 Cesare Cesariano, *Di Lucio Vitruvio Pollione de architectura libri dece* (Como: Gottardo de Ponte, 1521), fol. 6. Courtesy of HathiTrust, Getty Research Institute.

Very much like the Cesariano type, Quellinus's design seems to represent the Vitruvian idea of punishment on both a physical and emotional level, which suited the Tribunal's particular purpose. The reasons why the type of penitent and affected caryatid, as represented by Cesariano and later by Quellinus in the third dimension, was fairly uncommon in sixteenth- and seventeenth-century Western Europe were manifold. First, since the Erechtheion model was a popular Vitruvian illustration, it also became a popular ornament – from Pirro Ligorio's Casino built for Pius IV at the Vatican in 1562 to Jean Goujon's Tribune des Caryatides at the Louvre from circa 1550.[18] Second, the contexts in which caryatids were most often used left no other option than to use a beautiful caryatid. The Vitruvian caryatid is a type that publicly exhibits penitence, which is a very specific function that would clash with the order and grace of most façade designs.

Figure 6.5 Hans Vredeman de Vries, plate 15 of 16, as published in *Caryatidum* (Antwerp: Gerard de Jode, c. 1565). Courtesy Victoria and Albert Museum, London.

To understand the dominance of the Erechtheion type in Western Europe, and the historical significance of Quellinus's caryatids in breaking this dominance, the development of the French sixteenth-century caryatid is crucial. The work of Goujon and the French discourse that sparked it aimed to ground the Erechtheion model as an example of Greek art worthy of emulation. In addition to his illustrations in Martin's 1547 translation of Vitruvius, Goujon himself sculpted a group of grand caryatids adorning the Salle des Cent-Suisses of the Louvre Palace (Figure 6.6). The room was built by Pierre Lescot (1510–78) between approximately 1546 and 1550 and served as both a royal guardroom and occasional ceremonial hall. In the room, Lescot constructed a tribune for musicians, supported by four caryatids sculpted by Goujon – an Erechtheion model closely resembling his illustrations for the Vitruvius edition.[19] As examples of the Erechtheion type, their heads firmly point forwards, and all share the same idealized, anonymous, and expressionless face, characterized by bulging blank eyes. Rather than remembering viewers of enslaved and suppressed women, these sculptures would have reminded viewers of idealized antique marble sculptures. Moreover, Goujon did not need to show figures displaying pain or

Figure 6.6 Jean Goujon, two of the four caryatids in the Salle des Caryatides, 1546–1550. RMN, Musée du Louvre Paris, Public Domain.

shame, and such representations may not even have been appropriate or rhetorically convenient. Even though citizens were admitted to the Salle des Cent-Suisses, it did not serve the same political and judicial purpose that is key to the Vitruvian story, which must have strongly appealed to Quellinus. Most importantly, although Goujon knew Vitruvius's book very well and contributed to its first French translation, he would certainly not have wanted to manifest the idea of suppression to the degree of Quellinus's figures. Goujon's work, predating Quellinus's sculptures by a century, can be characterized by a strong emphasis on grace and delicacy. His goal was to translate known examples of classical antiquity into a more personal imagery, one of feminine gracefulness, showcasing a mix of classical Greek and modern ideals of beauty.

Figure 6.7 Theodoor van Thulden after Peter Paul Rubens, *The Temple of Janus,* as published in Gaspard Gevaerts, *Pompa Introitus Ferdinandi* (Antwerp: Van Thulden, 1639–41). Rijksmuseum Amsterdam, Public Domain.

This idea of feminine grace became a defining idea in the creation and theory of the caryatid in France during the seventeenth century. For instance, in the three-volume work *Histoire et recherches des antiquités de la ville de Paris,* French historian Henri Sauval (1623–76) praises Goujon's caryatids for giving them a classical perfection of femininity:

> [L]eurs coëfures & leurs cheveux viennent si bien à leur visage, qu'il ne se peut pas mieux; leur front uni & mollement vouté, une gorge ronde & pleine, leurs yeux à fleur de tête, leurs sourcils bien rangés, leur nés aquilin, leur bouche étroite, leur menton & leurs joues rondes, nous font bien voir que Goujon s'est efforcé de representer une beauté parfaite.[20]

> *Their head-dresses and their hair combine so well with their faces, that it cannot have been done better. Their united and softly rounded foreheads, a round and full throat, their bulging eyes, their well-arranged eyebrows, their aquiline noses, their narrow mouths, their round chins and cheeks, they all make it very clear that Goujon has endeavoured to represent a perfect beauty.*

This approach also returns in *Les oeuvres d'architecture* of Antoine Le Pautre (1621–79) from 1622, in which the architect elaborates on the use of caryatids and stresses that a caryatid should not carry too heavy a load ('si on regarde les Cariatides on remarquera qu'elles portent trop'), and therefore praises Goujon's figures at the Louvre.[21] Two years after Le Pautre's publication, architect Jacques Lemercier (1585–1654) started the construction of the Louvre's Pavillon de l'Horloge, adjacent to the Salle des Cent-Suisses, and included four pairs of caryatids by French sculptor Jacques Sarazin (1592–1660) on its façade, carrying the pavilion's pediment. The eight graceful figures closely resemble the caryatids in Le Pautre's engraving and they even seem to follow his advice; Sarazin's caryatids do not seem to carry anything at all, and their relaxed postures and interlocking glances evoke a sense of pleasant social interaction. Le Pautre's concern with the imbalance between the delicate female figure and the dominant architectural overload was shared by many French contemporaries. Later in the seventeenth century, the French engraver Sébastien Le Clerc (1637–1714) rejected perhaps most firmly the penitent type of caryatid in his theory on architecture, when he stated:

> On ne donne plus aux Cariates des representations d'esclavage & de servitude, comme autrefois; ces caracteres sont indignes & trop injurieux au beau sexe; on leur en donne de toutes opposées, & on ne les employe plus dans les Bâtimens, que comme des beautez respectables qui en doivent faire les plus riches Ornemens.[22]

> *We no longer represent Cariatides as representations of slavery and servitude, as before; these characters are unworthy and too abusive to this fair sex. We do exactly the opposite, and we only employ them in Buildings as respectable beauties, which make the richest of ornaments.*

Amidst this wave of rejection, however, there is one French writer whose ideal type of caryatid partly approached that of Quellinus. The theorist of art and architecture Fréart de Chambray (1606–76) argued in his *Parallèle de l'architecture antique avec la moderne* from 1650 against the use of female figures for caryatids altogether, deeming it 'a great outrage to this poor sex, and a shame to Architecture, for having so unreasonably used a weak and delicate object to act in a place where strength & hardness would actually be necessary'.[23] Nevertheless, he believed that contemporary architects should respect Vitruvius's *historia* of the caryatid. Because the Vitruvian role of the caryatid as an image of shame and political warning is so specific, Fréart de Chambray stated that 'there are few places where caryatids can be employed appropriately'. This is why he strongly condemned 'the majority of our moderns', architects who misuse caryatids by 'indifferently introducing them in all sorts of buildings'. He preferred the use of vicious figures, such as poor and miserable captives, instead of virtuous ones as caryatids, such as virtues, muses, graces and even angels.[24]

It is difficult to tell whether Fréart de Chambray would have approved of the four marble incarnations in the Amsterdam Tribunal, which Quellinus sculpted that very same year. To employ the caryatid appropriately ('judicieusement') one would need a space where the sculpted figure would, to quote Vitruvius, be 'weighted down forever by a burden of shame' and perform 'in public buildings as weight-bearing structures' the image of 'notorious punishment'. Actually, the Tribunal was such a place, where sculptures confronted the public with the price of disloyalty through their silent meditation on their own penitence.

Quellinus's unique approach to the caryatid, breaking a dominant mode that had been developed on paper and in marble for centuries, is not only evoked by his designs, but is also demonstrated by the voices of those who witnessed these sculptures during the seventeenth century. In contrast to the French emphasis on beauty and female grace, these Dutch accounts reflect on sensations such as sadness, pain, and fear. In fact, these contemporary reactions appear to be as Vitruvian as the caryatids themselves. An important aspect, in this regard, is the broader sculptural context that surrounds the caryatids: a complete programme that aimed at participating in the ritual itself. To fully imbue the viewer with the *gravitas* of the Tribunal's function, Quellinus and van Campen alternated the two pairs of caryatids with three narrative marble reliefs with scenes that expressed the same harsh reality of judgment and punishment.

The Tribunal caryatids: Lifelike participants

Whereas the Louvre caryatids framed the activities of the room as references to classical antiquity, the Amsterdam figures actually participated in the central narrative of the space's ritual. Quellinus placed the four figures in two pairs between three sculpted reliefs. These reliefs – scenes of sentences showing the Greek lawgiver Seleucus, the Biblical King Solomon, and the Roman consul

Lucius Junius Brutus – allude respectively to the notions of mercy, wisdom and justice. The four caryatids in between do not just frame these reliefs, but actually reinforce their message. The caryatids (when interpreted in the Vitruvian sense) further express the idea of justice by emphasizing the public function of the Tribunal: the emotions of remorse and shame of the condemned citizen should be made public, so that it may serve as a warning to all, regardless of status or high birth. They stress the central narrative of Quellinus's sculpted interior that is presented to the beholder, which comprises all stages of trial and execution.

When understood as participants in the exercise of power, these sculpted caryatids had few predecessors in early modern Europe. Perhaps the most notable example of earlier caryatids supporting the central narrative of the sculptural

Figure 6.8 Artus Quellinus, *The Judgement of Junius Brutus*, c. 1655, Courtesy Stichting Koninklijk Paleis Amsterdam. © The Royal Palace of Amsterdam, photograph: C. Messier.

programme and encompassing ritual is the Joyous Entry of the Cardinal-Infante Ferdinand into Antwerp in 1635. The ephemeral triumphal arches erected for these festivities, designed by Peter Paul Rubens (1577–1640), Gaspar Gevartius (1593–1666) and Theodoor van Thulden (1606–69), included a Temple of Janus (*Templum Jani*) that featured two pairs of caryatid terms, flanking a central scene with painted figures (Figure 6.7). The statues of Repose and Concord are situated on the right, and are mirrored on the left by their counterparts of Discord and Strife.[25] While both pairs carried the building's entablature, they also carried the temple's core meaning, evoking the sharp contrasts that characterize any war. And like Quellinus's Tribunal, the caryatids not only framed scenes with lively figures, but were also designed to appear lifelike itself. However, more strongly than the Antwerp figures – which were painted cut-outs of figures ending in tapering columns – the caryatids of the Tribunal reminded one of real human beings. Beyond the representation of myth, vice and virtue, their lifelike figures would also confront the seventeenth-century viewer with more basic feelings, such as pain and fear. Looking at these sculptures, one could actually relate to the uneasy pose of the figure and imagine the idea of a great weight resting eternally on one's shoulders. In other words, one does not even need to know Vitruvius, or anything else about these figures to be able to identify with them and to internalize their sculpted emotions. Here, we are not only concerned with iconographical meaning or with style, but also with qualities that are deeply human. Therefore, in addition to the aspect of iconography, we also need to consider the sculpture's anthropomorphic implications. As a matter of fact, a great number of seventeenth-century poems and descriptions of the Tribunal connected the caryatids with an array of human emotions, rendering them virtually 'alive'.

The caryatid and the condemned

During the pronouncement of the death sentence, the condemned would have been forced to look in the direction of the four caryatids, towering above the heads of the Sheriff and Magistrates sitting on the marble below. The inner two figures could confront the condemned with his penance. The outer two caryatids, holding their hands in front of their faces, could have imbued the criminal with the associated public humiliation.[26]

But instead of avoiding being seen, evoking the shame in the Vitruvian legend, seventeenth-century viewers could also easily interpret these outer caryatids as avoiding seeing what happens in front of them, thereby directly confronting the condemned with the severity and cruelty of the death sentence being pronounced. This shift from the caryatid's own punishment to that of the condemned, is clearly evoked in Melchior Fokkens's description of the Tribunal: 'Tusschen deze geschiedenissen staan vier groote Vrouwe beelden als weenende, beyde handen houdenze voor haar oogen, om de bedroefde ongelucken niet te zien.' ('Between these histories are four large female statues as if crying/ holding both hands in front of their eyes/ to avoid seeing these sad misfortunes.'[27])

Moreover, to the left, the condemned could have seen the marble relief depicting the lawgiver, Seleucus. Instead of executing the full penalty of putting out both eyes of his son, Seleucus, as a righteous lawgiver, but a merciful father as well, submitted himself to the loss of one of his own eyes. At this stage in the judicial procedure, however, the pathos evoked in the sculpted relief would not be able to influence the nine Magistrates, since they had already passed the judgement. Neither the tears of the screaming marble children sitting on top of the lectern of the town secretary, nor the apparent tears behind the folded hands of the caryatids (as evoked in Fokkens's description) would have been able to have an altering effect on the pronouncement of the verdict. The Dutch poet Jan Vos (1612–67), in his poem on the inauguration of the Town Hall, evokes this harsh reality by describing the crying marble figures of the Tribunal:

> Men weent hier overal, en mengt de laauwe beeken
> Van 't purperbloet, dat door de byl langs d'aard' komt leeken,
> Met zoute traanen, die langs doodtsche kaaken vliên.
> Men kan hier deerenis in steene beelden zien.[28]

> *Everywhere, here, they weep, and mix the lukewarm streams*
> *Of the purple blood, dripping from the axe upon the ground,*
> *With salty tears, flowing down dead jaws.*
> *Here, we can see pity in stone statues.*

The work of Fokkens and Vos demonstrates that the beholder connected the Tribunal caryatids with far more emotions than just the Vitruvian sensations of shame and remorse. Both writers attribute a sense of distress to Quellinus's caryatids, a distress in the face of death. For the condemned, who had now become a 'child of death', entering the Tribunal meant crossing a point of no return. Despite the distress these marble figures expressed, nothing would at this point work to the advantage of the person sentenced to death. The sadness would only appeal to the emotions of the condemned, and to the citizens watching the ritual through the barred windows. The emotion of distress joins that of sadness, pain and anxiety – and for the city's council members, this sensation would be an appropriate instrument of warning.

The caryatid and the citizen

Ultimately, this expression of distress and the function of these caryatids in their political and judicial context would not have been much different from that of their ancestors in the Vitruvian legend. Functioning as a public warning, the figures are personifications of defeat and just punishment. They were clearly visible to Amsterdam's citizens, who were always able to peer through the Tribunal's three windows. Whereas the Citizens' Hall, with its marble maps of the world, emphasized the city's control over the seas, the Tribunal demonstrated Amsterdam's control over life and death.[29]

For those citizens who knew Latin, the front of the Tribunal's heavy gate presented to them a warning from Virgil's *Aeneid*: the Greek hero Theseus, being condemned to the chair of oblivion in the underworld, tried to convince mankind to be righteous: 'Warned by me, learn justice, and not to despise the gods.'[30] The Tribunal's caryatids functioned in the same manner as Theseus's warning; they demonstrated what punishment entails and functioned as a frightening warning that confronts those people who are likely to follow the same path with an image of pain and defeat. While an image of a human being can cause its viewer to imitate or be attracted to what he or she perceives, it can just as well cause the viewer to strongly distance him- or herself from the object. The central figure of the righteous Solomon, for example, would have constituted an ideal mirror for the Magistrates sitting in front of it.[31] But as far as the caryatids were concerned, the opposite would ideally occur: as caryatids, they had to lead the viewer to internalize their pain and humiliation, thereby feeling what it is like to be captive or punished. This could provoke the viewer to avoid becoming what he or she perceived, like the female slaves and their stone caryatid copies in Vitruvius. The council members of the city of Amsterdam would not have wanted the citizens, gazing at the space and its ritual through the windows, to feel sympathy or even affective empathy. Ideally, the ritual and the surrounding space would instead cause an emphatic response of personal distress, which is primarily self-oriented.[32] In this case, the distress of another person does not elicit sympathy, but only makes oneself feel disturbed or warned. To this end, the condemned was even rendered more abject by means of public flagellation outside. A citizen of Amsterdam witnessing the entire ritual could easily equate the sentenced person with the sentenced caryatid in the background. Both figures would ideally function in the same manner and reinforce their role: as warnings in flesh and in marble.

This particular idea is evoked in the laudatory poem *Hemelsch Land-Spel*, written by Everard Meyster (1617–79) in 1655 in honour of the inauguration of the Town Hall. As pointed out in Chapter 4 of this book, Meyster's play features a conversation between Jupiter, other gods, and several renowned artists from the past – and among other things, the group discusses the interior of the new building. After the figure of Maarten van Heemskerck describes the relief depicting Brutus and the decapitation of his own sons, the figure of Jupiter states that this would be a righteous punishment for all who commit such a crime. One of Meyster's characters is none other than Vitruvius himself, who takes this idea even further: evoking the origin story of the caryatid from *De Architectura*, Meyster's Vitruvius exclaims that those who criticize the Town Hall itself should undergo the same painful punishment as the Tribunal's caryatids:

VITRUVIUS – Zoo moetens' oock geboeit, geparst, gepijnigt zijn,
Die'r oyt op dit *Gebouw* uyt-spouwen haer fenijn
Als de vier Beelden, die naer 't leeven uytgehouwen,
In d'Heyl'ge Vierschaer staen, zeer droevigh om t'aenschouwen,
Met d'Handen op de ruggh', met d'Handen voor haer Oogh,
Gelaen, getorst op 't Hooft; met swaeren Last om hoogh,
Tot elck eens Les en Leer, hoe Nemesis den quaden
Het quaed betaelen doet met straf en ongenaden.[33]

VITRUVIUS – *They should also be handcuffed, crushed, tortured,*
They, who would ever spit out their venom on this Building,
Like those four Statues, carved from life,
Standing in the holy Tribunal, very sad to behold,
With their hands behind their back, with their hands in front of their eyes,
Burdened, carrying on top of their Heads; this heavy Burden,
May it, to each, be a lesson to learn, that Nemesis makes evil
Pay the price of evil, through punishment and disgrace.

The idea that Meyster presents is that every citizen looking through the windows of the Tribunal was able to see what would eventually happen to them if they would do wrong. Regardless of the type of punishment, to commit a crime meant to be chained and surrendered to the decision of the Magistrates and Burgomasters, just like the caryatids are cuffed and fixed in the marble fabric of the building. And here, the use of the character of Vitruvius himself to describe the Vitruvian effect of sculpture on the viewer clearly evokes the significance in the social circle around van Campen – which included Quellinus – attached to the treatise. The creation of a truly Vitruvian caryatid as part of a permanent work of architecture was very rare and highly original in European public art, and Meyster was well aware of this significant role.

Mirroring gazes: The sculptural context

The different effects the Tribunal caryatids exerted – as described by their contemporaries – were only further enhanced by the multitude of sculptures that surrounded them. Quellinus and van Campen made sure that the other marble figures could also act on the viewer's role in the ritual – whether it be that of the citizen, the condemned, or the Magistrate.

In a similar manner to the equation of the condemned with the caryatids in the background, the public looking through the barred windows was also encouraged to draw another comparison. The marble reliefs of Seleucus, Solomon and Brutus were visible above the heads of the modern judges, the Magistrates, and this echoing effect ideally rendered the latter into the same grand examples, worthy of imitation (Figure 6.8). This particular idea returns in a rather obscure poem dedicated to the Tribunal itself, which has not yet received any attention by scholars. The poem, which bears the title 'Op de marmere Vierschaer van 't Stadthuys tot Amsterdam' ('On the marble Tribunal of the Town Hall of Amsterdam') and would probably have adorned the walls of the *Schepenzaal* (Aldermen's Hall), blurs the distinction between the marble Brutus and the real judges who would sit in front of these sculptures. The Brutus relief shows the unfortunate fate of Brutus's sons, who were relatives of the deposed and expelled king Tarquinus and had tried to bring him back to power. Their father, having to judge his own sons as consul, was left no choice as to sentence and execute them for this act of high treason by having their heads cut off. The poet establishes a relation between the coldblooded determination of Brutus, ordering the death of his own sons, and the coldness of the marble from which he is sculpted.[34]

Figure 6.9 Artus Quellinus, interior of the Tribunal with a portion of the eastern wall visible on the right, *c.* 1655, Courtesy Stichting Koninklijk Paleis Amsterdam. © The Royal Palace of Amsterdam, photograph: E&P Hesmerg.

> De Vader straft op 't strengst de misdaet in sijn Zoonen;
> Niet sonder reden is 't hier al van marmersteen,
> Ja tot de rechters toe,
> Hier sitten steene vaders,
> Die soo haer kind'ren oock veraerden tot verraders,
> Gebruyckten alsoo wel als Brutus byl en roê.[35]

> *The Father severely punishes the crime of his sons;*
> *It is not without reason that everything here is made of marble,*
> *Yes, even the judges,*
> *Here, stone fathers are seated,*
> *Who also reduce their children to traitors,*
> *And, like Brutus, also use the axe and rod.*

Like Brutus, the poet explains, the nine Magistrates would potentially do the same to their own sons, if the latter were to commit the same crime. Moreover, he continues, the judges, as 'fathers of stone', would subsequently use the same weapon as Brutus, the axe and bundle of rods. The poet immediately adds that the same judges, like Seleucus in the left relief, may also be inclined to be compassionate, when this would be more righteous:

> Niet dat men neycht tot straff,
> Maer veel eer tot medoogen;
> Hier sitten vaders die oock met haer eygen oogen,
> Waer 't recht daer meê gepayt, de misdaet kochten aff.[36]

> *Not that they are more inclined to punish,*
> *But rather to be compassionate;*
> *Here fathers are seated who, when deemed more just,*
> *Even expiate the crime with their own eyes.*

Whereas, according to the poet Vos, the marble caryatids above the Magistrates almost seemed to be alive, the anonymous writer renders the actual Magistrates as rigorous as marble. A good judge needs rigour to allow justice to prevail, but should also leave room for wisdom and compassion. These descriptions, how poetic they may be, testify to the powerful and extraordinary effects of sculpture when its visual rhetoric appeals to the viewer's emotions and sense of identity.

As we take into account the gaze of the Sheriff and Magistrates themselves, we are able to discover a scene that is strikingly similar to the perspective of the public looking inside. Although the viewers on Dam Square were able to peer through the window openings and look at the caryatids on the western wall, the Magistrates sitting on the marble bench during the ritual faced the opposite direction and were forced to look at the sculptures of the eastern wall: those of Justice and Prudence, each placed in a niche. As Katharine Fremantle had already pointed out, these two figures 'thus confront the Sheriff and Magistrates', and they 'force themselves on their notice (...) to guide the court's decisions'.[37] In this manner, they actually performed a task very similar to the opposite caryatids, which confronted citizens with themselves, and the path they were expected to walk in civil society.

Even though illustrated editions of Vitruvius served many early modern draughtsmen and sculptors who wanted to design and execute a caryatid, this did not necessarily make their end result thoroughly Vitruvian. What defined the Roman writer's aetiology was the sculpture's specific purpose and effect, and not so much its appearance. Quellinus must have been very aware, in this respect, of the similarities with his commission: it is the public purpose of sculpture where Vitruvius's original caryatid and his Town Hall figures overlap. This potential is reflected in their compelling presence, for they are executed larger than life. And rather than adopting the dominant Erechtheion model, Quellinus must have been more open to designs that evoked much more the Vitruvian sense of shame and punishment, such as Vredeman de Vries' bare-chested and hunched caryatids. This Vitruvian dimension returns in the writings of seventeenth-century poets. And more so, following these poets, Quellinus's sculptures confronted their viewers not only with the ideas of oppression, but also with emotions such as sadness and compassion. On a deeply human level, the Tribunal made the beholder witness and experience the serious consequences of power. First translated from text to marble, Quellinus's sculpted figures then became translated from marble to flesh, through the production of identification, wonder, and fear on the part of the spectator.

Notes

1. For the history of the Dutch Tribunal or *Vierschaar*, see Pieter Vlaardingerbroek, 'Dutch Town Halls and the Setting of the Vierschaar', in *Public Buildings in Early Modern Europe*, ed. Koen Ottenheym, Monique Chatenet, and Krista de Jonge (Turnhout: Brepols, 2010).
2. On the subject of the human tendency to endow images with life, see Caroline van Eck, *Art, Agency and Living Presence: From the Animated Image to the Excessive Object* (Berlin and Munich: De Gruyter, 2015).
3. Details about the pronouncement and execution ritual are derived from Olfert Dapper, *Historische Beschryving der Stadt Amsterdam* (Amsterdam: Jacob van Meurs, 1663), 512–13.
4. Dapper, *Historische Beschryving*, 346. He writes that the doors of the Tribunal 'ter weder zijde open gaen, en yzelijk op hare metalen pannen gieren'. All translations in this chapter are mine, unless stated otherwise.
5. Melchior Fokkens, *Beschrijvinge der wijdt-vermaarde koop-stadt Amstelredam...* (Amsterdam: Abraham and Jan de Wees, 1663), vol. 1, 112.
6. Here, I am indebted to the observations of Caroline van Eck on Primaticcio's vividly sculpted and non-traditional caryatids in the apartment of the Duchesse d'Étampes (1541–4) in the Château of Fontainebleau. See Caroline van Eck, 'Animation and Petrifaction in Rubens's Pompa Introitus Ferdinandi', in *Rubens's Introitus Pompa Ferdinandi*, ed. Anna Knaap and Michael C.J. Putnam (Turnhout: Brepols, 2014), 155.

7   For the influence of Scamozzi on the Town Hall's design, see Katharine Fremantle, *The Baroque Town Hall of Amsterdam* (Utrecht: Dekker & Gumbert, 1959), 113–14.
8   For De Laet's translation, see Koen Ottenheym, 'De Vitruvius-uitgave van Johannes De Laet (1649)', *Bulletin KNOB: tijdschrift van de Koninklijke Nederlandse Oudheidkundige Bond* 97, no. 2 (1998): 69–76.
9   See the letter written by Bannius to Huygens from 11 August 1636 in Jacob Adolf Worp, *De briefwisseling van Constantijn Huygens* (The Hague: Martinus Nijhoff, 1913), vol. 2, 182–3. Derived from Ottenheym, 'Vitruvius-uitgave', 73.
10 Leiden University Library, Hug 37, letter 41 (6 February 1642). From Ottenheym, 'Vitruvius-uitgave', 73.
11 Vitruvius, *Ten Books on Architecture*, trans. Ingrid D. Rowland (Cambridge: Cambridge University Press, 1999), 22.
12 Kathleen W. Christian, 'Raphael's Vitruvius and Marcantonio Raimondi's *Caryatid Façade*', *Bulletin of the John Rylands Library* 92, no. 2 (Autumn 2016): 107.
13 Alexandra L. Lesk, '"Caryatides probantur inter pauca operum": Pliny, Vitruvius, and the Semiotics of the Erechtheion Maidens', *Arethusa* 40, no. 1 (2007): 31.
14 Christian, 'Raphael's Vitruvius': 114. For Goujon's illustrations in Jean Martin's first French translation of Vitruvius (Jean Martin and Jean Goujon, *Architecture, ou art de bien bastir...* (Paris: J. Gazeau, 1547), see also Frédérique Lemerle, *Les Livres d'Architecture* (Tours: Centre d'Études Supérieures de la Renaissance, 2005), http://architectura.cesr.univ-tours.fr/Traite/Notice/ENSBA_LES1785.asp?param=#noticedetail (consulted on 14 August 2019). Moreover, see Vitruvius, *Vitruvius Teutsch: Nemlichen des aller namhafftigisten vn[d] hocherfarnesten, Römischen Architecti, und Kunstreichen Werck oder Bawmeisters, Marci Vitruuij Pollionis*, trans. Walter Hermann Ryff (Nuremberg: Johann Petreius 1548), fol. 14 r–v.
15 Vitruvius, *De Architectura libri dece traducti de latino in vulgare*, ed. Cesare Cesariano (Como: Gottardo de Ponte, 1521), vol. 1, 6.
16 Based on bills explaining the working relationship between van Campen and the sculptor Jan Jansz de Vos, we can assume that van Campen, as Frits Scholten writes, 'put his ideas about the compositions down on paper in simple sketches, which Quellien then modelled in clay.' See Frits Scholten, *Artus Quellinus. Beeldhouwer van Amsterdam* (Amsterdam: Nieuw Amsterdam, 2010), 39.
17 See Hans Vredeman de Vries, *Caryatidum (vulgus termas vocat) sive athlantidum multiformium ad quemlibet Architecture* (Antwerp: Gerard de Jode, 1565).
18 As Ciarán O'Neill mentions in his PhD dissertation on the caryatid in Britain, 'with the exception of the Vitruvian aetiology, the caryatid was notably absent from fifteenth- and sixteenth-century architectural discourse'. This meant that artists, looking for examples of caryatids, often resorted to the many Erechteion model illustrations of Vitruvius editions. See O'Neill's chapter on the history and theory of

the caryatid from Antiquity to 1914: Ciarán R. O'Neill, 'Bearing the Impossible: The Caryatid in Britain, 1790–1914' (York: PhD Diss., 2018), 58.
19 These details are provided by the research team of the Musée du Louvre. See http://www.louvre.fr/node/1725 (consulted on 14 August 2019).
20 Henri Sauval, *Histoire et recherches des antiquités de la ville de Paris* (Paris: Charles Moette and Jacques Chardon, 1724), 33. This book was not published until 1724 by Claude-Bernard Rousseau, who owned Sauval's manuscript.
21 Antoine Le Pautre, *Les oeuvres d'architecture* (Paris: Jombert, 1622), 4. 'Now, considering the exterior, the anterior façade is extraordinarily rich, though rustic, and the sculpture is not its least ornament. Nevertheless, if we look at the Caryatids, we will notice that they bear too much, and that it would have been better, either to place them on the first floor and carry the Attic in the centre of the wall, or to leave them where they are, moving them forward to carry a Balcony, like Jean Goujon Architect and Sculptor to Henry II has done at the old Louvre, to support a Tribune of Musicians.'
22 Sébastien Le Clerc, *Traité d'architecture avec des remarques et des observations tres-utiles...* (Paris: Pierre Giffart, 1714), 106.
23 Roland Fréart de Chambray, *Parallèle de l'architecture antique et de la moderne* (Paris, Edme Martin, 1650), 34. 'Et de vray bien tost aprés ont veid naistre l'ordre Caryatide, qui fut un tres-grand outrage à ce pauvre sexe, & une honte à l'Architecture, d'avoir si déraisonnablement employé une chose foible & delicate à faire office où la force & la dureté estoient entierement necessaires.'
24 See Chapter 22 ('De l'ordre des Caryatides') in Fréart de Chambray, *Parallèle*, 52. '... il y a peu d'occasions où elles puissent estre employées judicieusement, quoy que la pluspart de nos modernes se soient donné une tres-grande licence de les introduire indifferemment en toute sorte d'ouvrages (...) & bien souvent par une ineptie insupportable ils sont entrer en place de ces pauvres & miserables captives, des figures venerables, comme les vertus, les muses, les graces, & les anges mesme, au lieu que plustost il y faudroit attacher & emmenotter les vices'.
25 Stijn Bussels, 'Making the Most of Theatre and Painting: The Power of *Tableaux Vivants* in Joyous Entries from the Southern Netherlands (1458–1635)', *Art History* 33, no. 2 (2010): 244–45.
26 During the eighteenth century, the Dutch author Jan Wagenaar, in his book *Amsterdam in zyne opkomst, aanwas, geschiedenissen*, would equate the condemned in the Tribunal with the caryatid figure: 'De Vrouwenbeelden vertoonen de veroordeelde misdaadigen. De twee buitensten bedekken, uit schaamte, haare aangezigten met de handen. De handen der twee anderen zyn op den rug vastgeboeid.' ('The female figures represent the condemned criminals. The two outer figures cover their faces with their hands, out of shame. The hands of the other two are bound behind their backs.'). See Jan Wagenaar, *Amsterdam in zyne opkomst, aanwas, geschiedenissen...* (Amsterdam: Isaak Tirion, 1765), vol. 2, 9.

27 Fokkens, *Beschrijvinge*, vol. 1, 111. A similar description also returns in Philipp von Zesen's publication on the Town Hall from 1664, which was probably modeled on the text of Fokkens. See Philipp von Zesen, *Beschreibung der Stadt Amsterdam...* (Amsterdam: Joachim Noschen, 1664), 252.

28 Jan Vos, 'Inwyding van het Stadtshuis t'Amsterdam', in *Alle de gedichten van den Poëet Jan Vos* (Amsterdam: Jacob Lescailje, 1662), 341–42.

29 The Town Hall, and the 'Holy Tribunal' in particular, visualized, to quote Pieter Vlaardingerbroek, 'the highest right the city had, which was the right to decide over life and death'. See Pieter Vlaardingerbroek, 'An Appropriated History: The Case of the Amsterdam Town Hall (1648–1667)', in *The Quest for an Appropriate Past in Literature, Art and Architecture*, ed. Karl A.E. Enenkel and Koen Ottenheym (Leiden: Brill, 2018), 473.

30 The sentence 'discite justitiam moniti, et non temnere divos' is derived from the sixth book of Virgil's *Aeneid*. See Virgil, *Eclogues. Georgics. Aeneid: Books 1–6*, trans. Henry Rushton Fairclough (Cambridge, MA: Harvard University Press, 1916), 6.620, 574–577, https://doi.org/10.4159/DLCL.virgil-aeneid.1916 (consulted on 14 August 2019).

31 For an elaborate discussion on the Amsterdam Town Hall as a particularly overwhelming 'citizen mirror', see Stijn Bussels, 'Meer te verwonderen, als immer te doorgronden. Het Amsterdamse stadhuis, een overweldigende burgerspiegel', *Tijdschrift voor Geschiedenis* vol. 126, no. 2 (June 2013): 234–48.

32 Karsten Stueber, 'Empathy', *The Stanford Encyclopedia of Philosophy* (Fall 2019 Edition), https://plato.stanford.edu/archives/fall2019/entries/empathy (consulted on 22 December 2019).

33 Everard Meyster, *Hemelsch Land-Spel, Of Goden Kout, Der Amersfoortsche Landdouwen: Bevattende den buytensten Opstal van 't Nieuwe Stad-Huys: Eerste Deel* (Amsterdam: unknown publisher, 1655), 75-6.

34 Taking into account these lines, Quellinus's sculpted face of Medusa (accompanied by a Fury) comes to mind, which was situated above the marble bench of the judges. Its screaming face stared down at these judges, who only had to look upwards to turn into 'fathers of stone'.

35 Unknown author, *Den Herstelden Apollos Harp* (unknown publisher, 1663), fol. 66. This is the earliest known publication of this poem on the Tribunal and would probably have hung in the Town Hall's *Schepenzaal*. It returns in a publication *Collectio monumentorum rerumque maxime insignium* (vol. 1) from 1684, which describes buildings and their inscriptions in the Southern Netherlands and the Dutch Republic. Apparently, the poem in the *Schepenzaal* (Aldermen's Hall) was signed with the pseudonym 'Romane'. The name is mentioned under the poem in a description of the *Schepenzaal* from 1741 (see *Beschryvinge van 't stadhuis van Amsterdam* (Amsterdam: Erven J. Ratelband en Compagnie, 1741), 32–3, when the

poem was apparently still adorning its walls. But we already find a connection with this pseudonym in the commentary accompanying the poem in *Den Herstelden Apollos Harp* from 1663. 'Romane' was the pseudonym used by Romanus (or Roemer) van Wesel, a lawyer and poet, and son of Anna Roemer Visscher. However, in *Den Herstelden Apollos Harp*, the author/editor (who uses the pseudonym Trajanus Boccalini) writes that the judges of Amsterdam had written out the poem and placed it on the walls of the *Schepenzaal*, but without the knowledge of the author, whose name is not mentioned. Moreover, Boccalini writes, someone (perhaps Romanus van Wesel) had subsequently placed the name 'Romane' under the poem in the *Schepenzaal*, and a request by the real author to remove this name was apparently to no avail. Further research on this matter, certainly on the credibility of the commentary in *Den Herstelden Apollos Harp*, still needs to be conducted.

36 *Den Herstelden Apollos Harp*, b. fol. 66.
37 Katharine Fremantle, 'The Open Vierschaar of Amsterdam's Seventeenth-century Town Hall as a Setting for the City's Justice,' *Oud Holland* 77, no. 3/4 (January 1962): 216.

Bibliography

Unknown author. *Den Herstelden Apollos Harp*. Unknown publisher, 1663.
Bussels, Stijn. 'Making the Most of Theatre and Painting: The Power of *Tableaux Vivants* in Joyous Entries from the Southern Netherlands (1458–1635).' *Art History* 33, no. 2 (2010): 236–47.
Bussels, Stijn. 'Meer te verwonderen, als immer te doorgronden. Het Amsterdamse stadhuis, een overweldigende burgerspiegel.' *Tijdschrift voor Geschiedenis* 126, no. 2 (June 2013): 234–248.
Bussels, Stijn. 'Medusa's terror in the Amsterdam Town Hall, or how to look at sculptures in the Dutch Golden Age.' In *Idols to Museum Pieces. The Nature of Sculpture, its Historiography and Exhibition History, 1640–1880*, edited by Caroline van Eck, 85–102. Berlin: De Gruyter, 2017.
Christian, Kathleen W. 'Raphael's Vitruvius and Marcantonio Raimondi's *Caryatid Façade*.' *Bulletin of the John Rylands Library* 92, no. 2 (Autumn 2016): 91–127.
Dapper, Olfert. *Historische Beschryving der Stadt Amsterdam*. Amsterdam: Jacob van Meurs, 1663.
Eck, Caroline van. 'Animation and Petrifaction in Rubens's Pompa Introitus Ferdinandi.' In *Rubens's Introitus Pompa Ferdinandi*, edited by Anna C. Knaap and Michael C.J. Putnam, 143–65. Turnhout: Brepols, 2014.
Eck, Caroline van. *Art, Agency and Living Presence: From the Animated Image to the Excessive Object*. Berlin and Munich: De Gruyter, 2015.

Fokkens, Melchior. *Beschrijvinge der wijdt-vermaarde koop-stadt Amstelredam...* Amsterdam: Abraham and Jan de Wees, 1663.

Fréart de Chambray, Roland. *Parallèle de l'architecture antique et de la moderne.* Paris: Edme Martin, 1650.

Fremantle, Katharine. *The Baroque Town Hall of Amsterdam.* Utrecht: Dekker & Gumbert, 1959.

Fremantle, Katharine. 'The Open Vierschaar of Amsterdam's Seventeenth-century Town Hall as a Setting for the City's Justice.' *Oud Holland* 77, no. 3/4 (January 1962): 206–34.

Hersey, George L. *The Lost Meaning of Classical Architecture: Speculations on Ornament from Vitruvius to Venturi.* Cambridge, MA: MIT Press, 1988.

Le Pautre, Antoine. *Les oeuvres d'architecture.* Paris: Jombert, 1622.

Lesk, Alexandra L. '"Caryatides probantur inter pauca operum": Pliny, Vitruvius, and the Semiotics of the Erechtheion Maidens.' *Arethusa* 40, no.1 (2007): 25–42.

Le Clerc, Sébastien. *Traité d'architecture avec des remarques et des observations tres-utiles...* Paris: Pierre Giffart, 1714.

Lemerle, Frédérique. 'Les Livres d'Architecture.' Tours: Centre d'Études Supérieures de la Renaissance, Université François-Rabelais, 2005. http://architectura.cesr.univ-tours.fr/Traite/Notice/ENSBA_LES1785.asp?param=#noticedetail (consulted on 14 August 2019).

Martin, Jean and Jean Goujon. *Architecture, ou art de bien bastir...* Paris: J. Gazeau, 1547.

Meyster, Everard. *Hemelsch Land-Spel, Of Goden Kout, Der Amersfoortsche Landdouwen: Bevattende den buytensten Opstal van't Nieuwe Stad-Huys: Eerste Deel.* Amsterdam: unknown publisher, 1655.

O'Neill, Ciarán R. 'Bearing the Impossible: The Caryatid in Britain, 1790–1914.' PhD diss., University of York, York, 2018.

Ottenheym, Koen. 'De Vitruvius-uitgave van Johannes De Laet (1649).' *Bulletin KNOB: tijdschrift van de Koninklijke Nederlandse Oudheidkundige Bond* 97, no. 2 (1998): 69–76.

Sauval, Henri. *Histoire et recherches des antiquités de la ville de Paris.* Paris: Charles Moette and Jacques Chardon, 1724.

Scholten, Frits. *Artus Quellinus. Beeldhouwer van Amsterdam.* Amsterdam: Nieuw Amsterdam, 2010.

Stueber, Karsten. *The Stanford Encyclopedia of* Philosophy, Fall 2019 Edition, s.v. 'Empathy.' https://plato.stanford.edu/archives/fall2019/entries/empathy (consulted on 22 December 2019).

Virgil. *Eclogues. Georgics. Aeneid: Books 1–6.* Translated by Henry Rushton Fairclough. Cambridge, MA: Harvard University Press, 1916. https://doi.org/10.4159/DLCL.virgil-aeneid.1916 (consulted on 14 August 2019).

Vitruvius. *De Architectura libri dece traducti de latino in vulgare.* Edited and translated by Cesare Cesariano. Como: Gottardo de Ponte, 1521.

Vitruvius. *Ten Books on Architecture.* Translated by Ingrid D. Rowland. Cambridge: Cambridge University Press, 1999.

Vitruvius. *Vitruvius Teutsch: Nemlichen des aller namhafftigisten vn[d] hocherfarnesten, Römischen Architecti, und Kunstreichen Werck oder Bawmeisters, Marci Vitruuij Pollionis*. Translated by Walter Hermann Ryff. Nuremberg: Johann Petreius, 1548.

Vlaardingerbroek, Pieter. 'An Appropriated History: The Case of the Amsterdam Town Hall (1648–1667).' In *The Quest for an Appropriate Past in Literature, Art and Architecture*, edited by Karl A.E. Enenkel and Koen Ottenheym, 455–82. Brill: Leiden, 2018.

Vlaardingerbroek, Pieter. 'Dutch Town Halls and the Setting of the Vierschaar.' In *Public Buildings in Early Modern Europe*, edited by Koen Ottenheym, Monique Chatenet, and Krista de Jonge, 105–18. Turnhout: Brepols, 2010.

Vos, Jan. *Alle de gedichten van den Poëet Jan Vos*. Amsterdam: Jacob Lescailje, 1662.

Vredeman de Vries, Hans. *Caryatidum (vulgus termas vocat) sive athlantidum multiformium ad quemlibet Architecture*. Antwerp: Gerard de Jode, 1565.

Wagenaar, Jan. *Amsterdam, in zyne opkomst, aanwas, geschiedenissen...* Amsterdam: Isaak Tirion, 1765.

Zesen, Philipp von. *Beschreibung der Stadt Amsterdam...* Amsterdam: Joachim Noschen, 1664.

7

Jacob's Trowels: The Construction of the Amsterdam Town Hall and Its Ceremonial Objects (1648–present)

Minou Schraven

At the time of writing, on display at the Rijksmuseum is an ornate silver trowel, designed by silversmith Johannes Lutma (1584–1669): a fine example of the master's auricular style (Figure 7.1). The trowel is displayed next to a gold medal showing the coat of arms of Amsterdam with the characteristic three crosses, flanked by two lions and the date 1648 (similar to the medal in Figure 7.2). As the inscriptions on these objects make clear, they were made for the foundation ceremony of the Amsterdam Town Hall on 28 October 1648, when six-year-old Jacob de Graeff descended into the foundation pit on Dam Square and laid the first stone. This way, the displayed objects invite the museum visitor to connect to the beginning of perhaps the most ambitious building project in seventeenth-century Amsterdam.

This chapter will look closely at the ceremonies connected to the construction of the Town Hall. Which rituals were performed to mark the various stages of its construction, from the laying of the first stone in 1648 up to the inauguration seven years and seven months later? How do these rituals compare to other major building projects of this period, both in Amsterdam and elsewhere? Special attention will be given to the role of objects like the silver trowel, both during the ceremonies and afterwards, in constructing memories of these events. Reconstructing their use and tracing changes in ownership and institutional framings, this chapter aims to unlock the processes by which the ceremonial objects may have gained – and lost – layers of meaning and authenticity, from the moment they were first used until their present-day display in the Rijksmuseum.

Figure 7.1 Johannes Lutma, silver trowel with inscriptions used at the foundation ceremony of the Amsterdam Town Hall, 28 October 1648, 3.5 × 27.8 cm. Rijksmuseum Amsterdam, Public Domain.

According to the historian of religions Mircea Eliade, foundation ceremonies across all times and cultures contain the promise of making the world anew. Besides marking the beginning of a project, they ultimately all refer to a common archetype: the moment that God created the cosmos. From this premise follows the mythical role that communities often attribute to their 'founding fathers'.[1] Indeed, to those standing at the foundation pit at Dam Square, a new era seemed in the making. Their city was more prosperous than ever before. On top of that, the Eighty Years' War between Spain and the Dutch Republic had come to an end. The Peace of Münster, signed in early 1648, had been an outright victory for the merchants of Amsterdam, who had been longstanding advocates for peace. Yet the ambitious and costly building plans also came with risks, as not everybody

Figure 7.2 After Johannes Lutma, silver medal issued at the foundation ceremonies of the Amsterdam Town Hall, 28 October 1648, d. 4,7 cm. Courtesy Amsterdam Museum, Public Domain.

in the Amsterdam oligarchy was necessarily on board.[2] Besides marking the several stages of this building project, the carefully planned ceremonies therefore served just as much to project – at least to the outside world – an image of collective support for this massive undertaking.[3]

Towards a new Town Hall

As early as the first half of the seventeenth century, the city government had realized several successful expansion campaigns, developing living quarters and storehouses on newly created artificial islands. The third of these large expansion projects (1610–16) had created the Jordaan and the famous ring of canals around Dam Square.[4] The 1630s had witnessed the construction of many public buildings, such as the Citizens' Orphanage, the first permanent theatre and the Heiligewegpoort (a former city gate), all projects of architect Jacob van Campen. Compared to these magnificent buildings, the Gothic Town Hall at Dam Square was in a sorry and decrepit state. To replace it with a representative structure that matched Amsterdam's ambitions became felt as a matter of urgency in the aftermath of the Joyous Entry of Maria de' Medici (1575–1642), Queen Mother of France, in 1638.[5]

In his richly illustrated account of the event, Vondel praised the four 'weledelen, grootachbaren, eerentvesten, en voorzichtigen' ('honourable, venerable, respectable and prudent') Burgomasters of Amsterdam for bearing the expenses with magnanimity.[6] Against the spectacular backdrop of the newly created parts of town, triumphal arches and *tableaux vivants* were built for the Joyous Entry. Besides treating Maria to a waterborne theatre festival in the river Amstel, the Burgomasters proudly took her round to witness the recent building spree. The Queen Mother visited the headquarters of the Dutch East Indian Company for a banquet with Asian dishes, the newly built theatre, and the Western Church, then the largest Protestant church in the world.[7] At Dam Square, the Queen Mother visited the Weigh House and the Stock Exchange of Hendrick de Keyser. It is highly unlikely that Maria's itinerary included the unimpressive medieval Town Hall, yet Vondel's poem mentioned it nonetheless, with a focus on its decrepit state. In Vondel's words, this structure was, at best, a memorial of Amsterdam's humble past, and of the city government's desire not to show off.[8]

Just a few months after Maria's Joyous Entry, the Burgomasters started to develop plans for a more representative town hall. Although it was not immediately clear what form and shape it would take, the City Council started to acquire plots on Dam Square to accommodate a building of large dimensions. But then disaster struck. In January 1645, a massive fire destroyed the New Church, next to the old Town Hall on Dam Square. Now the City Council was confronted with two expensive building projects. The Church was rebuilt in the Gothic style, as befitting a house of worship. The plans also included the addition of an impressive tower 112 metres high, designed by Jacob van Campen. Had it been built, it would have been the tallest building of Amsterdam, surpassing even the tower on Utrecht's Dom Church.[9]

As was the custom, the start of the construction of this new tower called for a public ceremony. So, after drilling thousands of wooden poles in the soil, particularly soft in this part of Amsterdam, the first stone of the tower was laid on 26 June 1647. The honour fell to fourteen-year-old Cornelis Backer, son of Burgomaster Willem Cornelis Backer (1595–1652), leader of the Calvinist faction of the City Council, and actually the main instigator of the project. Along with the foundation stone, Backer Senior made a building deposit 200 guilders in the hope of securing a positive outcome to the project.[10] For the festive banquet later that day, a ceremonial wine glass was made, a rummer, studded with prunts for a safe grip, so that it could be passed from one greasy hand to the other during the banquet (Figure 7.3). The rummer was inscribed with the date, the names of Cornelis and Willem Backer, plus the grid (not visible on the image) used to drill the impressive number of 6,363 wooden piles in the foundations of the tower.[11] Now in the collection of the Amsterdam Museum, the drinking glass is

Figure 7.3 Rummer of green glass with inscriptions commemorating the foundation of the tower of the New Church, 26 June 1647, h. 27 cm. Amsterdam Museum, Public Domain.

preserved to keep the memory of the foundation ceremony alive, just as the silver trowel and medal for the foundation ceremony of the Town Hall.

As often happens with projects for an important part backed by just one patron, the construction of the tower would be aborted soon after Willem Backer's death in 1652.[12] In the meantime, though, work on the new Town Hall had started in earnest. In January 1648, the first of the 13,659 wooden foundation poles was driven into the soil. Tellingly, the laying of the foundations coincided with the signing of the Treaty of Münster, after five years of tough negotiations. Amsterdam celebrated this Peace that Spring with a series of *tableaux vivants* on Dam Square and the staging of a play in the City Theatre.[13] The connection between the Peace and the construction of the new Town Hall was made evident in the publication of the *Olyfkrans der Vrede* in 1649: a collection of celebratory texts and poems on both the peace and the foundation ceremony of the new Town Hall.[14]

Two trowels and a medal: The foundation ceremony of October 1648

During the Summer of 1648, the drilling of the foundation poles on Dam Square was nearing completion and moreover, the four Burgomasters finally approved van Campen's designs for the new Town Hall.[15] This meant that preparations for the public foundation ceremony could start. On 28 October of that year, thousands gathered at the building site on Dam Square facing the Kalverstraat, to witness the laying of the first stone. Present were the four Burgomasters in office, the members of the City Council, and architect Jacob van Campen. The task of laying the first stone was given to four children, the sons and nephews of the reigning Burgomasters. Aged between five and fourteen years, they were Gerbrand Pancras, nephew of Gerbrand Claesz. Pancras (1591–1649), Jacob de Graeff, son of Cornelis de Graeff (1599–1664), driving force behind the building project, Sybrant Valckenier, son of Wouter Valckenier (1589–1650), and Pieter Schaep, nephew of Gerard Simonsz. Schaep (1598–1666).[16]

Children often played a prominent role in foundation ceremonies in the Low Countries. In other parts of Europe, the task of laying the first stone was usually performed by the patron of the building, or a representative. This much becomes clear if we look at the foundation ceremony of Lyon Town Hall, a building project on an equally impressive scale.[17] Throughout the difficult years of the *Fronde*, Lyon had remained faithful to the king. The public foundation ceremony of the new Town Hall in 1646 was designed to show the Magistrates' ongoing support of the royal cause. As the date for this ritual, the Magistrates made a point of choosing 5 September, the seventh birthday of Louis XIV. The ritual was performed by Abbot Camille de Neufville (1606–93), future archbishop of Lyon, who had just been appointed as lieutenant-general of the young king for the Lyonnais region. The Abbot's elder brother Nicolas (1598–1685) acted as the young King's tutor, so the ceremony of laying the first stone was given a distinct royal touch.

In contrast, in seventeenth-century Amsterdam, the laying of the first stone of public buildings was often performed by sons of magistrates. In August 1603, the son of Burgomaster Gerrit Pietersz Bicker (1554–1604) had laid the Southern Church's first stone.[18] Likewise, we have seen that the son of Burgomaster Willem Backer laid the first stone of the tower of the New Church in 1647. For the laying

Figure 7.4 Chamois apron used at the foundation ceremonies of the Amsterdam Town Hall, 28 October 1648, 69 × 68 cm. Rijksmuseum Amsterdam, Public Domain.

of the first stone of the Town Hall, the four children were all relations of the Burgomasters in office at that moment, to show the collective character of the undertaking. In this respect, there is a striking analogy with the foundation ceremony of the Haarlem Orphanage in 1660, when four sons of Haarlem Magistrates laid the first stone.[19]

As we know from a poem of Reyer Anslo (1626–69) written to celebrate the laying of the first stone of the Amsterdam Town Hall, the four children were outfitted as stonemasons with trowels and chamois aprons of which one has been preserved (Figure 7.4).[20] During the ceremonies, a small gold medal with the municipal coat of arms was pinned to their chests: we have already encountered the one worn by Jacob (Figure 7.2).[21] Far more medals were issued for distribution amongst the participants that day: the Amsterdam Museum has two silver medals of this type in its collection.²² It had become standard practice to commission commemorative medals of foundation ceremonies for large building projects since the late fifteenth century.²³ Typically, some of these foundation medals were deposited along with the foundation stone. There is no documentation that this happened in the case of the foundation ceremony of the Amsterdam Town Hall. In any event, the medals made for this foundation ceremony were rather plain and inconspicuous, certainly when compared to those issued for the consecration seven years later (see below).

By far the most conspicuous object connected to the foundation ceremony of the Town Hall was Jacob's silver trowel (see Figure 7.1). The reverse of the blade bears an image with four boys engaged in the laying of a first stone in a rather pristine environment, compared to the bustle on Dam Square (Figure 7.5). Below

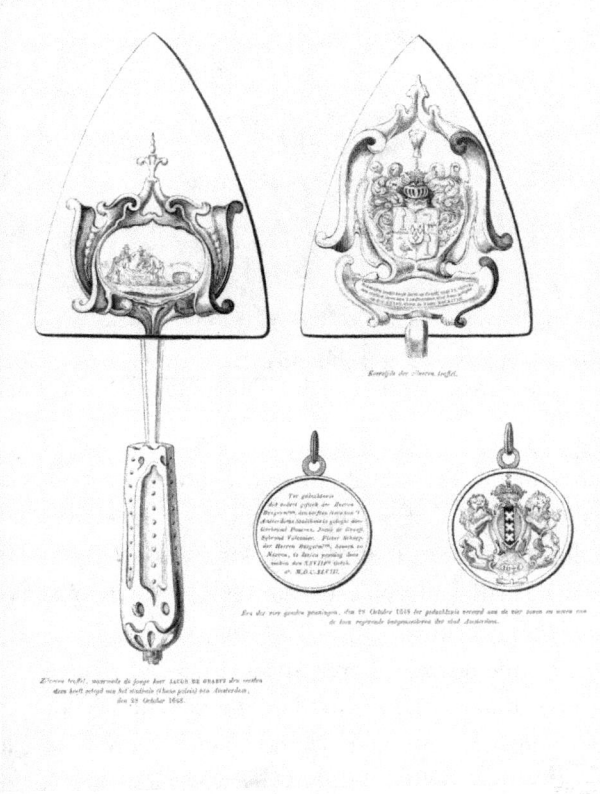

Figure 7.5 Illustration showing the obverse and reverse of Lutma's silver trowel (Figure 7.1), as published in *Bouwkundige Bijdragen* 5 (1849): 330–2. Also printed as separate engraving, Rijksmuseum Amsterdam, Public Domain.

the coat of arms of the de Graeff family on the obverse, the inscription identifies this specific object as the one used by six-year-old Jacob de Graeff for laying the first stone of the Town Hall. However, it is far more likely that the actual first stone was laid with a less ornate trowel, presently in the collection of the Amsterdam Museum. Its blade is inscribed with the name of Philips de Vos, the city's master mason who had assisted the children during the foundation ceremony. According to the inscription on the less ornate trowel, Jacob's family donated this trowel as sign of gratitude to de Vos, reserving Lutma's luxurious trowel for themselves.[24]

Amongst the many ceremonial silver trowels that have come down to us, Lutma's trowel stands out for its beauty, and for being amongst the earliest preserved in the Netherlands.[25] This is not to say that they were not used in other regions, too. A silver trowel was also used during the foundation ceremony of the Lyon Town Hall: once the marble foundation stone had been lowered into the foundation pit, the master mason of Lyon handed the Abbot a silver trowel to pour some cement in the foundation. Accompanied by the sound of trumpets, drums and the firing of canons, the four Aldermen of Lyon repeated this ceremonial act, 'and then all the previous consuls of said city', thus symbolizing the collective support for the undertaking.[26] In October 1666, Louis XIV used a silver trowel for laying the first stone of Bernini's extension to the Louvre. Chantelou informs us in his diaries that, after the ceremonies, the trowel was hot property amongst members of the nobility; everyone wanted to have it.[27]

Compared to the silver trowel, it is far more unusual that the chamois leather apron worn by Jacob has been preserved. To my knowledge, the only case in which similar items have been preserved together is the foundation of *Het Hofje van Staets* (a courtyard with almshouses) in Haarlem on 29 July 1730. Patron Cornelis Staets decided to leave the ceremonial objects to the almshouses's board 'in order to preserve the memory of its origins'. In contrast, the objects of Jacob de Graeff were kept within his family, as heirlooms. In the eighteenth century, the family would use Jacob's trowel for the ceremonial laying of the first stone of a church in Ilpendam.[28] Only towards the end of the nineteenth century would the family hand over the objects to the Amsterdam-based *Koninklijk Oudheidkundig Genootschap* (Royal Antiquarian Society), as we will see below.

The inauguration on 29 July 1655

Seven years after the foundation ceremony, construction of the new Town Hall proceeded swiftly. The Tribunal on the ground floor and the majestic Citizens'

Hall were nearing completion, but there was no sight as yet of a roof. This did not stop the Burgomasters officially taking possession of the Town Hall on 29 July, exactly seven years and seven months after the laying of the first stone. It was well known that Salomon's Temple had also been inaugurated seven years and seven months after its foundation. This biblical analogy with the new Town Hall and its promise of peace was too precious to miss.[29] Certainly, as we can read in the essay of Pieter Vlaardingerbroek in this book, the Temple had indeed been an important model for the design of the Town Hall. So, as we have already seen in case of the foundation of the Town Hall of Lyon, dates marking the major stages in building processes of this magnitude were carefully chosen to inscribe the event within a larger history. The Town Hall, the most ambitious building project of seventeenth-century Amsterdam, is no exception.[30] Organizing a festive inauguration, a second ritual moment in the construction process of their Town Hall, the Magistrates demonstrated that the collective support for this building project was unwavering.

On this carefully established day, the Magistrates attended a religious service and then went for a consistory to the Prinsenhof, that functioned as interim town hall (after the burning of the Gothic Town Hall).[31] From there, they walked in procession to the new Town Hall to take formal possession of the building. Whilst the crowd at Dam Square enjoyed a parade of civic guard companies, the college of Magistrates feasted on a banquet inside the building. To add lustre to this inauguration banquet, a number of objects were made. Firstly, a large green rummer to be passed around during the banquet, similar to the one produced for the foundation ceremony of the tower (Figure 7.3). This rummer was engraved with the inauguration date and the first lines of a poem composed for the occasion.[32] Moreover, Johannes Lutma produced a luxury silver ewer and basin for the banquet, so that hands could be washed in style between courses. The basin's rim was decorated with the names and coats of arms of the four Burgomasters in office that year. The ewer bore the coats of arms and names of Nicolaes Tulp and Cornelis van Dronckelaar: the two treasurers who had supervised the building project from its very beginning.[33] Finally, silver spoons engraved with the image of the (finished) Town Hall and the date of the inauguration were produced as gifts for the civic guard members who had stood on guard that day (Figure 7.6). None of these spoons survive, but as can be seen in an early nineteenth-century drawing, the handle of the spoon was designed as a musket topped by the helmeted head of a guard.[34]

And of course, there were the well-known gold and silver medals issued for the inauguration, designed by silversmith Jurriaan Pool (I) (1618-69), an immigrant from Silesia (Figure 7.7).³⁵ The obverse shows the procession of the Amsterdam Magistrates entering the (already finished) Town Hall. Above them in the sky, Mercury carries a caduceus and a golden hat with the words OMNIBUS IDEM ('the same for everyone'), alluding to the supposed egalitarian rule of Amsterdam. In the foreground, Amphion plays the golden lyre, a gift from the

Figure 7.6 Gerrit Lamberts, drawing of a silver spoon given to the citizens standing on guard during the inauguration ceremony of the Amsterdam Town Hall, c 1810. Courtesy of Stadsarchief Amsterdam, Public Domain.

Figure 7.7 Jurriaan Pool, silver medal commemorating the inauguration ceremony of the Amsterdam Town Hall, 29 July 1655, d. 70 mm. Rijksmuseum Amsterdam, Public Domain.

god Mercury. According to Greek mythology, Amphion would have played it during the miraculous construction of the citadel of Thebes, making the stones glide effortlessly into place.[36] By Amphion's feet, lies a slab with the names of the Burgomasters in office that year: Joan Huydecoper (1599–1661); Cornelis de Graeff (who had also served as Burgomaster in 1648); Jan van de Poll; and Hendrik Dirkszn. Spiegel (1598–1667). The names of treasurers Tulp and van Dronckelaar are also mentioned. The reverse of Pool's medal shows the personification of Amsterdam seated on a throne and flanked by two lions. Behind her is a city under siege; around them we see all thirty-six coats of arms of the members of the City Council. The medals were originally placed in circular boxes (ivory for the gold medals, palm wood for the silver ones), along with a short poem written by Vondel.[37]

Commemorating the foundation ceremony: 1748 and 1848

As we have seen, the construction of the new Town Hall was linked to the Peace of Münster from the very start. How did this combination play out in commemorations of these events? For the first centenary in 1748, the volume *Olyfkrans der Vrede* was republished in a far more prestigious quarto format. The connection with the Town Hall was enforced thanks to twelve newly created poems on the centenary of the building. However, as the political situation of the Dutch Republic was threatened both by the War of Austrian Succession (1740–8) and internal unrest, there was little ground for grand celebrations.[38]

The same was true during the revolutionary year 1848. In November of that year King Willem II (1792–1849) would sign the constitution that would turn the Netherlands into a constitutional monarchy. On 5 June, the king and his son had attended the unveiling of a statue of William of Orange, ringleader of the Dutch Revolt, at the Plein in The Hague. For the first time, the Catholic part of the population openly voiced discontent: why would they have to pay for the statue of a Calvinist? Ever since the Peace of Münster, the Catholic population had been marginalized in Dutch society. They could not run for office and were not represented in the Dutch government.[39]

While the commemoration of the Peace of Münster was thus politically sensitive at best, the bicentenary of the foundation ceremony of the Amsterdam Town Hall provided a welcome auto-celebratory opportunity for a relatively new professional group: that of architects. The *Maatschappij tot Bevordering der Bouwkunst* (Society for the Advancement of Architecture) had been instituted just five years earlier. The professional role model of the architects was Jacob van Campen: the image of the Amsterdam Town Hall would grace the cover of their journal, *Bouwkundige Bijdragen* (*Architectural Contributions*), for decades.[40]

For the bicentenary, the Society organized a commemorative lecture and small exhibition at the Odeon in Amsterdam. Obviously, their journal reported the proceedings of that evening at length.[41] The festive oration held by architect and chair Daniel David Büchler (1787–1881), standing next to a bust of Jacob van Campen, was printed in full. Büchler praised the Burgomasters, but the architect even more for having overcome obstacles and criticisms during the construction of the Town Hall. And what joy now to see it still standing, 'as a sign of what architecture, and, by extension, the Society for the Advancement of Architecture, could achieve!'. After this oration the poet Willem Hendrik Warnsinck (1782–1857) pronounced a celebratory poem he had composed for the occasion, with a profusion of exclamation marks and mentioning Van Campen's name as many as ten times.

The issue of *Bouwkundige Bijdragen* also listed the forty-six objects on display that evening. Amongst them are objects we have come to know so well by now: the silver trowel (number 19); the chamois leather apron (number 20); and the gold medal worn by Jacob de Graeff (number 21). Both trowel and gold medal were reproduced in the journal, erroneously attributing the laying of the first stone to Cornelis de Graeff; not Jacob. This error shows how in the nineteenth century it was automatically assumed that the Burgomasters had led the ceremony. Interestingly, the objects had been lent by Gerrit de Graeff van Polsbroek, who was serving on the Amsterdam city council, just as his forebears Cornelis and Jacob had done.

Apart from these objects, the exhibition included, besides various paintings of the Dam and its historical buildings, engravings of the Joyous Entry of Maria de' Medici of 1638.[42] So, already in the nineteenth century, historians were aware that this event played a crucial role in the start of the building process of the Town Hall. Seals and documents related to the further history of the Town Hall were also on display. Traditionally, objects like these had been kept in the Room of the Treasurers at the Town Hall. But now that the Town Hall had become a royal palace, everything had been moved to the Prinsenhof. Curated by the city archivist, the municipal collection was arranged in a Cabinet of Curiosities that was open to the public.[43]

The ceremonial objects move to museum collections

The exhibition mounted by the members of the Society for the Advancement of Architecture fits into the wider developments of heritage preservation. At the time this was still considered a matter for private initiative, not the state. In 1840, the Dutch government had blocked state museums' acquisition budgets. On the death of Willem II in 1849, the state did not lift as much as a finger to preserve at least part of his art collection during the auction of the late king's assets: the largest ever held in the Netherlands.[44]

Given this lack of interest for art and culture on state level, the Dutch heritage and museum world relied heavily on private initiatives. In 1854, an exhibition of about 800 historical objects was held in the society of artists and art collectors *Arti et Amicitiae* at the Rokin. All objects on display were lent by private collectors, amongst them King Willem III (1817–90).[45] And once again, we encounter Jacob's silver trowel, the gold medal, plus the chamois apron, all lent by Gerrit de Graeff van Polsbroek (1797–1870).

Four years later, an even larger exhibition with 2,650 historical objects from the Netherlands was organized in Arti. The catalogue mentions the silver ewer and basin used for the inauguration banquet of the Town Hall in 1655 (listed as item number 83), lent from the Municipality of Amsterdam. There were also three ceremonial silver trowels on display, but not those related to the foundation of the Town Hall.[46] In the wake of this successful exhibition, the Royal Antiquarian Society was founded, the aim of which was to 'foster the interest in antiquities, especially as sources for history, art and the applied arts'. The founding members aspired to bring together a collection of these objects to be displayed in a public museum. To make a start with this collection, they asked those who had loaned items to the 1858 exhibition to consider donating their objects to the Society, either permanently or in a long-term arrangement.[47] The collection of the Society was growing year by year and got its first permanent exhibition space at Spuistraat in 1876.[48] When the new Rijksmuseum opened in 1885, the collection and offices of the Society moved to this building at Stadhouderskade.[49] This prestigious permanent location must have convinced many owners to bestow their objects to the Society, amongst them the De Graeff family. Their family heirlooms (trowel, medal and apron) now became part of the museum collection. By this time, Lutma's trowel had gone down as 'the' authentic trowel used during the foundation ceremony of the Town Hall.

The opening of the Rijksmuseum also had consequences for the municipal collection of art objects, which were now given on loan to the Rijksmuseum. In

1975, when the Amsterdam Historical Museum (now Amsterdam Museum) moved to its current location, the former Citizens' Orphanage, many of the objects from the old municipal collection would be reunited in this new venue.[50] While the Amsterdam Historical Museum took it as its mission to show the historical and material culture of Amsterdam, the Rijksmuseum would move towards a presentation that divided the objects over the departments of painting, sculpture, decorative arts, prints and drawings. In this scheme, Jacob's trowel and the ewer and basin were displayed together as exemplary works of silversmith Johannes Lutma, in the Decorative Arts section. Only after the extensive renovation of the Rijksmuseum between 2004 and 2013, in which the building was restored to match Cuypers' original vision, the museum opted to display the objects thematically. And that is why Jacob's silver trowel and medal are today displayed in a room dedicated to the Peace of Münster, as visible testimonies of the connection between the Treaty and the foundation of the Amsterdam Town Hall.

Notes

1. Mircea Eliade, *The Eternal Return. Cosmos and History* (Princeton: Princeton University Press, 1954), first published as *Le mythe del'éternel retour. Archétypes et répétition* (Paris: Gallimard, 1949); Maarten Delbeke and Minou Schraven (eds), *Foundation, Dedication and Consecration in Early Modern Europe* (Leiden: Brill, 2013).
2. Gabri van Tussenbroek, *De toren van de Gouden Eeuw. Een Hollandse strijd tussen gulden en God* (Amsterdam: Prometheus, 2017), 38–52.
3. Delbeke and Schraven, *Foundation, Dedication and Consecration*.
4. Maarten Prak, *The Dutch Republic in the Seventeenth Century: The Golden Age* (Cambridge: Cambridge University Press, 2005); Marjolein 't Hart, 'The Glorious City. Monumentalism and Public Space in Seventeenth-Century Amsterdam', in *Urban Achievement in Early Modern Europe. Golden Ages in Antwerp, Amsterdam and London*, ed. Patrick O'Brien (Cambridge: Cambridge University Press, 2001): 128–50, with a graph of the expenditure for public works.
5. Pieter Vlaardingerbroek, *Het Paleis van de Republiek. Geschiedenis van het Stadhuis van Amsterdam* (Zwolle, Waanders: 2011), 15–23. Cf. 't Hart, 'The Glorious City', 21 and D. P. Snoep, *Praal en propaganda. Triumfalia in de Noordelijke Nederlanden in de 16de en 17de eeuw* (Alphen a/d Rijn: Canaletto, 1975), 39–63.
6. Joost van den Vondel, *Blyde Inkomst der allerdoorluchtighste Koninginne Maria de Medicis, t'Amsterdam, vertaelt uit het Latijn des hooghgeleerden heeren Kasper van Baerle* (Amsterdam: Johan and Cornelis Blaeu, 1639), 8. Perhaps because the

States-General had been so explicit in containing costs, Vondel profusely justified the Burgomasters' expenditure.

7   The Latin original was written by Kasper van Baerle (or Caspar Barlaeus), *Medicea hospes, sive Descriptio publicae gratulationis, qua Mariam de Medicis excepit* (Amsterdam: Johan and Cornelis Blaeu, 1638).

8   Vondel, *Blyde Inkomst*, 47.

9   Van Tussenbroek, *De toren van de Gouden Eeuw*.

10 Van Tussenbroek, *De toren van de Gouden Eeuw*, 129–33, for more examples of money deposits in foundations of church towers in the Low Countries. For a wider discussion of building deposits, see Minou Schraven, 'Out of Sight, Yet Still in Place: On the Use of Italian Renaissance Portrait Medals as Building Deposits', *Res* 55/56 (2009): 183–93.

11 Amsterdam Museum, inv.nr. KA 13951. In 1886, the rummer was given to the museum by a private owner. The Amsterdam Museum also owns the small copper commemorative medal worn by Cornelis during the ceremony: Amsterdam Museum, inv.nr. PB 22.

12 The unfinished walls of the tower were demolished by the end of the eighteenth century, integrating them in the west façade of the New Church: Van Tussenbroek, *De toren van de Gouden Eeuw*, 293.

13 Snoep, *Praal en propaganda*, 77. There is a close parallel between the topics of the *tableaux vivants* and those of the paintings chosen for the decoration of the Town Hall, see Katharine Fremantle, *The Baroque Town Hall of Amsterdam* (Utrecht: Haentjens Dekker & Gumbert, 1959).

14 *Olyfkrans der Vrede door de doorluchtigste geesten en geleerdste mannen deesens tyd gevlochten*, ed. Reyer Anslo (Amsterdam: Tymen Houthaak, 1649). The book contained the text of the Treaty of Münster; and a range of encomiastic poems written in honor of the Peace and the foundation of the Town Hall. In 1748, the book would be published once more (with a slightly adjusted title: *Olyfkrans der vrede…van dien tyd gevlochten*), including 12 new poems about the first centenary of the Town Hall's foundation.

15 Vlaardingerbroek, *Het Paleis van de Republiek*, 41–93.

16 Reyer Anslo composed a lengthy poem on the foundation ceremony, 'Het Gekroonde Amsterdam met het nieu Stadthuis gegrontvest door Gerbrandt Pancras, Jacob de Graaf, Sybrandt Valkonier, Pieter Schaap, der Burgemeesteren zonen en neven onder het gezag der zelven Heeren', in Reyer Anslo, *Poezy* (Rotterdam: de Hoes, 1713), 223–44.

17 T. Desjardins, *Histoire de l'Hotel-de-Ville de Lyon depuis l'epoque de sa construction jusqu'aux nos jours* (Lyon: Louis Perrin, 1871), 22–4; Yann Lignereux, *Lyon et le Roi. De bonne ville a l'absolutisme municipal, 1594–1654* (Seyssel; Champ Vallon, 2003). There is an analogy with the foundation ceremony of the Bentivoglio tower in Bologna: after laying the first stone in 1497, Giovanni Bentivoglio shovelled earth in the foundation pit, after him, his sons and then members of the noble families of the

city: see Minou Schraven, 'Foundation Rituals and Material Culture in Renaissance Italy. The Bentivoglio Tower in Bologna', in *Ritual Dynamics*, vol 5: *Ritualised Space and Objects of Sacrosanctity*, ed. A. Michaels (Wiesbaden: Harrassowitz, 2010), 339–57.

18 Dirk de Vries, *Bouwen in Nederland 600-2000. Vol II: Middeleeuwen* (Zwolle: Waanders, 1995), 19–29.

19 Bert Sliggers en P. van den Wijngaarden, *De eerste steen gelegd door. . . . Geschiedenis en inventarisatie van de Haarlemse eerste stenen* (Haarlem: de Vrieseborch, 1984), 21. In the nineteenth and twentieth centuries, first stones of middle-class homes in the Netherlands were typically laid by a child from the owners: a tile placed a little from the street level typically commemorates the date, the name of the child, and its age at the moment of the ceremony.

20 Anslo, 'Het Gekroonde Amsterdam', 233. The chamois apron worn by Jacob de Graeff is currently in the collection of the Rijksmuseum, inv.nr. NG-KOG-1491-1.

21 Rijksmuseum, inv. nr. KOG, MP 2-0025. The medal is 5.4 cm in diameter.

22 Amsterdam Museum, PA 462 (with the coat of arms in relief); and PA 518 (the coat of arms is engraved, making it less elegant).

23 The connection between foundation stone and foundation medal became customary from the foundation ceremony of the Ponte Sisto onwards: Minou Schraven, 'Founding Rome Anew. Pope Sixtus IV and the Foundation of Ponte Sisto (1473)', in *Foundation, Dedication and Consecration*, 129–51; Mary Quinlan-McGrath, 'The Foundation Horoscope(s) for St Peter's Basilica in Rome, 1506. Choosing a Time, Changing the Storia', *Isis* 92, no. 4 (2001): 716–41.

24 Amsterdam Museum, inv.nr. KA 15679. *Goud en Zilver met Amsterdamse keuren. De verzameling van het Amsterdams Historisch Museum*, ed. Hubert Vreeken (Zwolle: Waanders, 2002), 118.

25 M.B. de Roever, 'Metselen met zilverwerk. Troffels voor de eerste steen', *Ons Amsterdam* 55 (2003): 68–71; Anthony Bernbaum, 'Silver ceremonial trowels', *The Silver Society* 31 (2014): 99–116, citing mainly British examples from the eighteenth century onwards. A silver trowel was used by the pope to close the Holy Door at the conclusion of the Jubilee of 1575; A. Pientini, *Le pie narrationi dell'opere più memorabili fatte in Roma l'anno del Giubileo* 1575 (Viterbo, 1576), 346. The young Louis XIII of France also used silver trowels for his foundation acts, such as that or that of the Medici aqueduct at Grand Regard de Rungis in July 1613, an initiative of his mother Catherine de' Medici aimed at improving the water quality in Paris.

26 See note 17.

27 "[After the King and Bernini had left the scene], il s'est mu une contestation pour tous ces utils [. . .]. J'ai dit que M. Colbert réglerait cela, qu'ils laissassent ces outils aux gens du Cavalier [Bernini], ce qu'ils refusaient de faire'; Paul Fréart de

Chantelou, *Journal du voyage du Cavalier Bernin en France*, edited by Ludovic Lalanne (Paris: Gazette des Beaux-Arts, 1885), 240–2.
28 Johan ter Molen, 'Zilver', *Leids Kunsthistorisch Jaarboek* 10 (1995): 105–24.
29 Vlaardingerbroek, *Het Paleis van de Republiek*, for the building history and a discussion of models used by van Campen.
30 Mary Quinlan McGrath, *Influences. Art, Optics and Astrology in the Italian Renaissance* (Chicago: Chicago University Press, 2013), particularly chapter 5: 'The City, the Building, the Patron'. Delbeke and Schraven, *Foundation, Dedication, Consecration*.
31 The Prinsenhof was traditionally used to house important guests, such as Maria de' Medici in 1638. It would assume the function of town hall, when the Old Town hall burnt down in a fire in 1652. In 1806, when Lodewijk Napeoleon transformed the Town Hall on the Dam into his royal palace, the Prinsenhof acted once again as town hall of Amsterdam.
32 Amsterdam Museum, inv.nr. KA 13952.
33 Amsterdam Museum, inv. nr. KA 13 981. Vreeken, *Goud en Zilver*, 124–5. *Beschrijvinge van het Stadhuis*, 1761, p. 81. Until 1806, the ewer and basin were kept in the Room of the Treasurers in the Town Hall; the chimney of that room was decorated with the coats of arms of Tulp and Dronckelaar.
34 The drawing is made by Gerrit Lamberts, clerk at the Amsterdam Town Hall. He would become curator of the Rijksmuseum in 1824, when it was still located at the Trippenhuis.
35 At the end of 1655, however, his colleague Simon Valckenaar somehow won the monopoly to issue this particular Town Hall medal: from then on, his marker, a small falcon, appears on the medal's rim; Jan Pelsdonk, 'Van Pool tot Valckenaer. De Stadhuispenning van 1655', *De Beeldenaar* 3 (2013): 111–18.
36 One of the *tableaux vivants* in honour of the Peace of Münster on the Dam in June 1648 had also been a scene with Amphion and the lyre; and a relief with this subject would decorate the entrance to the Chamber of the City Council in the new Town Hall of Amsterdam.
37 One of these boxes is in the collection of the Amsterdam Museum, inv.nr. PE 015969.
38 H. De Schepper and J. de Vet, 'De herdenking van de Vrede van Munster in 1748 en 1948', *De Zeventiende Eeuw* 13 (1997): 11–29.
39 Albert van der Zeijden, *Katholieke Identiteit en historisch bewustzijn. W.J.F. Nuyens (1823–1894) en zijn 'nationale' geschiedschrijving* (Amsterdam: PhD diss., 2002), 234–9.
40 C.P. Krabbe, *Ambacht, kunst, wetenschap. Bevordering van de bouwkunst in Nederland 1775–1880* (Zwolle: Waanders, 1988). The society had been founded in 1842 and would fuse in 1919 with the *Bond van Nederlandse architecten*. The *Maatschappij* would petition for a statue of van Campen for years on end, but without result.

41 'Het tweede eeuwgetijde van het leggen van den eersten steen van het Stadhuis (thans Paleis) van Amsterdam herdacht door de Maatschappij tot Bevordering der Bouwkunst', *Bouwkundige Bijdragen* 5 (1849): 310-38; 'Lijst van hetgene door den Heer G. Lamberts op den 28. October 1848, bij gelegenheid der tweehonderd-jarige herdenking aan het leggen van den eersten steen van het Raadhuis dezer stad, ter bezigtiging is aangeboden', 335-8.

42 Item 28 on the 'Lijst' was a sheet of calligraphy made by Lieven Coppenol, featuring the poem composed by Constantijn Huygens for the inauguration banquet of 1655.

43 Vreeken, *Goud en Zilver*, 11-12, with an illustration of the Cabinet of curiosities at the Town Hall in the late nineteenth century.

44 Erik Hinterding and Femy Horsch, 'A Small but Choice Collection. The Art Gallery of King Willem II of the Netherlands (1792-1849)', *Semiolus* 19, no. 1 (1989): 4-122.

45 *Catalogus tentoonstelling van voorwerpen van kunst en nijverheid uit vroegeren tijd in het gebouw der Maatschappij Arti et Amicitiae te Amsterdam 1 februarij tot 15 maart 1854* (Amsterdam, 1854). The objects in the catalogue are ordered by material (gold and silver; copper; wood; ivory, pottery, textiles).

46 *Catalogus van voorwerpen uit vroegeren tijd, tentoongesteld in het gebouw van Maatschappij Arti et Amicitiae te Amsterdam ten behoeve van het Weduwen-en Wezenfonds, April en mei 1858* (Amsterdam, 1858).

47 J.F. Heijbroek, 'Het Koninklijk Oudheidkundig Genootschap (1858-1995)'.

48 The museum was opened daily and received that year 3,000 paying visitors. David van der Kellen jr, engraver and first curator of KOG, wrote the *Catalogus van het museum van het Koninklijk Oudheidkundig Genootschap* (Amsterdam, 1876), with some 1000 objects. Earlier, he had published the illustrated *Nederlands-Oudheden* (Den Haag, 1861-86), see Frans Grijzenhout, *Erfgoed. De geschiedenis van een begrip* (Amsterdam: Amsterdam University Press, 2007), 109-32.

49 Many paintings, sculptures and applied arts objects owned by the KOG were integrated with the collections of the Rijksmuseum, as it is still the case today.

50 Vreeken, *Goud en Zilver*, 20-2.

Bibliography

Anslo, Reyer (ed.). *Olyfkrans der Vrede door de doorluchtigste geesten en geleerdste mannen deesens tyd gevlochten*. Amsterdam: Tymen Houthaak, 1649.

Anslo, Reyer. 'Het Gekroonde Amsterdam met het nieu Stadthuis gegrontvest door Gerbrandt Pancras, Jacob de Graaf, Sybrandt Valkonier, Pieter Schaap, der Burgemeesteren zonen en neven onder het gezag der zelven Heeren'. In Anslo Reyer, *Poezy,* 223-44. Rotterdam: de Hoes, 1713.

Baerle, Kasper van (or Caspar Barlaeus). *Blijde Inkomst der allerdoorluchtighste Koninginne Maria de Medicis t'Amsterdam*. Amsterdam: Johan en Cornelis Blaeu, 1639.

Bernbaum, Anthony. 'Silver ceremonial trowels.' *The Silver Society* 31 (2014): 99–116.

Delbeke, Maarten, and Schraven, Minou (eds). *Foundation, Dedication and Consecration in Early Modern Europe*. Leiden: Brill, 2013.

Eliade, Mircea. *The Eternal Return. Cosmos and History*. Princeton: Princeton University Press, 1954.

Fremantle, Katharine. *The Baroque Town Hall of Amsterdam*. Utrecht: Haentjens Dekker & Gumbert, 1959.

't Hart, Marjolein. 'The Glorious City. Monumentalism and Public Space in Seventeenth-Century Amsterdam.' In *Urban Achievement in Early Modern Europe. Golden Ages in Antwerp, Amsterdam and London*, edited by Patrick O'Brien, 128–50. Cambridge: Cambridge University Press, 2001.

Hinterding, Erik, and Femy Horsch. 'A Small but Choice Collection. The Art Gallery of King Willem II of the Netherlands (1792–1849).' *Semiolus* 19, no. 1 (1989): 4–122.

Krabbe, C.P. *Ambacht, kunst, wetenschap. Bevordering van de bouwkunst in Nederland 1775–1880*. Zwolle: Waanders, 1988.

Molen, Johan ter. 'Zilver.' *Leids Kunsthistorisch Jaarboek* 10 (1995): 105–24.

Pelsdonk, Jan. 'Van Pool tot Valckenaer. De Stadhuispenning van 1655.' *De Beeldenaar* 3 (2013): 111–18.

Prak, Maarten. *The Dutch Republic in the Seventeenth Century: The Golden Age*. Cambridge: Cambridge University Press, 2005.

Quinlan-McGrath, Mary. 'The Foundation Horoscope(s) for St Peter's Basilica in Rome, 1506. Choosing a Time, Changing the Storia.' *Isis* 92, no. 4 (2001): 716–41.

Quinlan-McGrath, Mary. *Influences. Art, Optics and Astrology in the Italian Renaissance*. Chicago: Chicago University Press, 2013.

Schepper, H. de, and de Vet, J. 'De herdenking van de Vrede van Munster in 1748 en 1948.' *De Zeventiende Eeuw* 13 (1997): 11–29.

Schraven, Minou. 'Out of Sight, Yet Still in Place. On the Use of Italian Renaissance Portrait Medals as Building Deposits.' *Res* 55/56 (2009): 183–93.

Sliggers, Bert, and van den Wijngaarden, P. *De eerste steen gelegd door. . . . Geschiedenis en inventarisatie van de Haarlemse eerste stenen*. Haarlem: de Vrieseborch, 1984.

Snoep, D. P. *Praal en propaganda. Triumfalia in de Noordelijke Nederlanden in de 16de en 17de eeuw*. Alphen a/d Rijn: Canaletto, 1975.

Tussenbroek, Gabri van. *De toren van de Gouden Eeuw. Een Hollandse strijd tussen gulden en God*. Amsterdam: Prometheus, 2017.

Vlaardingerbroek, Pieter. *Het Paleis van de Republiek. Geschiedenis van het Stadhuis van Amsterdam*. Zwolle, Waanders: 2011.

Vondel, Joost van den. *Blyde Inkomst der allerdoorluchtighste Koninginne Maria de Medicis, t'Amsterdam, vertaelt uit het Latijn des hooghgeleerden heeren Kasper van Baerle*. Amsterdam: Johan and Cornelis Blaeu, 1639.

Vondel, Joost van den. *Inwijdinge van 't Stadhuis t'Amsterdam*, edited by Saskia Albrecht, Otto de Ruyter, Marijke Spies and Frank Elsing. Muiderberg: Coutinho, 1982.

Vreeken, Hubert (ed.). *Goud en Zilver met Amsterdamse keuren. De verzameling van het Amsterdams Historisch Museum*. Zwolle: Waanders, 2002.

Zeijden, Albert van der. *Katholieke Identiteit en historisch bewustzijn. W.J.F. Nuyens (1823-1894) en zijn 'nationale' geschiedschrijving*. Amsterdam: PhD diss., 2002.

8

Under Discussion: Eighteenth-Century Reactions to the Town Hall

Freek Schmidt

'Well, thank Heaven! Amsterdam is behind us.' These were the words William Beckford (1760–1844), Earl of Fonthill and famous art collector, wrote in his journal in the city of Utrecht in July 1780, on his way to Augsburg, Venice, Rome and Naples. For many British travellers and wealthy tourists, the city of Amsterdam was a stopover on the continent. The heat probably influenced Beckford's impression of what was considered one of the city's most frequented attractions, the Town Hall. Beckford could not skip the building, and on the day of his visit, it was 'the only cool place' in the city: 'I repaired thither, as fast as the heat permitted, and walked in a lofty marble hall, magnificently covered, till the dinner was ready at the inn.'[1]

Almost all visitors to Amsterdam in the early modern age went to the Town Hall and mentioned it in their accounts. A traveller of a century earlier, William Montague, did just that in his *Delights of Holland* of 1696:

> This Stadthouse, or Guild-Hall, is a most noble and magnificent Pile of Building, all after the modern Italian Architecture; 'tis the stateliest Piece we ever saw, 'tis the Wonder and Discourse of all the World, the Pride of Amsterdam, and the Glory of the Seven Provinces: The Entrance is mean, and contemptible, under seven small Piazza's, or Arches, which wonderfully abate its Beauty, which we told the Dutch, and which they own'd, for there is nothing that gives a great and noble Piece of Building more Advantage, than a large Portico, or Entrance, which makes the approach Magnificent.[2]

Throughout the eighteenth century, the building maintained this strong reputation, including this often mentioned architectural flaw – the entrance – that diminished its grandeur or magnificence, as the largest town hall ever built, located in a prominent place, contrasting in scale, material and decoration with its environment. Everyone arriving in Amsterdam would find the Town Hall on the only large open space in the city, which also featured the Stock Exchange, the New Church, as well as the Weigh House (Figure 8.1).

Figure 8.1 Daniel Marot, civil guard on Dam Square, presenting themselves to the Burgomasters of the city, on the occasion of the Amsterdam fair, 1686, engraving, 640 × 940 mm. Rijksmuseum Amsterdam, Public Domain.

Montague's quote is emblematic of the regular appreciation of the Amsterdam Town Hall, voiced by the 'average' visitor or tourist throughout the long eighteenth century, until the moment it was appropriated by King Louis Napoléon in 1806 as his royal palace. It can be contrasted with another, quite different, characterization from the late eighteenth century, in 1790, by Carl Gottlieb Kuettner (1755–1805) from Saxony, a courtier turned civil servant in England, who travelled with an English company to Amsterdam, noted: 'The world-famous Town Hall of Amsterdam ... is, in the end, an awful, tasteless thing, and in spite of its spectacular size, extremely small.'[3]

In this chapter on eighteenth-century reactions to the Amsterdam Town Hall, I will look more closely at how perceptions of the building were changing, and how we can account for some of the more outspoken views voiced by different consumers of the building. Besides the continuing praise of magnificence, from the earliest days of the building's existence, two different approaches surface in the eighteenth century: a critical assessment in terms of both architecture and aesthetics, and an outspoken historical view, which inscribes the building in the nation's recent glorious past, its 'Golden Age'.

But before we focus on some prominent viewers, we can ask ourselves how visitors arrived at their judgments of the Amsterdam Town Hall. A simple answer would be, from their own personal observation, but that seems too simple. Not only is the building, as an object, to paraphrase Michael Baxandall 'sensitive to the kinds of interpretative skill – patterns, categories, inferences, analogies – the mind brings to it'[4], but perception of familiar and unfamiliar buildings was steered by several factors. Travellers often inspected foreign sites in person. However, they also borrowed heavily from a vast body of travel texts, ranging from instructive guidebooks and treatises to popular and fictionalized journals, and on location were informed by local guides and other people who added novel information. The genre of the travelogue is, therefore, 'a highly intertextual and diffuse genre, parroting and reworking earlier materials', in which there is always some form of 'discursive overlap'.[5]

In addition, in the eighteenth century, a mass of polemic and essayistic periodicals was available, which often in their titles – with the word *Spectators* borrowed from Joseph Addison and Richard Steele's *The Specator* (1711) – already point to the fact that they are considering other, innovative and different ways of interpreting existing phenomena. But we may also include other kinds of literature that rewrite the city as it is experienced. The impact of what can be interpreted as orchestrated attempts to create historical narratives of the Dutch nation and the proud city of Amsterdam that surface around the middle of the eighteenth century, greatly affected the appreciation for particular institutions, places and buildings. And then there is the increase in visual representations – especially drawings and prints. The rise of print culture in general seems to feed into the perception of buildings and changes the ways in which these were encountered, understood and experienced.

In what follows, we will follow more closely a few outspoken critics of the Amsterdam Town Hall, and find explanations for their varied appreciation of the building. These critical architectural, aesthetic and historical views demonstrate original, independent standpoints that form an intriguing contrast to the 'average', more common accounts of the Town Hall.

Sturm

The first critic who is interesting for our focus on eighteenth-century responses to the Town Hall, is German *Baudirektor* Leonhard Christoph Sturm (1669–1719), who made three longer trips (in total twenty-one weeks) to the Low Countries, in 1697, 1699 and 1712 (Figure 8.2).[6] In 1719, he published a large folio volume of *Architectonische Reiseanmerkungen* (*Architectural Travel Accounts*) organized in

Figure 8.2 Martin Bernigeroth, portrait of Leonhard Christoph Sturm, 1707, engraving, 267 × 167 mm. Courtesy Rijkmuseum Amsterdam, Public Domain.

the form of a series of letters written from Rostock to an anonymous young nobleman making an educational trip through northern Europe. Sturm was a very prolific writer, which in some way compensated for the lack of opportunity he had to build. During his life, he published ninety-eight titles, of which fifty-three were devoted to architecture. He is best known for his edited version of *Vollständige Anweisung zu der Civil Bau-Kunst* (*Complete Survey of Civil Architecture*) (Wolfenbüttel 1696), based on the manuscript of the architecture theoretician and mathematician Nicolaus Goldmann (1611–65), who had worked most of his life in Leiden.[7] This book, republished several times, guaranteed the dissemination of Goldmann's ideas in a manner that was appreciated by eighteenth-century audiences, to which he would return in a number of his other publications.

Sturm's most original contribution to architecture, however, lies in his travel accounts, in which he took a special interest in contemporary buildings, and practised an outspoken architectural criticism.[8] Sturm's criticism can be seen as the work of an educator: he uses examples of existing buildings to illustrate practical solutions and adds alternatives to instruct his readership. It is an early modern version of what later became known as 'operative criticism' – the detailed study of historical architecture and analysis of architectural precedent to inform contemporary design.[9] It is a case study in professional judgment. As an architect, Sturm is particularly interested in fairly recent architecture, which he analyses in terms of *Angemessenheit* (propriety), emphasizing practical use over aesthetic (classicist) ideals.[10]

This approach becomes clear when he turns to the Amsterdam Town Hall. There, he not only voices and repeats the general criticism of the Town Hall's inconspicuous entrance with its low arcade, but he observes that the central hall is too dark, that the inner courtyards are too sober, that the windows of the staircases disrupt the regularity of the facades and that the columns of the Citizens' Hall are badly jointed. He presents, in print, an alternative solution to the entrance problem! He projects a double flight of steps in front of the building, leading to the main floor, and by flooring the void above the Tribunal, creates a domed and decorated portal in front of the passage to the Citizens' Hall. In Sturm's plate X (Figures 8.3 and 8.4) we see this arrangement, to which were

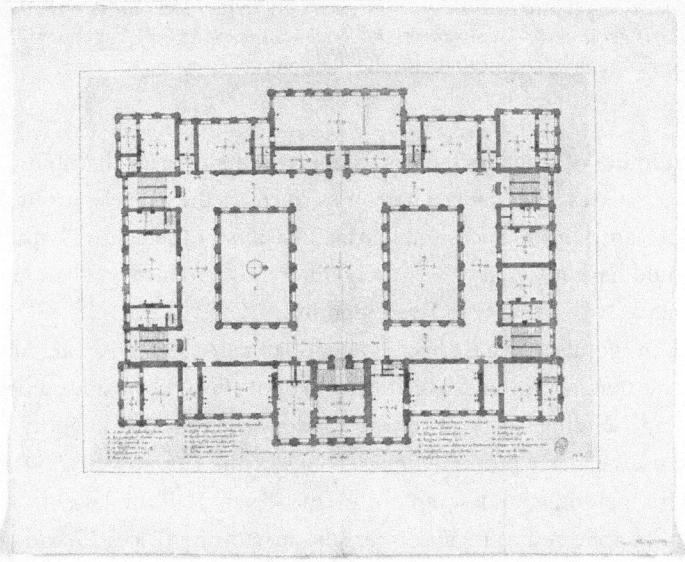

Figure 8.3 Dancker Danckerts (?) after Jacob Vennekool, ground plan of the main floor of Amsterdam Town Hall, 1661, engraving, 402 × 507 mm. Rijksmuseum Amsterdam, Public Domain.

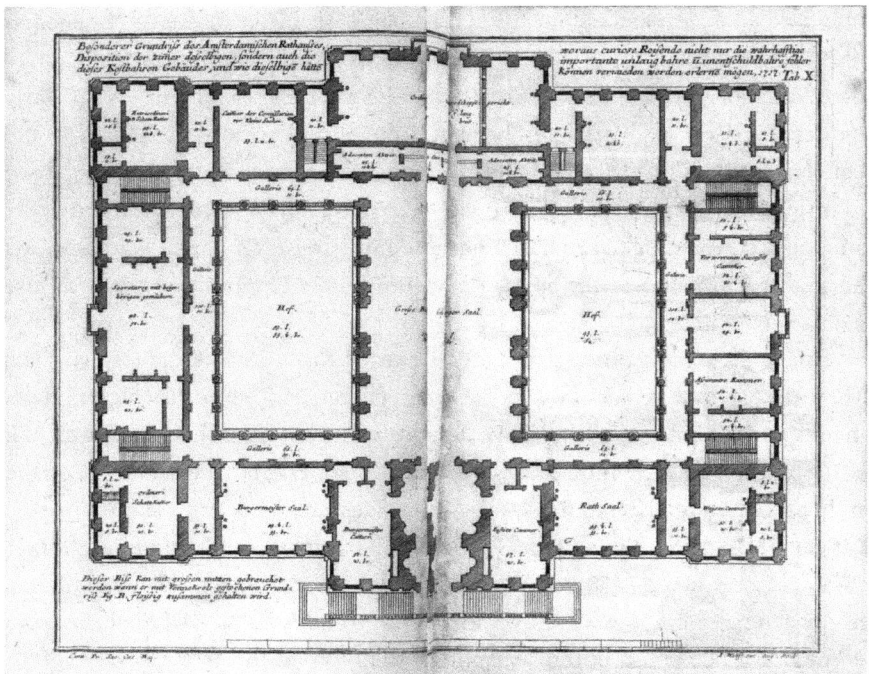

Figure 8.4 Leonhard Christoph Sturm, ground plan of the main floor of Amsterdam Town Hall, with Sturm's proposal for new external staircases, as published in Leonhard Christoph Sturm, *Eine grossen Theil von Teutschland un den Niederalnden bis nach Paris gemachete Architectonische Reise-Anmerckungen* (Augsburg: Hertel, 1760). Bayerische Staatsbibliothek, Public Domain.

added a number of smaller changes to improve the interior distribution. Sturm readjusts staircases, adds central balconies, narrows the galleries around the two inner courtyards and replaces the marble pilasters of the central with columns, which would have resulted in a entirely differently proportioned and decorated interior space, with a totally different lighting.

Sturm's proposals may have been noted by some readers in Amsterdam, but we do not know that for certain. His criticism did not affect the positive judgement of the existing building that continued to dominate in the majority of other publications. Regularly published guidebooks of the city, special guidebooks on architecture, paintings and sculpture of the Town Hall, or lavishly illustrated volumes that appeared at regular intervals, are not the places to find vehement architectural criticism. Yet, the Town Hall was no longer what it had been in the seventeenth century. On the one hand, we can see that the original idea of the building, as Montague phrased it, 'the wonder of the world, the pride of Amsterdam, the glory of the seven provinces', is being upheld; on the other hand, its architectural language is increasingly becoming the subject of criticism or even ridicule, an example of bad taste, inappropriate and being re-evaluated historically. In short, the building and its meaning are considered from alternative viewpoints.[11]

Wagenaar

The explosion of history writing in Amsterdam in the 1750s also seems to have nuanced the relationship between the construction of an architectural image, the actual site, its history and the way in which these are perceived. Growing self-interest in the image of Amsterdam was certainly amongst the motives of the city council in 1758 to commission the historian Jan Wagenaar (1709–73) to write the first official history of the city (Figure 8.5). Between 1760 and 1768 he published

Figure 8.5 Jacob Houbraken, *Portrait of Jan Wagenaar*, 1766, engraving, 179 × 188 mm. Rijksmuseum Amsterdam, Public Domain.

a three-volume history of Amsterdam of some 1,850 pages.¹² This project took off when Wagenaar was reaching the end of his twenty-one-volume history of the *Vaderlandsche Historie* (*National History*) (1749–59). Wagenaar's method included antiquarian subjects and observations, and emphasized the role of old documents as source material.¹³ Throughout his history of Amsterdam he added illustrations with detailed historical reconstructions of convents in the city, thus bringing together the historian's scholarship with the antiquarian interest and craft of the eighteenth-century draughtsman and topographer that had been en vogue since the 1730s in publications by Abraham Rademaker and others.¹⁴

Two years later, the production of a series of topographical views of the city started, by the art collector Pierre Fouquet (1729–1800) (Figures 8.6 and 8.7). Between 1760 and 1783, he commissioned several draughtsmen – such as Hendrik P. Schouten, Reinier Vinkeles, Hendrik Keun and Caspar Philipsz. Jacobsz – to create images of the city, with a special interest in portraying municipal buildings in their urban settings. The works of these draughtsmen seem to set a new standard in topographical drawing, especially in their attention to detail, a genre that had been popular since the early seventeenth century.¹⁵ These eighteenth-century drawings and prints, sometimes characterized as

Figure 8.6 Simon Fokke, *View of Amsterdam Town Hall with the New Church and the Weigh House on Dam Square*, c. 1770, engraving, 267 × 385 mm. Rijksmuseum Amsterdam, Public Domain.

Figure 8.7 C. Bogerts after Hendrik Keun, *Interior of the central hall of Amsterdam Town Hall*, c. 1770–8, engraving. Amsterdam Municipal Archive, Public Domain.

urban self portraits, map the city in numerous views that, at the same time, form the backdrop to everyday life.[16] We see a constantly changing, somewhat weathered, irregular and picturesque whole, portrayed in a friendly way. The drawings and prints together form a condensed version of the city that is alive, and shows all its scars. It is as if history creeps into these images, in that we are looking not at a perfect metropolis, but rather an ageing capital with a story attached to it that is described and documented. Aspects of antiquarianism and picturesque taste merge in the depiction of the contemporary city portraiture.

Fouquet's project forms an ideal companion to Wagenaar's series.[17] In fact, the descriptions of buildings in Fouquet's *Atlas*, a first edition of all prints appeared in 1780, were based on Wagenaar's second volume of his Amsterdam history, in which he devotes more than 400 pages to the buildings of the city. It comes as no surprise that the Town Hall is discussed in detail.[18] Critical remarks are absent in this text, reflecting both traditional civic pride and the general appraisal of the average tourist. But there are sparse reflexions, suggesting the arts of the previous century as superior to contemporary developments. When discussing the costs of the building for instance, Wagenaar states:

> And as painting, sculpture and architecture had, in the middle of the previous century, when this town hall was founded, reached the highest stage of perfection; artists and workers of all kinds, came hither in such abundance that it made it possible to complete the building faster and at lower costs than would have been possible today.[19]

Included in the architectural description is an engraving of the facade of the Town Hall on Dam square, by Frans de Bakker after a drawing by Reinier Vinkeles from the art collection of Cornelis Ploos van Amstel (1726–98) (Figures 8.8 and 8.9). In this way, texts and printed views combined could strengthen civic pride and urban patriotism. It is tempting to read the printed views as the recordings of antiquarians, documenting the buildings of a particular civilization, not unlike the historical impulse that led travelling architects to ancient ruins and forgotten civilizations elsewhere in Europe and beyond, at exactly the same time.[20] A brief look at some texts by architects and virtuosi who were leading

Figure 8.8 Simon Fokke, *Dam Square with the Town Hall, New Church and Weigh House*, 1762, engraving. Amsterdam Municipal Archive, Public Domain.

Figure 8.9 Reinier Vinkeles, *Amsterdam Town Hall and Weigh House*, c. 1764–7, coloured drawing, 230 × 345 mm. Rijksmuseum Amsterdam, Public Domain.

experts in circles of art collectors may help to clarify the increasing uneasiness with the architecture of the building, which at the same time should still be valued as a symbol of a successful city and Republic.

Laugier

In 1766, we find one of the most popular critics of architecture in France, the Jesuit priest Marc-Antoine Laugier (1713–69), visiting Amsterdam and its Town Hall. And his manuscript account *Détail de tout ce que nous avons observé et éprouvé dans notre voyage de Hollande* (*Overview of everything we have seen and experienced on our travels in Holland*) is quite terse:

> The Amsterdam town hall appeared to us quite below its reputation: it is a great cube-like mass, completely built of grey stone. On a base, two levels are erected with an architecture of pilasters. The first order is composite, with bizarre singularities in the capitals. The second order is Corinthian. At each level, there are two ranges of square windows, separated by garlands of heavy and unwieldy workmanship.... The middle pavilions are crowned by pediments of which the tympanum is sculpted in a confusing design and barbaric execution.[21]

Laugier continues by following the accounts of so many visitors before him by writing that he is not pleased with the entrance. However, he goes on by stating that the ground floor was 'obscure like a cave'. He only had words of praise for the Citizens' Hall (Figure 8.10). This hall was 'august, because of its grandeur', but badly lit, and the ceiling 'decorated in bad taste'. In fact, the paintings are more to his liking, although he thinks that Rembrandt's large painting that today is known as *The Night Watch*, which shortly after 1715 had been installed in the small war council chamber on the second floor used by the civic guard, is too dark to make out the details.[22]

In contrast with the travel account left in manscript, Laugier's *Essai sur l'architecture* of 1753 and his *Observations sur l'architecture* published in 1765,

Figure 8.10 Reinier Vinkeles, *Ball in Amsterdam Town Hall in 1768, on the occasion of the entry of Prince Willem V and Princess Wilhelmina*, 1771, engraving, 434 × 359 mm. Rijksmuseum Amsterdam, Public Domain.

the year before his visit to Amsterdam, reached a large non-professional audience and allowed his readers to understand, appreciate and value the architectural production of their day.[23] He was one of the very few writers who distanced himself from treatises that concentrated on the exact measurement of the orders, antique monuments or Vitrivius, but was looking for alternative principles and rules by which talent and taste would be governed.[24] Although some of his views divided professional architects in France, which they considered typical for an outsider, the *Essai* in particular was welcomed by a wide audience.[25] As a critic he argued that reason, taste and experience were needed to guide the architect on his obscure path to find new principles. The column, the entablature and the pediment should again form the basis of good architecture, other features should not contribute to the beauty of a building, but are admitted because they are indispensable.[26] Walls were thus *licenses*, but so were pilasters, 'the bastard child of architecture', while other features, such as strangely shaped pediments, niches, arcades were labelled as '*caprice*'.[27] It is not difficult to see that in Laugier's eyes, the Amsterdam Town Hall contained many aspects he considered in conflict with good architecture.

Camper

Almost simultaneously to Laugier's visit to Amsterdam, we find another forceful critic sharpening his pen in front of Amsterdam Town Hall, but this time not a foreigner, but a Dutch citizen, writing anonymously, in the 1767 October issue of *De Philosooph* (*The Philosopher*), a spectatorial magazine. Later, this author was identified as none other than the internationally renowned scientist and scholar Petrus Camper (1722–89) (Figure 8.11).[28] Known for his versatility – Goethe called him 'ein Meteor von Geist, Wissenschaft, Talent und Thätigkeit' ('a meteor of spirit, science, talent and activity'[29]) – his concern with architecture was more than a onetime digression from his work as a professor in medicine, anatomist, natural scientist, prolific publicist and amateur draughtsman.[30] He lectured on (architectral) aesthetics more than once and also initiated and supervised the competition for a new Town Hall for the city of Groningen.[31] His interest in one of the very few buildings in the Republic that could be considered magnificent seems to have been profound, but is also extremely critical, when he starts his letter with a strongly worded statement: 'When we consider the nature of our Republic and especially the intellectual faculties of its inhabitants, we must be surprised that we, who in general do not have to bow for other nations

Figure 8.11 Reinier Vinkeles. *Portrait of Petrus Camper*, 1776, black and white drawing, 200 × 146 mm. Rijksmuseum Amsterdam, Public Domain.

of the world, are extremely backward when it comes to that special ability of the soul called taste.'[32]

In eight pages, Camper raises the question of the Dutch lack of taste, which he sees especially reflected in architecture. He sketches a brief history since the late sixteenth century, in which he mentions the thoughtless imitation of Italian models. Thus, his views contrast with William Montague's admiration for 'the Italian Architecture' as applied to the Amsterdam Town Hall. Our polemic then continues, stating that to demonstrate 'this passion for imitation and lack of taste is most clearly demonstrated' in the Amsterdam Town Hall, the building that for most Dutch people and certainly for Amsterdammers, was still one of their most cherished buildings, the pride of the city and the glory of the seven provinces, or in Wagenaar's words: 'the first and foremost of all civic buildings that enrich this city, and which, in terms of art and lustre, outshines all others.'[33]

Of course, our author finds the Town Hall's exterior plain and the low entrance lacking grandeur, arguing that the architect was unable to design a building of this scale and magnificence. In his walk through the building, there is hardly any space that he considers right. The small but high Tribunal is sumptuous but as far as beauty is concerned, it is 'without any taste in both the order and the sculpture details' (Figure 8.12).[34] The four caryatids placed there may have been acceptable in Greek buildings, but in the Amsterdam setting they are highly inappropriate and incomprehensible, and the iconography of three reliefs is too far-fetched.[35] Only the interior space of the great hall receives praise. In all, these judgements have a severity not unusual in eighteenth-century spectatorial literature. But the letter also shows how our critic considers architecture as an

Figure 8.12 Anonymous, *Tribunal in the Amsterdam Town Hall,* undated photograph. Amsterdam Municipal Archive, Public Domain.

instrument of cultural expression and a barometer of taste, and clearly finds there is no balance between the two. It does not have to be like this, and so the author presents a remedy. He notices the positive recent turn in the manner of speaking, spelling and writing, in particular in the 'pure and manly style' of the Amsterdam town historian Jan Wagenaar (1709–73), author of one of the most popular histories of the Netherlands, and the introduction of reason and a purity of language by spectators and preachers.[36] In conclusion, he recommends that his compatriots improve their taste independently from other nations, by studying the great *philosophes* of the age, who will be able to guide the Dutch to improve their sense of taste and take control of design. This should then improve taste, and as a result, sound judgment in matters of art and architecture would automatically follow.

Although there is no recipe for this architecture included, as in Sturm's print, we can reconstruct Camper's ideas in detail by looking at his involvement with architecture on other occasions. Camper lectured on taste and beauty at the university of Groningen in 1766, and again in 1782 at the Amsterdam *Stadstekenacademie* (Drawing Academy), a lecture that would be published richly annotated in 1792 and translated in French and German.[37] There, he reflects on French and English architectural and archaeological publications of the 1750s and 1760s, but also refers to Claude Perrault's 1673 annotated Vitruvius edition and concludes that preferences for the orders and their proportions are based on notions of authority and custom. The beauty in buildings is 'a beauty of agreement' and that which is considered beautiful in art and architecture is often simply dictated by the greatest artists and accomplished architect.[38] Not unlike Laugier, Camper was a compassionate but critical lover of the arts and studious virtuoso. Through lectures and letters to cultural societies he was able to share his views on the benefits of architecture to society with a well-informed group of scholars, amateurs, artists and well-educated craftsmen. In Amsterdam, he knew Fouquet, who advised him on his art collections.[39] In the Amsterdam *Stadstekenacademie* especially, he encountered many who were as passionate about architecture as he was. There, he probably first met Jacob Otten Husly, who would become his soulmate, according to Husly's biographer, and one of the most successful architects of the later eighteenth century in the Republic, best known today for his Felix Meritis building.[40] Although Camper did not design himself, he would later preside a commission for the first international architectural competition in the Republic, for a new Town Hall for the city of Groningen in 1774, won by Husly.[41]

Ploos van Amstel

Camper's letter in *De Philosooph* was soon answered by a reply in the form of an anonymously published pamphlet of more than forty pages by Cornelis Ploos van Amstel, one of the most renowned art collectors of his day and a director of the *Stadstekenacademie*, Amsterdam's drawing school.[42] Ploos' interests were varied and concentrated around the art of drawing. He published prints, was an avid amateur draughtsman, a collector with great interests in drawings and prints and a special collection of Amsterdam topography, the *Atlas van Amsterdam*.[43] In 1767, he designed an allegorical frontespice for Jan Wagenaar's history of Amsterdam, and ten years later, had a frontespice drawn by Jan Stolker for his own atlas.[44] Although the exact content of his collected drawings of more than 7,200 sheets, auctioned and dispersed after 1800, remains unclear, he possessed various drawings of *stadgezigten* (cityscapes) by De Beyer, Vinkeles and Schouten amongst others, and may well have included drawings used previously for Fouquet's prints. He was promoting a 'Dutch' iconography by focusing on seventeenth-century and contemporary Dutch work, and opening artists' eyes to various alternative, non-classicist genres of painting.[45]

At the time, Ploos was unaware that Camper was his opponent, but found this out later, and concluded that, since his reply was never answered, he had convinced Camper of his mistake. But there is strong doubt that this was the case. In fact, this polemic demonstrates how two authors who shared a passion for drawing, could uphold completely different opinions in terms of architecture and Dutch architecture in particular. In his defence, Ploos found Camper's interpretation of the Amsterdam Town Hall as a product of lack of taste and blind imitation totally unacceptable, but his retort suggests that he was living in a different world. Everything on the building that Camper had dared to question, was interpreted by Ploos as completely in accordance with the absolute principles of architecture. But because Camper had nowhere questioned the general rules and techniques that had to be observed to arrive at a satisfactory building, Ploos could only disagree, without force of argument. His reaction remains rather emotional, worshipping the greatness of the Dutch past:

> But we think we have said enough, to have shown the weakness of this critic, as well as his thoughtless zeal or inexperience; which are all the more inexcusable because he thereby has tried to stain the honour of the whole nation, of his own homeland as an unworthy citizen; while it should have been his duty, to conceal its shortcomings in a decent manner.[46]

For Ploos, Dutch art and architecture were beyond dispute. Maybe he applauded a revival of architecture parallel to his active promotion of seventeenth-century painting and subjects from national history.[47] Supporting Camper meant questioning significant examples of Dutch seventeenth-century cultural dominance, such as the Amsterdam Town Hall, and admitting that architecture had been led astray by assimilating Italianate classicism in Amsterdam's Golden Age. For him, it had already become part of national architecture and an inviolable, proud patriotic symbol. The Amsterdam Town Hall was still a functioning building and a celebration of the peace of Münster, but had – a century after its completion – also become a monument perpetuating the memory of past glory. It was, in other words, historicized, a building able to recall an era from the past to be identified within the present, as an object of architectural history.[48]

Building – Monument – Symbol

With his suggestion to judge a worldly building in direct relation to the society that erected it, Ploos added a new layer to the variety of meanings that had already been ascribed to the Town Hall and were influencing its observers and their attitudes towards the building. The agency of the building, 'the non-artistic, and almost purely social influence of art on its observers', became more varied in the sense that the building was perceived as a real presence, reminding the beholder 'of the powers and reputation of identifiable persons or groups, and eventually gives this awareness a place in his social behaviour'.[49] Thus, Ploos observes the building which incites him to identify with the group that founded it. The ancestors thus inspire his patriotism. Even representations of the building could instill in the eighteenth-century beholder the conviction to follow in the footsteps of their forefathers, to uphold the implicit values radiating from the *monumentum*.[50] The large number of paintings and drawings that were produced from the moment that the building was being erected and which increased substantially after its completion in 1665, not only indicates a curiosity amongst painters and draughtsmen to reproduce the building or be inspired by it, but also points towards the meaning the building was expected to transmit, in terms of civic pride, now and in the future.[51]

But we can even wonder if, contrary to Sturm's strictly architectural observation, for Ploos there was already a new 'emotionalist aesthetic' attached to the Town Hall, supported by nationalist feelings.[52] Although there was certainly nothing picturesque, sublime or romantic about the building for Ploos – it was still considered a contemporary building in classicist style – he was, in fact, defending a style of building that was increasingly considered unfashionable, or even inappropriate. Yet, he simply could not allow himself to criticize it, because the building was so strongly connected with a glorious era of the nation from the recent past.

Ploos' perception of the building as one with important monumental or commemorative value seems to form part of a wider awareness of patriotism as a positive force to celebrate Dutch identity. In a lecture at the Amsterdam Drawing Academy in 1769, he stressed the importance of picturing prominent *vaderlanders* (patriots) and their actions – rather than mythological or biblical figures – as subjects in contemporary art.[53] Ploos' assessment of the Amsterdam Town Hall becomes clearer when related to similar notions ventilated by his brother Jacob in a special lecture at the society of *Concordia et Libertate* in 1774, to present the idea to raise a monument to the jurist and writer Hugo de Groot.[54] On the occasion, he presented a paper memorial ['papieren gedenkstuk'] of a temple designed by Husly, which should replace the despised castle of Loevestein, in which de Groot had been imprisoned in 1622 after having been falsely accused of high treason.[55] We are less concerned here with the new monument.[56] Our concern focuses on the old castle that sparks the historical sensation.

Jacob, in his lecture, described in detail how his visit to Loevestein gave him the sense of suddenly being in the company of De Groot at the time of his predicament. This can be interpreted as the historical sensation, which is often described following the famous Dutch historian Johan Huizinga (1872–1945). According to Huizinga: 'This contact with the past that cannot be reduced to anyting outside itself, is the entrance into a world of its own, it is one of the many variants of *ekstasis*, of an experience of truth that is given to the human being.'[57] This sensation can be aroused by any fragment of the past and make it seem very real to the beholder, but is not something created by the historian. 'It is "behind" and not "in" the book the past has left us.'[58] In the words of Frank Ankersmit: 'All spatial and temporal demarcations have been temporarily lifted. . . Historical experience pulls the faces of past and present together in a short but ecstatic kiss.'[59]

The Ploos brothers were thus engaged in similar processes of *memoria*, the recollection of a thing from the past in its materiality in the present, and of *narratio*, the (historical) narration in which it is included and used.[60] In these processes, buildings are instrumental in different ways: the old castle of Loevestein sparks the historical sensation in Jacob and provides a kind of timeless perception in which the site is meaningful and the architecture of the castle indifferent, while the Amsterdam Town Hall for Cornelis becomes the main figure and embodies the historical narrative about the Golden Age and great forebears. The Town Hall is at once an historic yet operational building, a piece of architecture and a *monumentum* to the nation.

Clearly, what is happening in different ways in both instances, is the stirring up, through the emotions, of a living memory, as Françoise Choay has described. Monuments mobilize and engage memory through the mediation of affectivity, in such a way as to recall a past that is localized and selected to directly contribute 'to the maintenance and preservation of the identity of an ethnic, religious, national, tribal or familial community'.[61] We find Ploos and his brother fully aware of art and architecture as 'patrimoine', 'heritage', inherited property. They considered the monument, with its commemorative role, useful to trigger certain public memories or evoke political and nationalist values. In bringing their opinion on memory to print, the Ploos brothers were producing heritage in the way it is considered today, signifying not only the buildings that are the object of preservation, but also the processes by which they are understood, contextualized, perceived, managed, modified, destroyed or transformed.[62] In fact, the brothers are contributing to 'a cultural and social process, which engages with acts of remembering that work to create ways to understand and engage with the present'.[63] Thus, the brothers were 'doing' heritage, as defined in terms of current debate in heritage studies, a contemporary practice dealing with memory.[64]

Around the same time, in other areas, antiquarians were trying to find the origins of the Dutch 'nation', or traces of a prehistoric civilization on Dutch soil, by looking for the 'Batavian' hut.[65] These investigations provided a long history of settlement with a distinct art of building. Heaped up boulders and *hunebedden* (dolmens) were regarded as the oldest burial grounds of the Nordic tribes in the territory of the Republic from a stone age. This adoration for local and national *Antiquitates*, a combination of eighteenth-century sensibilities and notions of the picturesque interest in the ruin, was combined with thinking about a prehistoric past and the foundations of the nation. Places and buildings were increasingly considered reliable sources for the construction of the earliest past of the Netherlands, and should therefore be exempt of all blemishes. Here, we have heritage in the making, long before the words *erfgoed* (heritage) or *patrimonium* (patrimony) would surface in the Dutch language.[66] It is a form of commemoration, the passing on of knowledge, asserting cultural values and expressing identity, by attributing specific meaning through history and historical narratives to monuments and architecture that starts to compete with, or overshadow, the aesthetic appreciation of architecture.

It is interesting to see that the two brothers both focus on the representational qualities of the buildings, how Loevestein reminds the visitor of a location with historic significance centred around an intellectual hero, and how the Amsterdam Town Hall refers to Republican greatness and autonomy. Both buildings could act as symbols of the nation and both can stand for the ideological aspirations of the Dutch people. The appreciation for both buildings during these years was probably strengthened by Republican feelings as opposed to Orangist sentiments, which surfaced in the late 1750s and 1760s in Holland circles, before turning more radical during the Patriot Revolt of 1781–7.[67] With appeals to a glorious or noteworthy past, and attaching this to exemplary buildings, architecture was employed to construct or reinforce parts of a national and political identity. It is a far cry from the formalist approach demonstrated by the professional architect Sturm half a century earlier, but also from the aesthetic judgments by Camper and Laugier, who both ignored the nationalist meaning attached to architecture, when they concentrated on taste.

Conclusion

We have seen, by concentrating on a limited number of texts, how perceptions of architecture varied over the eighteenth century. There is common praise for the Amsterdam Town Hall in ego documents and in guide books and other publications. We encountered notions of civic pride, national and urban patriotism in travelogues and polemics, and we have understood how historical narratives were created to defend specific architectures, supported by images and texts, to strengthen ideas about national identity and belonging. But the Town Hall could also serve to criticize architectural or Dutch taste. All of these different opinions, interpretations and associations circled around one building in the eighteenth-century city of Amsterdam. Rather than taking for granted the renown of the Town Hall – a must-see attraction in most guidebooks to the city that appeared every few years during the eighteenth century, and followed the usual 'tourist gaze' – the writers discussed above considered the building as modern day professionals and critics. The arguments used to evaluate the building could be conflicting. We find ideas about what is good architecture and taste juxtaposed. The building is approached historically, not beyond critique (any more). In fact, these views, descriptions, interpretations, reinterpretations and misprisions of the Amsterdam Town Hall show an eighteenth-century urge for redescription. The building was no longer what it had been in the seventeenth century. In these novel approaches, we can recognize two basic elements of early architectural historiography: architectural analysis and aesthetic criticism on the one hand, as a means to study precedent to inform contemporary design practice and style, and on the other, the historical understanding of a building becoming a monument in the construction of national heritage.

In the later nineteenth century, long after the Town Hall had become a royal palace, it would again be judged differently in terms of heritage and architecture. Around the middle of the century, the Amsterdam Town Hall and its designer were firmly inscribed in architectural history, canonized by architects united in the *Maatschappij tot Bevordering der Bouwkunst* (Society for the Advancement of Architecture) who, in establishing themselves as professionals, identified their predecessors from the past, with Jacob van Campen with 'his' Town Hall as a key figure, both depicted on the frontispice of the Society's journal *Bouwkundige Bijdragen* (Architectural Contributions). Even the bicentenary of the laying of the first stone of the Town Hall was commemmorated in 1848 with a ceremonial that did not leave room for criticism: 'This building, of which we today commemmorate the laying of the foundations, still stands in complete splendor, and continues to proclaim the honour of this great building artist.'[68] But this appraisal of the building must be understood within the context of the Dutch architect's efforts to defend his art from being undermined by the building industries and in competition with the increasing demand for engineers. The sculptor-architect Hendrick de Keyser and the painter-architect Jacob van Campen became role models for the professional, nineteenth-century architect as an artist. Thus, the lobby of architects created their own professional heritage.

In the meantime, outside this circle, the Amsterdam Town Hall as a monument was re-evaluated in a broader understanding of Dutch culture. An independent critic could again question the status of the building on the basis of its architecture, but this time without being criticized for being unpatriotic as had happened to Petrus Camper. The opinion of Conrad Busken Huet (1826–86) is well known, describing the Town Hall in his studies on Dutch seventeenth-century culture as 'that gloomy dice with the many eyes, whose sight reminds of neither the history of the Netherlands before the Reformation, nor of its history afterwards, but only of the portfolios of drawings of native architects who, after having spent ample time in Italy on the Arno or Tiber, found it interesting to transplant a palazzo Farnese, Borghese of Strozzi to the banks of the Y.'[69] By then, the magnificence that, in the eighteenth century, had overwhelmed general visitors but had already been questioned by Sturm, Camper and Laugier, was considered inappropriate and out of place, and the building could no longer automatically function as a monument to unite the nation.

Notes

1 Guy Chapman (ed.), *The travel-diaries of William Beckford of Fonthill*, 2 vols. (Cambridge: Cambridge University Press, 1928), I, 26: Letter VI, Utrecht, 2 July 1780.
2 William Montague, *The delights of Holland [or A Three Months' Travel about that and the other Provinces]* (London: John Sturton and A. Bosvile, 1696), 123-4.
3 Author's translation. 'Das weltberümte Stadthaus zu Amsterdam ... ist denn doch an Ende ein elendes, geschmackloses Ding, und seiner ungeheuren Grösse ungeachtet kleinlich.' Julia Bientjes, *Holland und der Holländer im Urteil deutscher Reisender (1400-1800)* (Groningen: Wolters, 1967), 162; Carl Gottlieb Kuettner, *Beyträge zur Kenntnis vorzüglich des gegenwärtigen Zustandes von Frankreich und Holland, met untermischten Vergleichungen verschiedener Orte und Gegenstände unter einander. Aus den Briefen eines in England wohnenden Deutschen auf seinen Reisen durch Frankreich und Holland in den Jahren 1787, 1790 und 1791* (Leipzig: Hrsg. von Johann Gottfried Dijk, 1792), 329.
4 Michael Baxandall, *Painting and Experience in Fifteenth Century Italy: A Primer in the Social History of the Pctorial Style*, 2nd ed. (Oxford: Oxford University Press, 1988), 34.
5 Alan Moss, 'Comparing Ruins: National Trauma in Dutch Travel Accounts of the Seventeenth Century', in *The Roots of Nationalism: National Identity Formation in Early Modern Europe, 1600-1815,* ed. Lotte Jensen (Amsterdam: Amsterdam University Press, 2016), 217-333: 21.
6 Thomas H. von der Dunk, 'Sturm en het stadhuis. Een Duits architectuurdocent corrigeert het werk van Jacob van Campen en Jacob Roman', *Bulletin KNOB* 100 (2001): 133-57.
7 Jeroen Goudeau, *Nicolaus Goldmann (1611-1665) en de wiskundige architectuurwetenschap* (Groningen: Philip Elchers, 2005).
8 Goudeau, *Nicoaus Goldmann*, 460.
9 Manfredo Tafuri, *Theories and History of Architecture* (New York: Harper & Row, 1980), 141-70; Peter Collins, *Architectural Judgment* (London: Faber & Faber, 1971).
10 Christian Schädlich, 'Leonhard Christoph Sturm (1669-1719)', in *Grosse Baumeister*, ed. Adalbert Behr (Berlin: Henschel, 1990), 91-139: 117-18.
11 Pieter Vlaardingerbroek, *Het paleis van de Republiek. Geschiedenis van het stadhuis van Amsterdam* (Zwolle: Waanders, 2011), 12.
12 Jan Wagenaar, *Amsterdam, in zyne opkomst, aanwas, geschiedenissen, voorregten, koophandel, gebouwen, kerkenstaat, schoolen, schutterye, gilden en regeeringe, / beschreeven, door Jan Wagenaar* (Amsterdam: Yntema en Tieboel/Isaak Tirion, 1760-5).
13 Eco O.G. Haitsma Mulier, 'Between Humanism and Enlightenment: The Dutch writing of history', in *The Dutch Republic in the Eigtheenth Century. Decline,*

Enlightenment, and Revolution, ed. Margaret C. Jacob and Wijnand W. Mijnhardt (Ithaca/London: Cornell University Press, 1992), 170-87: 173.

14 Bert Gerlagh, 'Veranderingen en continuïteit in de topografie', in *Kijk Amsterdam 1700-1800. De mooiste stadsgezichten*, ed. Bert Gerlagh et al. (Amsterdam: Thoth, 2017), 52-65: 60.

15 Freek Schmidt, 'Amsterdam's Architectural Image from Early-Modern Print Series to Global Heritage Discourse', in *Imagining Global Amsterdam: History, Culture, and Geography in a World City*, ed. Marco de Waard (Amsterdam: Amsterdam University Press, 2012): 219-21.

16 Boudewijn Bakker, *Amsterdam in de achttiende eeuw. Een keuze uit de tekeningen in het gemeentearchief* (Delft: s.n., s.d. [1974]); See also *Kijk Amsterdam 1700-1800. De mooiste stadsgezichten*, ed. Bert Gerlagh et al. (Amsterdam: Thoth, 2017). This detailed catalogue of a rich selection of Amsterdam topographical drawings, many by artists whose work was then engraved by Fouquet, analyses in great detail everything depicted, but hardly discusses the specific nature of representing the city and the reasons behind it, beyond general observation.

17 The fact that Jan Wagenaar's publisher, Isaac Tirion, received a printing privilege of the States of Holland to protect Wagenaar's illustrated history of Amsterdam, did not prevent Fouquet from issuing his own prints. Ester Wouthuysen and Erik Ariëns Kappers, 'De Atlas Fouquet opnieuw bekeken. Pierre Fouquet jr. (1729-1800), prentuitgever en kunsthandelaar', in Gerlagh, *Kijk Amsterdam*, 34-45.

18 Wagenaar, *Amsterdam*, II: 2: 'Wy beginnen met de eersten, en geeven, onder de menigvuldige aanzienlyke weereldlyke gebouwen, waarmede de stad verrykt is, met regt, den voorrang aan 't stadhuis, welk, in konst en luister, boven alle de anderen uitmunt.' The complete description: 3-28.

19 Author's translation. 'En gelyk de schilder-, bouw- en beeldhouwkunst in 't midden der voorgaande eeuwe, toen 't stadhuis gestigt werdt, den hoogsten trap van volkomenheid bereikt hadden; zo vloeiden de konstenaars en arbeiders van allerlei soorte, in zulk eene menigte, herwaards, dat zulks gelegenheid gaf, om het gebouw, spoediger, en zelfs met minder kosten, te volmaaken, dan tegenwoordig zou konnen geschieden.' Wagenaar, *Amsterdam*, II, 28. See also: L.H.M. Wessels, *Bron, waarheid en de verandering der tijden. Jan Wagenaar (1709-1773), een historiografische studie* (Den Haag: Stichting Hollandse Historische Reeks, 1997), 47.

20 Françoise Choay, *The Invention of the Historic Monument*, trans. Lauren M. O'Connell (Cambridge: Cambridge University Press, 2001), 40-62; Janine Barrier, *Les architectes européens à Rome: 1740-1765. La naissance du goût à la grecque* (Paris: Monum, 2005); John A. Pinto, *Speaking Ruins: Piranesi, Architects and Antiquity in Eighteenth-Century Rome* (Ann Arbor: University of Michigan Press, 2012); Dora Wiebenson, *Sources of Greek Revival architecture* (London: Zwemmer, 1969); Freek Schmidt, 'Beschavende bouwkunst voor Burgers. Jacob Otten Husly's

redevoeringen over de architectuur van de Oudheid', in *De Oudheid in de achttiende eeuw/Classical Antiquity in the Eighteenth Century*. Congresreeks Werkgroep 18e eeuw nummer 1, ed. A.J.P. Raat, W.R.E. Velema and C. Baar-de Werd (Utrecht: Werkgroep 18e Eeuw, 2012), 179–99.

21 Author's translation. 'L'hôtel de ville d'Amsterdam nous a paru bien au-dessous de sa réputation: c'est une grande masse carrée, toute bâtie en pierre gros bleu. Sur us soubassement qui a 12 pieds de haut, s'élèvent deux étages d'architecture en pilastres. Le Ier ordre est composite avec des singularités bizarres dans les chapiteaux. Le 2ième ordere est corinthien; à chaque étage, il y a deux rangs de fenêtres carrées, séparées par des guirlandes dont le travail est lourd et pesant.... Les avant-corps du milieu sont couronnés par un grand fronton dont le tympan est taillé de sculpture d'un dessin confus et d'une exécution barbare.' Marc Antoine Laugier, 'Detail de tout ce que nous avons observé et éprouvé dans notre voyage de Hollande' [1766] (manuscript Bibliotheque Nationale Paris, Bréquigny 66), from: Madeleine van Strien-Chardonneau, *'Le voyage de Hollande': récits de voyageurs français dans les Provinces-Unies, 1748–1795* (Oxford: The Voltaire Foundation, 1994), 370–72.

22 Jan B. Bedaux, 'A discussion on Rembrandt in eighteenth-century Amsterdam: Petrus Camper versus Cornelis Ploos van Amstel', *Hoogsteder-Naumann Mercury* (1986): 38–56. The Nightwatch, the group portrait of militiamen was originally made for, and hung in the Arquebusiers' Headquarters (Kloveniersdoelen) in Amsterdam; in (or soon after) that year it was moved to the Small War Council room in the Town Hall. J. Bruyn et al., *A Corpus of Rembrandt Paintings. III: 1635–1642*, Dordrecht etc. 1989, 484.

23 On Laugier: Wolfgang Herrmann, *Laugier and Eighteenth-century French Theory* (London: Zwemmer, 1962), and Barry Bergdoll, *European Architecture 1750–1890* (Oxford: Oxford University Press, 2000), 10–13.

24 Herrmann, *Laugier*, 36.

25 As has been studied by Herrmann and recently by Richard Wittman, *Architecture, Print Culture, and the Public Sphere in Eighteenth-century France* (New York/London: Routledge, 2007).

26 Herrmann, *Laugier*, 50.

27 Herrmann, *Laugier*, 51.

28 [Petrus Camper], [Untitled], *De Philosooph* 2, no. 93 (1767): 321–28. The original letter: University Library, Leiden (BPL 247/133).

29 Miriam Claude Meijer, *Race and aesthetics in the anthropology of Petrus Camper (1722–1789)* (Amsterdam: Rodopi, 1999), 26. Johann Wolfgang von Goethe, *Goethes Werke, herausgegeben im Auftrag der Grossherzogin Sophie von Sachsen* (Weimar: Herman Böhlau, 1887–1919), v. 61, p. 18.

30 Bedaux, 'A discussion', first identified Camper as the mysterious 'C'. Bedaux stressed the significance of the letter's discussion of seventeenth-century painting, while the architecture part was first discussed by Thomas H. von der Dunk and Freek Schmidt,

"Petrus Camper en Jacob van Campen. Een polemiek met Cornelis Ploos van Amstel inzake het Stadhuis van Amsterdam uit 1767", *Bulletin KNOB* 100 (2001): 158–77, slightly edited and republished in: Thomas H. von der Dunk, *Een Hollands heiligdom. De moeizame architectonische eenwording van Nederland*, Amsterdam 2007, chapter 3, and subsequently by Lex Hermans, 'Alles wat zuilen heeft is klassiek'. *Classicistische ideeën over bouwkunst in Nederland 1765-1850* (Rotterdam: NAi, 2005), 130–8; Jan K. van der Korst, *Het rusteloze bestaan van dokter Petrus Camper (1722-1789)* (Houten: Bohn Stafleu van Loghum, 2008), 84–8.

31 Freek Schmidt, 'A Passion for Architecture: Petrus Camper and the Groningen Town Hall', in *Petrus Camper in Context: Science, the Arts and Society in the Eghteenth Century Dutch Republic*, ed. : Klaas van Berkel and Bart Ramakers (Hilversum: Verloren, 2015), 275–307; Thomas H. von der Dunk (with contributions by Eva Roëll), *De eerste prijs. Twee eeuwen stadhuis van Groningen. De eerste Nederlandse architectuurprijsvraag en de bouw van het ontwerp van Husly* (Amsterdam: Architectura & Natura, 2010).

32 [P. Camper], Letter in *De Philosooph* 2 (1767) no. 93, 321–8. The original letter: University Library, Leiden (BPL 247/133): 321. 'Wanneer wij onze Republiek in haren aart beschouwen, en byzonderlyk op de verstandelyke vermogens der Ingezetenen letten, moeten wy ons verwonderen, dat wy, die ten deze opzichte voor de meeste Volkeren des Werelds geenzints behoeve te wyken, echter zo achterlyk zyn in dat byzonder vermogen der Ziel, 't welk men SMAAK noemt.'

33 Author's translation. 'de eersten ... onder de menigvuldige aanzienlyke weereldlijke gebouwen, waarmede de stad verrykt is, ... welk in konst en luister, boven alle de anderen uitmunt.' Wagenaar, Amsterdam, II, 3.

34 [Camper], 325.

35 [Camper], 325.

36 [Camper], 327. Wagenaar was also the author of one of the publications in support of the plea for a more communicative way of preaching: Jan Wagenaar, *Zeven lessen over het verhandelen der Heilige Schriftuur in Godsdienstige Vergaderingen* (Amsterdam: Jacob ter Beek, 1752). Jelle J. Bosma, *Woorden van een gezond verstand. De invloed van de Verlichting op de in het Nederlands uitgegeven preken van 1750 tot 1800* (Kampen: PhD diss., 1997), 306.

37 Jacob van Sluis and Sybren Sybrandy, 'Petrus Camper over schoonheid, of: het leerzame van de analogie', in *Onderwijs en onderzoek: studie en wetenschap aan de academie van Groningen in de 17e en 18e eeuw*, ed. A.H. Huussen (Hilversum: Verloren, 2003), 208–10; Petrus Camper, *Redenvoeringen over de wyze, om de onderscheidene hartstogten op onze wezens te verbeelden; over de verbaazende overeenkomst tusschen de viervoetige dieren, de vogelen, de visschen en den mensch; en over het gedaante schoon* (Utrecht: B. Wild and J. Altheer, 1792), 60; Meijer, *Race and aesthetics*, 228.

38 Schmidt, 'A passion', 283-7; Freek Schmidt, *Passion and Control. Dutch Architectural Culture of the Eighteenth Century* (Aldershot, Ashgate, 2016), 131.
39 Wouthuysen and Ariëns Kappers, 'De Atlas Fouquet', 37.
40 Roeland van Eijnden and Adriaan van der Willigen, *Geschiedenis der Vaderlandsche schilderkunst, sedert de helft der XVIII eeuw*, 3 vols. (Haarlem: A. Loosjes, Pz, 1817-40), 161.
41 Schmidt, *Passion and Control*, 145-53.
42 Cornelis Ploos van Amstel, *De bouworde van 't stadhuis van Amsterdam, en de smaak der Nederlanderen, ten opzigte der konsten en weetenschappen, verdedigd, tegen de ongegronde berispingen van den heer C., in zynen brief aan Den philosooph* (Amsterdam: Yntema en Tieboel, 1767).
43 Th. Laurentius, J.W. Niemeijer and G. Ploos van Amstel, *Cornelis Ploos van Amstel, 1726-1798, Kunstverzamelaar en prentuitgever* (Assen: Van Gorcum, 1980); G. van Ploos van Amstel, *Portret van een koopman en uitvinder: Cornelis Ploos van Amstel. Maatschappelijk, cultureel en familieleven van een achttiende eeuwer* (Assen: Van Gorcum, 1980), 6-29.
44 Boudewijn Bakker, 'Cornelis Ploos van Amstel en het stadsgezicht als kunst', in Bert Gerlagh et al., *Kijk Amsterdam 1700-1800. De mooiste stadsgezichten*, Amsterdam/Bussum 2017, 20-33: 24-6.
45 Eveline Koolhaas & Sandra de Vries, 'Terug naar een roemrijk verleden. De zeventiende-eeuwse schilderkunst als voorbeeld voor de negentiende eeuw', in *De Gouden Eeuw in perspectief. het beeld van de Nederlandse zeventiende-eeuws schilderkunst in later tijd*, ed. : Frans Grijzenhout and Henk van Veen (Nijmegen: Sun, 1992), 107-38: 114-15; Paul Knolle, 'Cornelis Ploos van Amstel, pleitbezorger van een "Hollandse" inconografie', *Oud Holland* 98 (1984), 43-53.
46 Ploos, *bouworde*, 38-9. 'Maar wy meenen genoeg gezegd te hebben, om de zwakheid van de bewyzen van onzen berisper, nevens zynen onbedagten yver of onbedrevenheid, in een helder daglicht te stellen: welke te overschoonlyker zyn, om dat hy daar door de Eer van eene gantsche Natie, ja van zyn eigen Vaderland, als een onwaardig Medeburger, heeft poogen te bevlekken; daar het veel eer zyn pligt was, dezelve, op eene betaamelyke wyze, op te houden, en de gemeene gebreken te bedekken.'
47 Knolle, "Cornelis"; Koolhaas and De Vries, 'Terug', 114-16. For Ploos' lectures, see Cornelis *Ploos van Amstel, Redenvoeringen gedaan in de Teken-Academie te Amsterdam* (Amsterdam: J. Yntema, 1785) and Laurentius, *Cornelis*, 304-07.
48 On the interest in 'historical' architecture throughout the past, see: Wim Denslagen, *Memories of Architecture: Architectural Heritage and Historiography in the Distant Past* (Amsterdam: Het Spinhuis, 2009).
49 L. Hermans, 'Perpetual presenses. Some remark on the agency of buildings and images in Renaissance Italy', in *The secret lives of artworks. Exploring the boundaries*

between art and life, ed. : C. van Eck, J. van Gastel and E. van Kessel (Leiden: Leiden University Press, 2014), 56–74: 60.
50 Hermans, 'Perpetual', 65.
51 Jan Peeters, 'Het hart van Amsterdam als inspiratiebron', in *Het Paleis in de schilderkunst van de Gouden Eeuw*, ed. : Jan Peeters et al. (Amsterdam/Zwolle: Waanders, 1997), 6–17: 9.
52 Miles Glendinning, *The Conservation Movement: A History of Architectural Preservation – Antiquity to Modernity* (London/New York: Routledge, 2013), 49.
53 Koolhaas and De Vries, 'Terug', 114.
54 Jacob Ploos van Amstel, *Het uitmuntend karakter en de zonderlinge lotgevallen van Hugo de Groot herdagt bij de beschouwing van het slot Loevestein in de maand Julij 1772* (Amsterdam s.a.); Schmidt, *Passion and Control*, 140–4; Von der Dunk, *Een Hollands heiligdom*, 21–38 (previously published in *Grotiana* 19 (1998), 25–81). Previously discussed by Ploos van Amstel, *Portret*, 39–40; Frans Grijzenhout, *Feesten voor het vaderland. Patriotse en Bataafse feesten 1780–1806* (Zwolle: Waanders, 1989), 29–30; Niek van Sas, 'Gedenck aan Loevesteyn', in *Waar de blanke top der duinen en andere vaderlandse herinneringen*, ed. N.C.F. van Sas (Amsterdam: Contact, 1990), 70–80 (reprinted in N.C.F. Sas, *De metamorfose van Nederland. Van oude orde naar moderniteit 1750–1900*, Amsterdam 2004, 567–75), describes how Loevestein became the object of a cult in terms of politics and was mobilized by the 'Patriotten' in the 1780s, before becoming nationalized in the nineteenth century.
55 Freek Schmidt, '"Het eenige en zeldzame Wonderstuk van de geheele wereld". Een architectonische fantasie voor een illustere vaderlander", in *Een tempel voor Hugo de Groot. Een rede van Jacob Ploos van Amstel uit 1774*, ed. Jan Bloemendal and H.K. Ploos van Amstel (Amersfoort: Florivallis, 2010), 63–75.
56 The temple with the statue to worship Hugo de Groot, and its paper *monumentum* refer to classical mausoleums, but also to the commemoration of the virtue and ideals of a visionary that transcends the individual person. In fact, this architectural rendering of Enlightenment ideals is similar to slightly later attempts by French 'revolutionary' architects, such as the monuments designed for heroes of the Revolution and the creation of the French Panthéon dedicated 'aux grands hommes' in 1790–1 as revolutionary symbol. It is a study for an architectural monument not unlike the ones Etienne Louis Boullée studied, such as his famous design for a cenotaph for Newton (1784), celebrating the discovery of the laws of nature on a scale that should arouse sublime sensations. *Les architectes de la Liberté 1789–1799*, Paris [Ecole Nationale Supérieure des Beaux-Arts] 1989; Barry Bergdoll et al., *Le Panthéon. Symbole des révolutions. De l'Eglise de la Nation aux Temple des grands hommes*, Paris 1989; Emil Kaufmann, *Three Revolutionary Architects: Boullée, Ledoux and Lequeu*, Philadelphia 1952 [Transactions of the American Philosophical Society; new series; vol. 42, Pt 3, 431–564]; Günter Metken and Klaus Galwitz (eds.),

Revolutionsarchitektur. Boullée, Ledoux, Lequeu (Baden-Baden: Staatliche Kunsthalle, 1970); Bergdoll, *European Architecture*, 86–8.

57 Frank Ankersmit, *De sublieme historische ervaring* (Groningen: Historische uitgeverij, 2007), 115. Translation by Frank Ankersmit, *Sublime Historical Experience* (Stanford: Stanford University Press, 2005), 120.

58 'Dit niet geheel herleidbare contact met verleden is een ingaan in een sfeer, het is een der vele vormen van buiten zichzelf treden, van het beleven van waarheid, die den mensch gegeven zijn.' 'Het ligt achter en niet in het geschiedenisboek. De lezer brengt het den schrijver tegemoet, het is zijn respons op dien roep.' Johan Huizinga, 'De taak der cultuurgeschiedenis', in: Johan Huizinga, *Verzamelde werken. VII: Geschiedwetenschap, Hedendaagsche cultuur* (Haarlem: Tjeenk Willink, 1950), 35–94: 71–2. First published in: Johan Huizinga, *Cultuurhistorische verkenningen* (Haarlem: H.D. Tjeenk Willink & Zoon, 1929), 1–85.

59 'Alle ruimtelijke en temporele demarcaties zijn tijdelijk opgeheven... De historische ervaring verenigt verleden en heden in een korte extatische kus.' Ankersmit, *De sublieme*, 116; Ankersmit, *Sublime*, 121.

60 Caroline van Eck, *Inigo Jones reconstrueert Stonehenge. Architectuurgeschiedenis tussen memoria en narratio* (Amsterdam: Architectura & Natura, 2009), 43–6. See also Caroline van Eck, *Art, Agency and Living Presence: From the Animated Object to the Excessive Object* (Boston: De Gruyter; Leiden: Leiden University Press, 2015), 191–4.

61 Françoise Choay, *The invention of the historic monument*, transl. from the French by Lauren M. O'Connell (Cambridge: Cambridge University Press, 2001), 6.

62 Graham Fairclough, 'New Heritage Frontiers', in: *Heritage and Beyond, Council of Europe*, December 2009, 29–41: 29. https://rm.coe.int/16806abdea. See also: Marlite Halbertsma and Marieke Kuipers, *Het erfgoeduniversum. Een inleiding in de theorie en praktijk van cultureel erfgoed* (Bussum: Coutinho, 2014), 18. Another definition that is much in use, is of 'a contemporary product shaped from history', David C. Harvey, 'The History of Heritage', in *The Ashgate Research Companion to Heritage and Identity*, ed. Brian Graham and Peter Howard (Aldershot: Ashgate, 2008), 19–36: 20, referring to J.E. Tunbridge and G.J. Ashworth, *Dissonant Heritage: The Management of the Past as a Resource in Conflict* (Chichester: Wiley, 1996), 20. See also: David C. Harvey, 'Heritage pasts and heritage presents: Temporality, meaning and the scope of heritage studies', *International Journal of Heritage Studies* 7, no. 4 (2001): 319–38.

63 Laurajane Smith, *Uses of Heritage* (London: Routledge, 2006), 2.

64 Heritage Studies as an expanding interdisciplinary field of study, tends to focus on contemporary developments, yet it is acknowledged that it is part of the human condition. Although histories of the 'heritage' and 'patrimoine' exist, heritage discourse as a 'discursive construction' has not attracted serious scholarly attention

for its own past or previous manifestations. Cf. Glendinning, *The Conservation movement*.
65 Sandra Langereis, 'Antiquitates: voorvaderlijke oudheden', in *Erfgoed. De geschiedenis van een begrip*, ed. Frans Grijzenhout (Amsterdam: Amsterdam University Press, 2007), 57–83: 78–83; Auke van der Woud, *De Bataafse hut. Denken over het oudste Nederland (1750–1850)* (Amsterdam/Antwerpen: Contact, 1998).
66 Frans Grijzenhout, 'Inleiding', in Grijzenhout, *Erfgoed*, 1–20: 8; Coert Peter Krabbe, 'Monumenten: architectonische overblijfselen', in Grijzenhout, *Erfgoed*, 151–74.
67 Van Sas, *De metamorfose*, 572–3.
68 Coert Peter Krabbe, *Ambacht, kunst, wetenschap. De bevordering der bouwkunst in Nederland (1775–1880)* (Zeist/Zwolle: Waanders, 1998), 176–7: '"Het gebouw, welks eerste grondlegging wij heden herinneren, [staat] nog in vollen luister daar, en verkondigt nog bij voortduring den lof van den voortreffelijken bouwmeester."'
69 Author's translation. Conrad Busken Huet, *Het land van Rembrand. Studies over de Noordnederlandse beschaving in de zeventiende eeuw*, 2 vols. (Haarlem: H.D. Tjeenk Willink, 1882–4), II, 748: 'Het is alsof men genoeg is gaan krijgen van die zwaarmoedige dobbelsteen met de vele ogen, wiens aanblik noch aan de geschiedenis van Nederland vóór de hervorming doet denken, noch aan zijn geschiedenis daarna, maar alleen aan de teeken-portefeuilles van vaderlandsche bouwmeesters die geruimen tijd in Italie hadden vertoefd, aan den Arno of den Tiber, en het eigenaardig vonden aan de boorden van het Y een palazzo-Farnese, een palazzo-Borghese, of een palazzo-Strozzi over te planten.'

Bibliography

Ankersmit, Frank. *De sublieme historische ervaring*. Groningen: Historische uitgeverij, 2007.
Ankersmit, Frank. *Sublime Historical Experience*. Stanford: Stanford University Press, 2005.
Bakker, Boudewijn. *Amsterdam in de achttiende eeuw. Een keuze uit de tekeningen in het gemeentearchief*. Delft: Elmar, 1974.
Bakker, Boudewijn. 'Cornelis Ploos van Amstel en het stadsgezicht als kunst.' In *Kijk Amsterdam 1700–1800. De mooiste stadsgezichten*, edited by Bert Gerlagh et al., 20–33. Amsterdam, Bussum: Thoth, 2017.
Barrier, Janine. *Les architectes européens à Rome: 1740–1765. La naissance du goût à la grecque*. Paris: Monum, 2005.
Baxandall, Michael. *Painting and Experience in Fifteenth Century Italy. A primer in the social history of the pictorial style*, 2nd ed. Oxford: Oxford University Press, 1988.

Bedaux, Jan B. 'A discussion on Rembrandt in eighteenth-century Amsterdam: Petrus Camper versus Cornelis Ploos van Amstel', *Hoogsteder-Naumann Mercury* (1986), 38–56.

Bergdoll, Barry, et al., *Le Panthéon. Symbole des révolutions. De l'Eglise de la Nation aux Temple des grands hommes*. Paris: Editions A. et J. Picard, 1989.

Bergdoll, Barry. *European Architecture 1750–1890*. Oxford, Oxford University Press, 2000.

Bientjes, Julia. *Holland und der Holländer im Urteil deutscher Reisender (1400–1800)*. Groningen: Wolters, 1967.

Bosma, Jelle J. *Woorden van een gezond verstand. De invloed van de Verlichting op de in het Nederlands uitgegeven preken van 1750 tot 1800*. Kampen: PhD diss., 1997.

Bruyn J. et al., *A Corpus of Rembrandt Paintings. III: 1635–1642*. Dordrecht: Martinus Nijhoff, 1989.

Busken Huet, Conrad. *Het land van Rembrand. Studies over de Noordnederlandse beschaving in de zeventiende eeuw*, 2 vols. Haarlem: H.D. Tjeenk Willink, 1882–4.

[Camper, P.]. [Untitled]. *De Philosooph* 2, no. 93 (1767): 321–8.

Camper, Petrus. *Redenvoeringen over de wyze, om de onderscheidene hartstogten op onze wezens te verbeelden; over de verbaazende overeenkomst tusschen de viervoetige dieren, de vogelen, de visschen en den mensch; en over het gedaante schoon*. Utrecht: B. Wild and J. Altheer, 1792.

Chapman, Guy (ed.). *The travel-diaries of William Beckford of Fonthill*, 2 vols. Cambridge: Cambridge University Press, 1928.

Choay, Françoise. *The Invention of the Historic Monument*, trans. Lauren M. O'Connell. Cambridge: Cambridge University Press, 2001.

Collins, Peter. *Architectural Judgment*. London: Faber & Faber, 1971.

Denslagen, Wim. *Memories of Architecture: Architectural Heritage and Historiography in the Distant Past*. Amsterdam: Het Spinhuis, 2009.

Dunk, Thomas H. von der. 'Sturm en het stadhuis. Een Duitsarchitectuurdocent corrigeert het werk van Jacob van Campen en Jacob Roman', *Bulletin KNOB* 100 (2001): 133–57.

Dunk, Thomas H. von der, and Freek Schmidt, 'Petrus Camper en Jacob van Campen. Een polemiek met Cornelis Ploos van Amstel inzake het Stadhuis van Amsterdam uit 1767', *Bulletin KNOB* 100 (2001): 158–77.

Dunk, Thomas H. von der. *Een Hollands heiligdom. De moeizame architectonische eenwording van Nederland*. Amsterdam: Bert Bakker, 2007.

Dunk, Thomas H. von der, with contributions by Eva Roell. *De eerste prijs. Twee eeuwen stadhuis van Groningen. De eerste Nederlandse architectuurprijsvraag en de bouw van het ontwerp van Husly*. Amsterdam: Architectura & Natura, 2010.

Eck, Caroline van. *Inigo Jones reconstrueert Stonehenge. Architectuurgeschiedenis tussen memoria en narratio*. Amsterdam: Architectura & Natura, 2009.

Eck, Caroline van. *Art, Agency and Living Presence: From the Animated Object to the Excessive Object*. Boston: De Gruyter, 2015.

Eijnden, Roeland van, and Adriaan van der Willigen. *Geschiedenis der Vaderlandsche schilderkunst, sedert de helft der XVIII eeuw*, 3 vols. Haarlem: A. Loosjes, Pz, 1817-40.
Fairclough, Graham. 'New Heritage Frontiers.' In *Heritage and Beyond, Council of Europe*, 29-41. Strasbourgh: Council of Europe, 2009.
Gerlagh, Bert et al. *Kijk Amsterdam 1700-1800. De mooiste stadsgezichten*. Amsterdam: Thoth, 2017.
Gerlagh, Bert. 'Veranderingen en continuïteit in de topografie.' In *Kijk Amsterdam 1700-1800. De mooiste stadsgezichten*, edited by Bert Gerlagh et al., 52-65. Amsterdam: Thoth, 2017.
Glendinning, Miles. *The Conservation movement: A history of architectural preservation. Antiquity to Modernity*. London and New York: Routledge, 2013.
Goethe, Johann Wolfgang von. *Goethes Werke. Herausgegeben im Auftrag der Grossherzogin Sophie von Sachsen*, Weimar: Herman Böhlau, 1887-1919.
Goudeau, Jeroen. *Nicolaus Goldmann (1611-1665) en de wiskundige architectuurwetenschap*. Groningen: Philip Elchers, 2005.
Grijzenhout, Frans. *Feesten voor het vaderland. Patriotse en Bataafse feesten 1780-1806*. Zwolle: Waanders, 1989.
Grijzenhout, Frans. 'Inleiding.' In *Erfgoed. De geschiedenis van een begrip*, edited by Frans Grijzenhout, 1-20. Amsterdam: Amsterdam University Press, 2007.
Halbertsma, Marlite, and Marieke Kuiper. *Het erfgoeduniversum. Een inleiding in de theorie en praktijk van cultureel erfgoed*. Bussum: Coutinho, 2014.
Haitsma Mulier, Eco O.G. 'Between Humanism and Enlightenment: The Dutch writing of history', In *The Dutch Republic in the Eigtheenth Century: Decline, Enlightenment, and Revolution*, edited by Margaret C. Jacob and Wijnand W. Mijnhardt. 170-87. Ithaca/London: Cornell University Press, 1992.
Harvey, David C. 'Heritage pasts and heritage presents: Temporality, meaning and the scope of heritage studies', *International Journal of Heritage Studies* 7, no. 4 (2001): 319-38.
Harvey, David C. 'The history of heritage.' In *The Ashgate Research companion to heritage and identity*, edited by Brian Graham and Peter Howard, 19-36. Aldershot: Ashgate, 2008.
Herrmann, Wolfgang. *Laugier and Eighteenth-century French Theory*. London: Zwemmer, 1962.
Hermans, Lex. *'Alles wat zuilen heeft is klassiek.' Classicistische ideeën over bouwkunst in Nederland 1765-1850*. Rotterdam: NAi, 2005.
Hermans, Lex. 'Perpetual presenses. Some remark on the agency of buildings and images in Renaissance Italy.' In *The Secret Lives of Artworks: Exploring the Boundaries Between Art and Life*, edited by C. van Eck, J. van Gastel and E. van Kessel, 56-74. Leiden: Leiden University Press, 2014.
Huizinga, Johan. *Cultuurhistorische verkenningen*. Haarlem: H.D. Tjeenk Willink & Zoon, 1929.
Huizinga, Johan. *Verzamelde werken. VII: Geschiedwetenschap, Hedendaagsche cultuur*. Haarlem: Tjeenk Willink, 1950.

Kaufmann, Emil. *Three Revolutionary architects: Boullée, Ledoux and Lequeu*. Philadelphia: Transactions of the American Philosophical Society; new series; vol. 42, 1952.

Knolle, Paul. 'Cornelis Ploos van Amstel, pleitbezorger van een "Hollandse" inconografie', *Oud Holland* 98 (1984): 43–53.

Koolhaas, Eveline, and Sandra de Vries, 'Terug naar een roemrijk verleden. De zeventiende-eeuwse schilderkunst als voorbeeld voor de negentiende eeuw.' In *De Gouden Eeuw in perspectief. het beeld van de Nederlandse zeventiende-eeuws schilderkunst in later tijd*, edited by Frans Grijzenhout and Henk van Veen, 107–38. Nijmegen: Sun, 1992.

Korst, Jan K. van der. *Het rusteloze bestaan van dokter Petrus Camper (1722–1789)*. Houten: Bohn Stafleu van Loghum, 2008.

Krabbe, Coert Peter. *Ambacht, kunst, wetenschap. De bevordering der bouwkunst in Nederland (1775–1880)*. Zeist/Zwolle: Waanders, 1998.

Krabbe, Coert Peter. 'Monumenten: architectonische overblijfselen.' In *Erfgoed. De geschiedenis van een begrip*, edited by Frans Grijzenhout, 151–74. Amsterdam: Amsterdam University Press, 2007.

Kuettner, Carl Gottlieb. *Beyträge zur Kenntnis vorzüglich des gegenwärtigen Zustandes von Frankreich und Holland, met untermischten Vergleichungen verschiedener Orte und Gegenstände unter einander. Aus den Briefen eines in England wohnenden Deutschen auf seinen Reisen durch Frankreich und Holland in den Jahren 1787, 1790 und 1791*. Leipzig: Johann Gottfried Dijk, 1792.

Langereis, Sandra. 'Antiquitates: voorvaderlijke oudheden.' In *Erfgoed. De geschiedenis van een begrip*, edited by Frans Grijzenhout, 57–83. Amsterdam: Amsterdam University Press, 2007.

Laurentius, Th., J.W. Niemeijer and G. Ploos van Amstel. *Cornelis Ploos van Amstel, 1726–1798, Kunstverzamelaar en prentuitgever*. Assen: Van Gorcum, 1980.

Meijer, Miriam Claude. *Race and aesthetics in the anthropology of Petrus Camper (1722–1789)*. Amsterdam: Rodopi, 1999.

Metken, Günter, and Klaus Galwitz (eds). *Revolutionsarchitektur. Boullée, Ledoux, Lequeu*. Baden-Baden: Staatliche Kunsthalle, 1970.

Montague, William. *The delights of Holland [or A Three Months Travel about that and the other Provinces]*. London: John Sturton and A. Bosvile, 1696.

Moss, Alan. 'Comparing Ruins. National Trauma in Dutch Travel Accounts of the Seventeenth Century.' In *The Roots of Nationalism: National Identity Formation in Early Modern Europe, 1600–1815*, edited by Lotte Jensen, 217–33. Amsterdam: Amsterdam University Press, 2016.

Mouilleseaux, Jean-Pierre, and Annie Jacques (eds). *Les architectes de la Liberté 1789–1799*. Paris: Ecole Nationale Supérieure des Beaux-Arts, 1989.

Peeters, Jan. 'Het hart van Amsterdam als inspiratiebron.' In *Het Paleis in de schilderkunst van de Gouden Eeuw*, edited by Jan Peeters et al., 6–17. Amsterdam/Zwolle: Waanders, 1997.

Pinto, John A. *Speaking Ruins: Piranesi, Architects and Antiquity in Eighteenth-Century Rome*. Ann Arbor: University of Michigan Press, 2012.

Ploos van Amstel, Cornelis. *De bouworde van 't stadhuis van Amsterdam, en de smaak der Nederlanderen, ten opzigte der konsten en weetenschappen, verdedigd, tegen de ongegronde berispingen van den heer C., in zynen brief aan Den philosooph*. Amsterdam: Yntema en Tieboel, 1767.

Ploos van Amstel, Cornelis. *Redenvoeringen gedaan in de Teken-Academie te Amsterdam*. Amsterdam: J. Yntema, 1785.

Ploos van Amstel, G. van. *Portret van een koopman en uitvinder: Cornelis Ploos van Amstel. Maatschappelijk, cultureel en familieleven van een achttiende eeuwer*. Assen: Van Gorcum, 1980.

Ploos van Amstel, Jacob. *Het uitmuntend karakter en de zonderlinge lotgevallen van Hugo de Groot herdagt bij de beschouwing van het slot Loevestein in de maand Julij 1772*. Amsterdam: s.l., s.a. [1772].

Sas, Niek van. 'Gedenck aan Loevesteyn.' In *Waar de blanke top der duinen en andere vaderlandse herinneringen*, edited by N.C.F. van Sas, 70–80. Amsterdam: Contact, 1990.

Sas, N.C.F. van. *De metamorfose van Nederland. Van oude orde naar moderniteit 1750–1900*. Amsterdam: Amsterdam Univerity Press, 2004.

Schädlich, Christian. 'Leonhard Christoph Sturm (1669–1719).' In *Grosse Baumeister*, edited by Adalbert Behr, 91–139. Berlin: Henschel, 1990.

Schmidt, Freek. '"Het eenige en zeldzame Wonderstuk van de geheele wereld". Een architectonische fantasie voor een illustere vaderlander.' In *Een tempel voor Hugo de Groot. Een rede van Jacob Ploos van Amstel uit 1774*, edited by Jan Bloemendal and H.K. Ploos van Amstel, 63–75. Amersfoort: Florivallis, 2010.

Schmidt, Freek. 'Amsterdam's Architectural Image from Early-Modern Print Series to Global Heritage Discourse.' In *Imagining Global Amsterdam: History, Culture, and Geography in a World City*, edited by Marco de Waard, 219–38. Amsterdam: Amsterdam University Press, 2012.

Schmidt, Freek. 'Beschavende bouwkunst voor Burgers. Jacob Otten Husly's redevoeringen over de architectuur van de Oudheid.' In *De Oudheid in de achttiende eeuw/Classical Antiquity in the Eighteenth Century*, edited by A.J.P. Raat, W.R.E. Velema and C. Baar-de Werd, 179–99. Utrecht: Werkgroep 18e Eeuw, 2012.

Schmidt, Freek. 'A passion for architecture. Petrus Camper and the Groningen town hall.' In *Petrus Camper in context. Science, the arts and society in the eighteenth century Dutch Republic*, edited by Klaas van Berkel and Bart Ramakers, 275–307. Hilversum: Verloren 2015.

Schmidt, Freek. *Passion and Control: Dutch Architectural Culture of the Eighteenth Century*. Aldershot: Ashgate, 2016.

Sluis, Jacob van, and Sybren Sybrandy. 'Petrus Camper over schoonheid, of: het leerzame van de analogie.' In *Onderwijs en onderzoek: studie en wetenschap aan de academie van Groningen in de 17e en 18e eeuw*, edited by A.H. Huussen, 207–30. Hilversum: Verloren, 2003.

Smith, Laurajane. *Uses of Heritage*. London: Routledge, 2006.

Strien-Chardonneau, Madeleine van. "Le voyage de Hollande": récits de voyageurs français dans les Provinces-Unies, 1748–1795. Oxford: The Voltaire Foundation, 1994.

Sturm, Leonhard Christoph. *Leonhard Christoph Sturms durch Einen grossen Theil von Teutschland und den Niederlanden bis nach Paris gemachete Architectonische Reise-Anmerckungen zu der vollständigen Goldmannischen Bau-Kunst VIten Theil als ein Anhang gethan, Damit So viel in des Auctoris Vermögen stehet, nichts an der Vollständigkeit des Wercks ermangle*. Augsburg: Jeremias Wolff, 1719.

Sturm, Leonhard Christof. *Nicolai Goldmanns vollständige Anweisung zu der Civil-Bau-Kunst*. Wolffenbüttel; Leipzig: Sturm, 1699.

Tafuri, Manfredo. *Theories and History of Architecture*. New York: Harper & Row, 1980.

Tunbridge, J.E., and G.J. Ashworth. *Dissonant Heritage: The Management of the Past as a Resource in Conflict*. Chichester: Wiley, 1996.

Vlaardingerbroek, Pieter. *Het paleis van de Republiek. Geschiedenis van het stadhuis van Amsterdam*. Zwolle: Waanders, 2011.

Wagenaar, Jan. *Zeven lessen over het verhandelen der Heilige Schriftuur in Godsdienstige Vergaderingen*. Amsterdam: Jacob ter Beek, 1752.

Wagenaar, Jan. *Amsterdam, in zyne opkomst, aanwas, geschiedenissen, voorregten, koophandel, gebouwen, kerkenstaat, schoolen, schutterye, gilden en regeeringe, beschreeven*. 3 vols. Amsterdam: Yntema en Tieboel/Isaak Tirion, 1760–5.

Wessels, L.H.M. *Bron, waarheid en de verandering der tijden. Jan Wagenaar (1709–1773), een historiografische studie*. Den Haag: Stichting Hollandse Historische Reeks, 1997.

Wiebenson, Dora. *Sources of Greek Revival architecture*. London: Zwemmer, 1969.

Wittman, Richard. *Architecture, Print Culture, and the Public Sphere in Eighteenth-century France*. New York and London: Routledge, 2007.

Woud, Auke van der. *De Bataafse hut. Denken over het oudste Nederland (1750–1850)*. Amsterdam /Antwerpen: Contact, 1998.

Wouthuysen, Ester, and Erik Ariëns Kappers. 'De Atlas Fouquet opnieuw bekeken. Pierre Fouquet jr. (1729–1800), prentuitgever en kunsthandelaar.' In *Kijk Amsterdam 1700–1800. De mooiste stadsgezichten*, edited by Bert Gerlagh et al., 34–45. Amsterdam: Thoth, 2017.

Index

Page numbers for illustrations are given in *italics*.

Acropolis, 148, 150, 152
acroteria, 38
Aelst, Pieter Coecke van, 146
Aemilius Paullus, 68
Afbeelding van 't Stadt Huijs van Amsterdam (Campen/ Danckerts), *35*, *39*, *46*, *65*, *69*
affect, 158, 159–60, 212–13
   historical sensation, 213
   wonder, 14–17, 85–6, 87, 90, 102–4, 123–4
agency, of buildings, 65, 212
Albrecht, Count of Holland, 33
Alkmaar organ, 34
allegory, 6–7, 84, 101, 118, 211
   classical, 8, 10, 65, 67
   See also personification
amazement. *See* wonder
Amersfoort, 101
Amphion (builder of Thebes), 96, 183–4, *183*, 190 n.36
Ampzing, Samuel, *119*
Amstel, Cornelis Ploos van, 211–14
   Atlas van Amsterdam, 211
Amstel, Jacob van, 213–14
Amsterdam
   celebration of, 123
   as centre of creation, 46–7, 68
   City Maiden, 6, 10, *10*, 38, 51, 184
   classical models for, 8
   coat of arms, 173, *175*, *180*
   freedom of, 51
   global position of, 6–7
   growth of, 2, 29, 175
   identity of, 118
   laudatory poems to, 106–8
   official history of, 201–2, 203–4
   origins of, 29
   population, 2, 29, 118
   representations of, 117–18
   Rome, equated with, 11, 85
   symbols of, 72
   visitors to, 195
   wealth of, 10, 174
   William II's attack on, 107
Amsterdam Exchange bank, 38
Amsterdam Museum (Amsterdam Historical Museum), 187, 188 n.11
Amsterdam Town Hall
   Aldermans' Hall (Schepenzaal), 162
   as body politic, 129
   building materials, 49–50, 99–100
   building plots, 31–2, *31*
   Burgomasters' room, 49, 66, *66*, 69, 130, *131*
   Chamber of Justice, 145
   City Council chamber, 49, 190 n.36
   classical style in, 7
   commission for, 4
   construction, 47–50, 99–100, 177–8, 181–2
   cost of, 5–6, 48, 89, 93
   decoration, 4, 6–7, 206
   designs for, 32, *32*, 36–47, *39*, *44*, 55 n.31, *199*
   divine grace, manifestation of, 124–7
   emulation, subject of, 98–9
   entrance, 195, 199, 206
   European context of, 50–2, 107–8, 131–5
   façades, 38, 66
   first floor, 38–40, *39* (*See also* Citizens' Hall (Burgerzaal))
   functions of, 36–7
   ground floor, 38, *39* (*See also* Tribunal (Vierschaar))

immortality of, 129–31
interior design of, 46–7, 49–50
Krijgsraadzaal, 47
legitimization of, 17, 175
medieval, 30–1, *30*, 130–1, *130*, 175, 176
  destroyed by fire, 1, 47, 128, *128*
models for, 17, 45, 63
monumentality of, 120–1
peace, expression of, 29, 68, 184
planning of, 176–8
proposed redesigns of, 199–200, *200*
reactions to, 19–20, 195–216
  architectural criticism, 198–201, 206–12, 216
  and commemoration, 212–14
  historical accounts, 203–4
  sacer horror, 16–17
  travelogues, 205–6
  and visual culture, 202–4
roof, 47–8
as royal palace, 1, 52, 185
tower, 38, 45–6, 47
tympana, 6, 38, 51
uniqueness, 62
visual representations, 117–31
  by Beerstraaten, 128–9, *128*
  by Berckheyde, 11–12, *12*, *37*, 120–4, *120*, 125, 126, 132
  by Fokke, *202*, *204*
  imbrication with, 122
  by Keun, *203*
  by Marot, *196*
  medieval Town Hall, *30*, 128–31, *128*, *130*
  by Mommers, *14*
  by Saenredam, 118, *119*, 130–1, *130*
  by Ulft, 125–6, *126*, 127
  by Vinkeles, *205*, *206*
wonder, object of, 16–17
See also caryatids; ceremonies; Citizens' Hall (Burgerzaal); Tribunal (Vierschaar)
Angemessenheit (propriety), 199
animation, 120, 122–3
Ankersmit, Frank, 213
Anslo, Reyer, 33–4, 188 n.16
  Olyfkrans der Vrede, 177–8, 184, 188 n.14

anthropomorphism, 158
  See also personification
anti-strophe, 90, 91, 92–3
Apelles, 101
Apollodorus of Damascus, 97
appropriation, 64, 69, 72
aprons, ceremonial, 179, *179*, 181, 185, 186
arches, triumphal, 18, 63, 67–9, 158
  in Citizens' Hall (Burgerzaal), *67*
  representations of, *69*, *133*, *154*
architecture
  all'antica, 61–4, 86
  Catholic styles of, 5, 45, 61
  classical, 7, 17–18, 61–4, 86, 212
  criticism of, 198–201, 206–7, 215–16
  description of, 85–7
  fictional, 85–6
  and geometry, 35–6
  Gothic, 61–2
  historiography of, 146–7, 215–16
  Italianate, 33, 212
  other art forms, relation with, 123
  Palladian, 33
  as profession, 184–5, 216
  public, 42, 43
  religious symbols in, 45–6, *45*
  Roman, 11, 17–18
  rules of, 41, 207, 211
  Solomonic, 41, 50–2, 86
  in visual art, 12–14, 18–19, 202–3, 211 (*See also* portraits, of buildings)
  See also buildings; orders
Aristotle, 9–10
Asselijn, Thomas, 85
Athens, 90, 148, 150, 152
awe. *See* wonder

Backer, Cornelis, 176
Backer, Willem Cornelis, 125–6, 176, 177, 178
Bakker, Frans de, 204
Bank of Amsterdam, 50
Barbaro, Daniele, 146, 149–50
Barlaeus, Caspar, 30–1
  Blyde Inkomst der allerdoorluchtighste Koninginne Maria de Medicis, *30*
  Medicea Hospes, 30

Mercator Sapiens, 65
basilicas, 43, 63
basin and ewer, ceremonial, 182, 186, 187
Batavian people, 47
   Dutch identification with, 40, 65, 214
beauty, 151, 153, 210
Beckford, William, 195
Beerstraaten, Jan, *Ruins of the old Town Hall*, 128–9, *128*
Berckheyde, Gerrit, 11, 18–19, 118–21
   The Amsterdam Town Hall, *37*
   The Town Hall on Dam Square (1665–80), 11–12, *12*
   The Town Hall on Dam Square (1668), 120–4, *120*, 125, 126, 132
Bernigeroth, Martin, *198*
Beurs (Stock Exchange), 2, 176
biblical references, 41, 46–7
   See also Solomon
Bicker, Gerrit Pietersz, 178
Biondo, Flavio, 68
Blaeu, Willem, 105
bodies
   buildings, ascribed to, 122, 129–31
   natural/politic, 129
Bogerts, C., *Interior of the central hall*, *203*
Bol, Ferdinand, 4, 47
Bonaparte, Louis Napoléon (Louis I, King of Holland), 1, 52
Bouwkundige Bijdragen (Architectural Contributions, journal), 185, 216
Bray, Salomon de, 41
Brosterhui(j)sen, Johan, 41–2, 146
Brutus, Lucius Junius, 47, 148, 156–7, *157*, 161, 162–4
Büchler, Daniel David, 185
buildings
   agency of, 65, 212
   bodies, ascribed to, 122, 129–31
   characteristics of, 118, 121
   commemoration through, 212–14
   description of, 86, 87
   divine grace, manifested in, 87, 124–7
   identity of, 7, 212
   models for, 17
   performativity of, 117
   portraits of, 118–35
      animating power of, 122–3
   divine grace, manifestations of, 124–7
   European context of, 131–5
   laudatory poems to, 121–4, 128–9
   public, 42, 43, 65, 118, *119*, 178, 181
   See also architecture
Burckhardt, Jacob, 69
Burgerzaal. *See* Citizens' Hall (Burgerzaal)
Burgomasters, 1–4, 31, 36
   and body politic, 129
   commemorative ceremonies, celebrated in, 185
   and death sentences, 145
   in laudatory poems, 85, 89, 90–6, 108
   offices of, 49, 66, *66*, 69
   patronage of, 8–9
   power, display of, 6
   as religious leaders, 47
   representations of, 10–11, *10*
Burgomasters (individual)
   Backer, Willem Cornelis, 125–6, 176, 177, 178
   Graeff, Cornelis de, 47, 178, 184, 185, 188 n.11
   Maarsseveen, Johan Huydecoper van, 96, 103, 108, 184
   Pancras, Gerbrand Claesz., 178
   Poll, Jan van de, 184
   Schaep, Gerard Simonsz., 178
   Spiegel, Hendrik Dirkszn., 184
   Valckenier, Wouter, 178
Bussels, Stijn, 61

Calderón de la Barca, Pedro, 87
Calvinism, 5–6, 15–16
Campen, Jacob van, 4, 5, 11, 32–40, *35*, 175
   Afbeelding van 't Stadt Huijs van Amsterdam, *35*, *39*, 46, 65, 69
   Amsterdam Town Hall, designs for, 38–47, *39*, 166 n.16
   arches and festoons, use of, 18
   architectural influences on, 41–2
   capitals, transformation of, 71–2
   commemorative ceremonies, celebrated in, 185
   Coymans' houses, Keizersgracht, 33
   festoons, use of, 71–2, *72*
   at foundation ceremony, 178
   Girls' Courtyard, Civic Orphanage, 33

Huis ten Bosch, 4, 33, *34*
Huygens' house, 33
  in laudatory poems, 96–7, 100–2
Mauritshuis, 33–4
New Church (Nieuwe Kerk), proposed tower for, 61–2, 125–6, *126*, 176–7
Noordeinde Palace, 4, 33
role model, 216
Vitruvius, reading of, 146, 149
Campen, Nicolaas van, 4
Camper, Petrus, 207–10, *208*, 211, 215, 216, 219 n.30
canals, 175–6
capitals, 71–2, 146, 205
Capitoline Hill, Rome, 11, 17, 32, 65, 69, 132, *133*
Carrara marble, 49
caryatids, 143–69
  burdens, as bearers of, 146, 149, *154*, 155
  criticism of, 209
  in early modern Europe, 148–56
  emotional effect of, 159–60
  feminine, 153–5, *153*
  Forum of Augustus, *150*
  French use of, 152–6, *153*
  lifelike, 158, 164
  by Quellinus, in Tribunal (Vierschaar), 19, 143–51, *144*, 156–65, 209
  by Raimondi, *149*
  sculptural context of, 162–5
  symbolism of, 153–6
  types of, 148–56, *152*, 165, 166 n.18
  Vitruvian, 146–50, *151*, 161–2, 164–5
  as warning, 147–8, 155–6, 160–2
Castracane, Condottiere Castruccio, 68
Catholicism, 15–16, 184
ceremonial objects, 19, 173, 179–80, 182–4
  aprons, 179, *179*, 181, 185, 186
  basin and ewer, 182, 186, 187
  in commemoration ceremonies, 185
  in museum collections, 185–7
  preservation of, 181
  rummer (drinking glass), 176–7, *177*, 182, 188 n.11
  spoons, 182, *183*
  See also medals; trowels, ceremonial
ceremonies, 7, 47, 173–85

banquets, 176, 182
children's role in, 178–9, 188 n.17, 189 n.19
commemoration of, 184–5
commemorative, 216
foundation, 173–81, 189 n.19, 216
  Amsterdam Town Hall, 7–8, 19, 47, 90–3, 173, 177–81, *180*
  Louvre Palace, Paris, 181
  Lyon Town Hall, 178, 181
  New Church (Nieuwe Kerk), 176–7
inauguration, 7–8, *8*, 19, 47, 87–8, 93–100, 175–84
Cesariano, Cesare, 149, 151
  Di Lucio Vitruvio Pollione de architectura libri dece, 151
Chambray, Fréart de, 155–6
Charles I, King of England, 50
Charles II, King of England, 50
Charles V, Holy Roman Emperor, 68
Chaucer, Geoffrey, 85
chiaroscuro, 120–1
chimneypieces, 49–50, 66, *66*
Choul, Guillaume du, 73, 74
Christian IV, King of Denmark, 50
Chrysoloras, Manuel, 86
churches, 12–13, *13*, 34, 50, 176, 176–8
  descriptio templi (description of), 87
  See also New Church (Nieuwe Kerk)
cities
  planning of, 135
  praise of, 86, 87
  See also cityscapes
Citizens/Civic Orphanage, 33, 175, 187
Citizens' Hall (Burgerzaal), 2, *3*, 4, 6, 38–40, *105*, 209
  decoration, 44, 46, *203*, 206, *206*
  in laudatory poems, 104–6
  maps in, 16, 38, 46, *67*, 104–6, *105*
  positioning of, 43
  triumphal motifs in, 67, *67*
City Council, 36, 178, 184
  Chamber of, 49, 190 n.36
City Maiden, 6, 10, *10*, 38, 51, 184
cityscapes, 132–3, 136 n.6, 202–3, 211
City Theatre, 177
civic pride, 2, 37, 203–4
'civitas', 38

classical culture, 15, 46–7, 97–8
  allegory, 8, 10, 65, 67
  architectural, 7, 17–18, 61–4, 86, 212
  gods, 46, 65, 101–2, 161, 183–4, *183*
  and laudatory poems, 85–7, 90
  orders, 49, 50
  transfer, 63, 69, 71–4
coats of arms, 173, *175*, *180*, 181, 182, 184
colour, 12, 49, 126
columns, 78 n.31, 146, 207
  vs. caryatids, 147
  Composite, 61, 120, *120*
  pilasters, 44, *44*, 67, 205, 207
commemoration
  ceremonies, 184–5
  of past glory, 212
  through buildings, 212–14
  through objects, 180
commerce. *See* trade
Commissioner of Bankruptcy, 37
Commissioners of Insurance, 37
Commissioners of Petty Affairs, 37, 50
contrast, visual, 13, 120, 132, 158
Coppenol, Lieven, *103*, 191 n.42
courtyards, 38, 50
cupolas, 45–6, *45*

Dam Square, 2, 31–2
  by Berckheyde, 11–12, *12*, 120–4, *120*, 125, 126, 132
  by Fokke, *202*, *204*
  by Marot, *196*
  by Mommers, *14*, 127, *127*
  by Ovens, 10–11, *10*
  by Ulft, 125–6, *126*, 127
  by Vinkeles, *205*
Danckerts, Dancker, 46, 65, *199*
  Afbeelding van 't Stadt Huijs van Amsterdam, 35, *39*, 46, 65, 69
Danckerts de Rij, Cornelis, 31, 32, *39*
Dancx, François, *72*
Dapper, Olfert, 144–5
Darnell, Lorne, 61
decoration, 4, 6–7, 44, 46, *203*, 206, *206*
Dentatus, Manius Curius, 47
De Philosooph (The Philosopher, journal), 206, 211
description (*ekphrasis*), 18, 86, 87

designs, 32, *32*, 36–47, *39*, *44*, 55 n.31, *199*
  interior, 46–7, 49–50
  revisions, 199–200, *200*
divinity, 15–17, 87, 101–2, 124–9
Doetechum, Johannes or Lucas van, *119*
Doge's Palace, Venice, 66
doorways, 67, *67*, 195, 199, 206
Drawing Academy (Stadstekenacademie), 210, 213
drawings, 7, 10–11, 125–6, 197
  topographical, 202–3, 211
Dronckelaar, Cornelis van, 182, 184
Duchy of Burgundy, 64
Dunk, Thomas von der, 125
Duquesnoy, François, 4
Dutch East India Company, 176
Dutch Golden Age, 20, 65, 84, 212, 213
Dutch Republic, 184
  body politic in, 129
  classical tradition, part of, 65
  establishment of, 17–18, 29, 64, 64–5
  as successor state, 63, 74
Dutch Revolt, 64, 88

Edinburgh, Palace of Holyroodhouse, 50–1, *51*
Eggerts, Willem, 33
ekphrasis (description), 18, 86, 87
Eliade, Mircea, 174
emotion, 158, 159–60, 212–13
  historical sensation, 213
  wonder, 14–17, 85–6, 87, 90, 102–4, 123–4
entablature, 49, 145, 146, 149, 150, 158, 207
entrances, 67, *67*, 195, 199, 206
epistrophe, 90, 91–2, 93
Erechtheion, Acropolis, 148, 150, 152
Erynnis, 101–2
Escorial, Spain, 45, 50
etchings, 118, *119*
Europe, representations of, 45–6, *45*
Eusebius, 87

Fabius Maximus Cunctator, 66, *66*, 69
façades, 38, 43–4, 66
feeling, 158, 159–60, 212–13
  historical sensation, 213
  wonder, 14–17, 85–6, 87, 90, 102–4, 123–4

femininity, 153–5
festoons, 18, 49, 63, 71–4, 205
   representations of, *69*, *72*, 120, *120*
Flinck, Govert, 47
Fokke, Simon
   Dam Square with the Town Hall, *204*
   View of Amsterdam Town Hall, *202*
Fokkens, Melchior, 145, 159
Forum of Augustus, Rome, 148, *150*
foundation. *See* ceremonies
Fouquet, Pierre, 202–3, 210, 211, 218 n.17
France, 13–14, 33, 50, 132–5, 178, 181, 189 n.25
   See also Louvre Palace, Paris
Frederick Henry, Prince of Orange, 4, 33, *135*, 139 n.39
Fremantle, Katharine, 5, 62, 67, 117
Furies, 101–2

Galle, Philips, *The Temple of Diana at Ephesus*, *15*
Galle, Theodoor, *119*
garlands, 18, 49, 63, 71–4, 205
   representations of, *69*, *72*, 120, *120*
gaze/gazing, 37, 121, 160–5, 182
   viewpoint, 118, *119*, 121, 132
geometry, 35–6
Germany, 87
Gevaerts (Gevartius), Gaspar, 67, 158
Giocondo, Giovanni, 148
glass, drinking (ceremonial), 176–7, *177*, 182, 188 n.11
God
   grace of, 124–7
   providence of, 128–9
gods, 15–17
   classical, 46, 65, 101–2
      Jupiter, 101–2, 161
      Mercury, 183–4, *183*
   sacrificial rites, 72–3
Golden Age, 20, 65, 84, 212, 213
Goldmann, Nicolaus, 198
Goujon, Jean, 148, 151, 152–3, *153*, 154–5
grace
   divine, 87, 124–7
   feminine, 153–5
Graeff, Cornelis de, 47, 178, 184, 185, 188 n.11
Graeff, Jacob de, 173, 178, 180–1, 185

Graeff van Polsbroek, Gerrit de, 185, 186
Great Britain, 6, 33, 50–1, *51*, 64, 87, 107
Greece, 90, 148, 150, 152
Greill, Tomas, 87
Groningen, 207, 210
Groot, Hugo de, 213, 215
Grotius, Hugo, 17
Guicciardini, Lodovico, 86

Haarlem
   Grand Square, 118, *119*
   Guild of St Luke, 35
   Het Hofje van Staets, 181
   New Church, 34
   Orphanage, 179
   Town Hall, 118, *119*
Hague, The, 4, 33–4, 70
   Huis ten Bosch, 4, 33, *34*
   Mauritshuis, 33–4
   Plein, 135, 184
Heemskerck, Maarten van, 14, 101, 129, 161
   The Temple of Diana at Ephesus, *15*
Heiligewegpoort, 175
Henri IV, King of France, 135
heritage, 186–7, 214, 216, 223 n.62, 223 n.64
Herodotus, 86
Heyden, Jan van der, 132
hierarchies, 49–50
historical sensation, 213
historicization, 212
historiography, 201–2, 213–14
   architectural, 146–7, 215–16
Holbein, Hans, 101
Homer, 85, 122
Hooft, Pieter Corneliszoon, 64
Houbraken, Jacob, *201*
Huet, Conrad Busken, 216
Huis ten Bosch, 4
   Oranjezaal, 33, *34*
Huizinga, Johan, 213
Husly, Jacob Otten, 210, 213, 222 n.56
Huydecoper van Maarsseveen, Johan, 96, 103, 108, 184
Huygens, Constantijn, 4, 8–9, 17, 87, 146
   Campen, house built by, 33
   on classical style, 61

Congratulations to the Noble Lords (Geluk an de ee.heeren), 102–4, *103*, 124, 127, 191 n.42
   engraving of, 9, 66, *125*, 130
   On the Globe (Op de aerdtcloot), 16, 104–6
   On the heavenly vault (Op den hemelcloot), 104–6
Hofwijck, 18
Villalpando, reading of, 41

identity
   of Amsterdam, 118
   of buildings, 7, 212
   civic, 2
   classicizing, 62
   Dutch, 211–13, 214–15
inauguration. *See* ceremonies
incorruptibility, 47
intertexuality, 84–5, 197
Israelites, Dutch identification with, 40–1, 64–5, 73, 90
Italy, 65–6
   See also Rome

Jacobsz, Caspar Philipsz., 202
James I, King of England, 50, 64
James V, King of Scotland, 50–1
Jerusalem, 41–3, *42*, 50
   Dome of the Rock, 45
   Temple of, 7, 41–2, 45, 90
   See also Temple of Solomon
Jews, Dutch identification with, 40–1, 64–5, 73, 90
Jones, Inigo, 64
Jonson, Ben, 50, 87
Jordaens, Jacob, 4, 33, 47
   Peace of the Batavians and Rome, 67
Josephus, Titus Flavius (Yosef ben Matityahu), *Jewish War*, 73
Julius II, Pope, 68
justice, 90, 157
   death sentences, 144–5, 158–9, 160–1, 162–3
   historical exempla of, 46–7
   legal processes, 2–4, 36–7
   public display of, 37, 160–2
Justitia, 38, 164

Kantorowicz, Ernst, 129
Keizersgracht, 33
Keun, Hendrik, 202
   Interior of the central hall, 203
Keyser, Hendrick de, 48, 176, 216
Keyser, Willem de, 48
Kloveniersdoelen, 30
Koninklijk Oudheidkundig Genootschap (Royal Antiquarian Society), 181, 186, 191 n.48, 191 n.49
Kuettner, Carl Gottlieb, 196

Laet, Johannes de, 146
La Fontaine, Jean de, 87
Lamberts, Gerrit, 182, *183*, 190 n.34
Laugier, Marc-Antoine, 205–7, 215
   Essai sur l'architecture, 206–7
   Observations sur l'architecture, 206–7
Le Clerc, Sébastien, 155
legal processes, 2–4, 36–7
   death sentences, 144–5, 158–9, 160–1, 162–3
legitimization
   of Amsterdam Town Hall, 17, 175
   of the Dutch Republic, 64–5
Lemercier, Jacques, 155
Le Pautre, Antoine, 155
Lescot, Pierre, 152
liberality, 9
Lievens, Jan, 4, 47
life
   everyday, 86, 120–1, 203
   works of art, created by, 122–3
light/lighting, 13, 120–1, 127, 132–5, 200, 206
Ligorio, Pirro, 151
limestone, 49
liveliness, 120, 122–3
Livy (Titus Livius), 68
Loevestein castle, 213, 214–15, 222 n.54
London, Whitehall Palace, 33, 50, 107
Lorenzetti, Ambrogio, *The Allegory of Good and Bad Government*, 118
Louis I, King of Holland (Bonaparte, Louis Napoléon), 1, 52, 196
Louis XIII, King of France, 135, 189 n.25
Louis XIV, King of France, 50, 135, 178, 181
Louvre Palace, Paris, *13*, 107

caryatids, 151, 152–3, *153*
foundation ceremony, 181
Grand Galerie, *134*, 135, *135*
Pavillon de l'Horloge, 155
Salle des Cent-Suisses, 152–3, 155
Solomonic architecture in, 50
Lutma, Abraham, *Portrait of Jacob van Campen*, *35*, 36
Lutma, Johannes, 173, 180–1
    basin and ewer, ceremonial, 182, 186, *187*
    medals, *175*, *180*
    trowel, ceremonial, 173, *174*, 180, *180*, 186, 187
Lyon Town Hall, 178, 181

Maarsseveen, Johan Huydecoper van, 96, 103, 108, 184
Maatschappij tot Bevordering der Bouwkunst (Society for the Advancement of Architecture), 184–5, 186, 190 n.40, 216
Machiavelli, Niccolò, *Discorsi*, 66
Magistrates, 2–4, 36–7, 40, 49, 145, 163–4
    at inauguration ceremony, 182, *183*, 183
magnificence, 9–14, 15
Mantegna, Andrea
    Saint Sebastian, 68
    Triumphs of Caesar, 69–70, *70*
maps, in Citizens' Hall (Burgerzaal), 2, 16, 38, 46, *67*, 104–6, *105*
marble, 49–50, 163–4
Marot, Clément, 85
Marot, Daniel, *196*
Martin, Jean, 148, 152
Marvell, Andrew, 87
Mary, Princess Royal and Princess of Orange, 33
Mauritshuis, 33–4
medals
    exhibition of, 185, 186
    foundation, *175*, 179–80, *180*, 185, 186, 188 n.11, 189 n.23
    inauguration, 7–8, *8*, 182–4, *183*
    by Lutma, Johannes, *175*, *180*
    by Pool, Jurriaan (I), 7–8, *8*, 182–4, *183*
Medici, Cosimo III de', 132
Medici, Lorenzo de', 68
Medici, Maria de', Joyous Entry of, 29–30, 67, 175–6, 185

Medusa, 101–2, *101*
memoria, 213–14
memory, 173, 177, 213–14
    See also commemoration
metaphor, 36, 123
    See also personification
Meyster, Everard, 7, 78 n.35
    Heavenly Pastoral Play (Hemelsch Land-Spel), 84–5, 100–2, 161–2
Michelangelo, 11, 32, 84–5, 101–2
Milizia, Francesco, 35
Milton, John, 87
mirrors, 162–5
modesty, 5–6
Mommers, Hendrick, 13–14
    Market Scene before the Dam, *14*, 127, *127*
    View of the Louvre from the Pont-Neuf, *13*
Montague, William, 195, 200, *208*
monumentality, 120–1, 128–9, 212–14, 216, 222 n.56
Moses, 47
Mosyn, Michiel, *72*
museums, 185–7, 188 n.11, 190 n.34, 191 n.48, 191 n.49

narratio, 213–14
Nassau-Siegen, John Maurice of, 33
nationalism, 212–13, 214
Netherlands, Kingdom of, 52, 184
    See also Dutch Republic
Neufville, Abbot Camille de, 178, 181
New Church (Nieuwe Kerk), 2, 6, 31, 176
    by Berckheyde, 11, *12*, 120, *120*, 121
    by Fokke, *202*, *204*
    by Mommers, 127, *127*
    tower, proposed, 61–2, 125–6, *126*, 176–7, 188 n.12
    by Ulft, *126*
    by Vinkeles, *205*
Nieulandt, Willem van, *The Arch of Septimus Severus*, 132, *133*
Nieuwe Kerk. *See* New Church (Nieuwe Kerk)
Nolpe, Pieter, *32*
Noordeinde Palace, 4, 33
Noski, Elias, *125*

obelisks, 11
Office for Public Works, 48
'Op de marmere Vierschaer van 't
    Stadthuys tot Amsterdam' ('On
    the marble Tribunal of the Town
    Hall of Amsterdam') (poem),
    162–4, 168 n.35
Oranjezaal, Huis ten Bosch, 33, *34*
orders, 5, 38, 42, 207, 210
    classical, 49, 50
    of colour, 49
    Composite, 38, 49, 120, *120*, 205
        associations of, 61–2, 71, 97–8
    Corinthian, 38, 41, 43–4, 49, 71, 97–8,
        205
    Ionic, 49
    and marble, 49–50
Orpheus, 96
Ottenheym, Koen, 62
Ovens, Jürgen (Jurraien), 47
    Entry of the Amsterdam Burgomasters,
        10–11, *10*
Ovid, 85, 86

paintings, 4, 7
    architectural, 12–14, 18–19
    vedute, 132
    and wonder, 123–4
Palace Noordeinde, 4, 33
Palace of Holyroodhouse, Edinburgh,
    50–1, *51*
Palais du Louvre. *See* Louvre Palace,
    Paris
Palais du Luxembourg, Paris, 33
Palladio, Andrea, 41–2, 63, 74, 146
Pancras, Gerbrand, 178
Pancras, Gerbrand Claesz., 178
panegyrics. *See* poems, laudatory
Paris, 13–14, *13*, 33, 132–5
    See also Louvre Palace, Paris
patrimony, 214–15, 223 n.64
patriotism, 204, 212–13, 214, 215, 216
Patriot Revolt, 215
patronage, 8–9, 63
Paul II, Pope, 68
Paulus Silentiarius (Paul the Silentiary),
    87
peace
    allegory of, 10
    Amsterdam Town Hall, as expression
        of, 29, 68, 184
    symbols of, 38, 73
Peace of Münster, 1, 17, 174, 177–8, 187
Peace of Westphalia, 29
pedigree, historical, 64–5, 70, 84
pediments, 55 n.31, 62, 68, 205, 207
penitence, 144–5, 151, 155–6
performativity, of buildings, 117
periodical press, 185, 197, 206, 211, 216
Perrault, Charles, 50, 210
personification, 90, 122, 129–30
    Amsterdam City Maiden, 6, 10, *10*, 38,
        51, 184
    Justitia, 38, 164
    Prudentia, 38, 164
perspective, 13–14, 118, *119*, 121
Perugino, Pietro, *Christ giving the Keys to
    Saint Peter*, 69, *69*, 73
Petrarch (Francesco Petrarca), *Africa*, 68
Philip II, King of Spain, 50
phoenixes, 129–30
pilasters, 44, *44*, 67, 205, 207
Pius IV, Pope, 151
Pliny the Younger, 87
poems, laudatory, 7, 9–10, 16, 18, 33–4,
    83–108, 168 n.35
    anti-strophe, 90, 91, 92–3
    ceremonial, 90–9, 93–100, 188 n.16
    classical origins of, 85–7, 90
    commemorative, 184, 185
    dissemination of, 87
    and divine providence, 129
    epistrophe, 90, 91–2, 93
    form of, 90
    funeral elegies, 108
    laus urbium (praise of a city), 86, 87
    Olyfkrans der Vrede, 177–8, 184,
        188 n.14
    'Op de marmere Vierschaer van 't
        Stadthuys tot Amsterdam' ('On
        the marble Tribunal of the Town
        Hall of Amsterdam'), 162–4,
        168 n.35
    political value of, 87–8
    to portraits of buildings, 121–4
    as propaganda, 86
    strophe, 90–1, 92
    on the Tribunal (Vierschaar), 162–4

See also Huygens, Constantijn; Meyster, Everard; Rotgans, Lucas; Vondel, Joost van den; Vos, Jan; Zoet, Jan
Poll, Jan van de, 184
Pool, Jurriaan (I), 8, 182–4, *183*, 190 n.35
portraits, of buildings, 118–35
  animating power of, 122–3
  divine grace, manifestations of, 124–7
  European context of, 131–5
  laudatory poems to, 121–4
  monumentalizing, 128–9
Post, Pieter, *34*
power, display of, 6, 86
praise. *See* poems, laudatory; reactions, to Amsterdam Town Hall
press, 185, 197, 206, 211, 216
pride, civic, 2, 37, 203–4
Prinsenhof, 182, 185, 190 n.31
print culture, 185, 197, 206, 211, 216
prints, 7, 197
propaganda, 86
propriety (*Angemessenheit*), 199
Prudentia, 38, 164
public buildings, 42, 43, 65, 118, *119*, 178, 181
public space, 37, 38
punishment, 144–6, 147, 148–9, 151, 162–4
  death sentences, 144–5, 158–9, 160–1, 162–3

Quellinus, Artus, 4, 5, 19, 48, 70, 166 n.16
  arches and festoons, use of, 18
  Burgomasters' room, overmantle, 66, 66, 69
  Treasurers' office sculptures, 50
  Tribunal (Vierschaar), 144–5, *163*
    caryatids, 19, 143–51, *144*, 156–65, 209
    The Judgement of Junius Brutus, 156–7, *157*
    Medusa head, *101*
    reliefs, 148, *157*, 159, 161, 162–4, 209
  Vitruvius, influence of, 149–50, 164–5
Quellinus, Erasmus, 70
  Free Copy after Mantegna's Triumphs of Caesar Canvas II and IX, 71

Rademaker, Abraham, 202
Raimondi, Marcantonio, 148
  Façade with caryatids, 149

Raphael, 101, 148
reactions, to Amsterdam Town Hall, 19–20, 195–216
  architectural criticism, 198–201, 206–12, 216
  and commemoration, 212–14
  historical accounts, 203–4
  sacer horror, 15–17
  travelogues, 205–6
  and visual culture, 202–4
reflection, 132–5
reliefs
  Burgomasters' room, overmantle, 66, *66*, 69–70
  Citizens' Hall (Burgerzaal), 67
  on façades, 66
  northern gallery, 67
  pedimental, 62
  Tribunal (Vierschaar), 148, 156–7, *157*, 159, 161, 162–4, 209
religion
  biblical references, 41, 46–7 (*See also* Solomon)
  Calvinism, 5–6, 15–16
  Catholicism, 15–16, 184
  divine grace, manifested in buildings, 87, 124–7
  divine providence, 128–9
  factions of, 125–6
  festoons, use in, 72–4
  freedom of, 64
  pagan, 68, 72–3
  sacer horror, evocation of, 15–16
  supervision of, 47
  symbols of, 7, 45–6, *45*, 129–30
  See also God; gods
Rembrandt van Rijn, 4, 20 n.11
  Night Watch, 30, 206, 219 n.22
republicanism, 51–2, 215
resurrection, 128–31
Rij, Cornelis Danckerts de, 31, 32, 39
Rijksmuseum, 186–7, 190 n.34, 191 n.49
Ripa, Cesare, 45–6, *45*
ritual. *See* ceremonies
Rixtel, Pieter, *On the Town Hall of Amsterdam (Op het Stadthuys van Amsterdam)*, 121–4, 129–30, 131, 132
Rome, 65–6

Amsterdam as heir to, 11, 85
architecture of, 11, 61
Arch of Septimus Severus, 132, *133*
Capitoline Hill, 11, 17, 32, 65, 69, 132, *133*
Dutch Republic, equated with, 11
Forum of Augustus, 148, *150*
personification, 90
St Peter's, 12–13, *13*
symbolic associations with, 11, 17, 32
triumphs, 68–71
Vatican, 151
roofs, 47–8
Rotgans, Lucas, *Elegy on Joan Huydecoper van Maarsseveen*, 108
Rouge Royal marble, 49
Royal Antiquarian Society (Koninklijk Oudheidkundig Genootschap), 181, 186, 191 n.48, 191 n.49
Rubens, Peter Paul, 33
  Free Copy after Mantegna's Triumphs of Caesar Canvas II and IX, 71
  Joyous Entry of Cardinal-Infante Ferdinand into Antwerp, designs for, 67, 157–8
  The Temple of Janus, *154*
rummer (ceremonial), 176–7, *177*, 182, 188 n.11
Ryff's, Walter Hermann, 148

sacer horror (impact of divine presence), 15–17
Sachs, Hans, 86
Saenredam, Pieter, 120
  The Old Town Hall of Amsterdam, 130–1, *130*
  'View on the Grand Square with Town Hall of Haarlem', 118, *119*
sandstone, 49
Sarazin, Jacques, 155
Sauval, Henri, 154–5
Savery, Salomon Jacobsz, *30*
Scamozzi, Vincenzo, 33, 49, 63, 74, 101, 146
Schaep, Gerard Simonsz., 178
Schaep, Pieter, 178
Scharfenberg, Albrecht, 85
Schouten, Hendrik P., 202, 211
Schrevelius, Theodorus, 35–6

Scipio Africanus, 68
sculpture, 4, 67, 102
  See also caryatids; reliefs
Seleucus (Zaleucus), 47, 148, 156–7, 159, 162, 164
Semper, Gottfried, 69
sensation, historical, 213
Seven Wonders of the Ancient World, 14–15, *15*, 86, 104, 124
Sévigné, Madame de, 87
SGL (architect), 32, *32*
shade, 120–1
shame, 146, 147, 148–9, 155–6
Sheriffs, 145, 164
social class, 35
Society for the Advancement of Architecture (Maatschappij tot Bevordering der Bouwkunst), 184–5, 186, 190 n.40, 216
Solomon, 7, 156–7, 160, 162
  architecture of, 41, 50–2, 86
  judgment of, 46–7
  magnificence, example of, 9–10
  Palace of, 11, 17, 42–3, *42*, *43*, 51–2, 63, 86
  Temple of, 41–2, *42*, 182
    Amsterdam Town Hall, model for, 17, 45, 63
    influence of, 50, 86
songs, 88
Southern Church (Zuiderkerk), 178
Spain, 6, 18, 45, 50, 50–1
spectators, 10, 182
  of judicial process, 37, 160–2
Spiegel, Hendrik Dirkszn., 184
spoons, commemorative, 182, *183*
Stadholders, 4, 9
Stadstekenacademie (Drawing Academy), 210, 213
Stalpaert, Daniel, 46, 48, 96–7
star charts, 46, 104–6
Stock Exchange (Beurs), 2, 176
Stolker, Jan, 211
stone, 49–50, 163–4
St Peter's, Rome, 12–13, *13*
strophe, 90–1, 92
Sturm, Leonhard Christoph, 197–201, *198*, *200*, 215
sublime, 16–17, 86, 104–6

successor states, 63, 64, 74
Suger of Saint Denis, 87
Sun Palace (Ovid), 85, 86
symbols/symbolism
  of Amsterdam, 72
  of caryatids, 153–6
  of immortality, 129–30
  of justice, 144–5
  patriotic, 212–13
  of peace, 38, 73
  religious, 7, 45–6, *45*, 129–30
  Rome, associations with, 11, 17, 32
  of victory, 18

tableaux vivants, 177, 188 n.13, 190 n.36
Tacitus, 40
Tarquinius Superbus, 66
Tasso, Torquato, 85
taste, 20, 201, 203, 208, 209–10
Temple of Solomon (First Temple), 41–2, *42*, 182
  Amsterdam Town Hall, model for, 17, 45, 63
  influence of, 50, 86
Temple of the Grail, 85
Tengnagel, Mattheus Gansneb
  Amsterdam Linden Leaves (Aemsterdamsche Lindebladen), 89
  On the Future Town Hall (Op het toekomende Raedhuis), 18, 84, 89–90
terms/terminal figures, 150
Tertullianus, *De Corona*, 73
Theseus, 160
Thirty Years' War, 29
Thulden, Theodoor van, *The Temple of Janus*, *154*, 158
time, 133
  interconnectedness of, 90–1, 130–1
  past, 40–1, 84, 98, 212, 213
  present, 84, 86, 212, 213, 214
towers, 45–6, 50
  Amsterdam Town Hall, 38, 45–6, 47
  New Church (Nieuwe Kerk), 61–2, 125–6, *126*, 176–7, 188 n.12
town halls
  Haarlem, 118, *119*
  Lyon, 178, 181

  role of, 65
  See also Amsterdam Town Hall
trade, 8, 65
transfer, cultural, 63, 69, 71–4
travel writing, 197, 198–9
Treasurers, 31, 36, 49–50, 185
Tribunal (Vierschaar), 2–4, *3*, 7, 38, 46–7, 209
  criticism of, 209
  entrance gate, 144, 160
  in laudatory poems, 84, 90, 101–2, 162–4
  public nature of, 37
  sculpture in, 19, *163* (*See also* caryatids)
    Medusa head, 101–2, *101*
    reliefs, 148, 156–7, *157*, 159, 161, 162–4, 209
triumphs, 18, 66–71, *66*
  See also arches, triumphal
trowels, ceremonial, 19, 47, 179, 180–1, 189 n.25
  exhibition of, 185, *186*, *187*
  by Lutma, 173, *174*, 180, *180*, *186*, *187*
Trustees of Orphans, 36
Tulp, Nicolaes, 182, 184
Tussenbroek, Gabri van, 125
two bodies theory, 129
tympana, 6, 38, 51, 205

Ulft, Jacob van der, 127
  Market on Dam Square, 125–6, *126*, 127
Utrecht, Dom Church, 176

Valckenaar, Simon, 190 n.35
Valckenier, Sybrant, 178
Valckenier, Wouter, 178
Vanvitelli, Gaspare (Casper van Wittel), 132
  View on St. Peter's Square, 12–13, *13*
Vatican, Rome, 151
Velde, Jan van de, *119*
Venice, 65–6
Vennekool, Jacob, *199*
Verhulst, Rombout, 48
Verwer, Abraham de, 132–5
  Galerie du Louvre and the Porte Neuf, *134*

The Louvre Grande Galerie, view of Paris from the Barbier bridge, 134, 139 n.39
The Louvre Grande Galerie, view of Paris from the Barbier bridge (upstream), 135, *135*, 139 n.39
victory. *See* triumphs
Vierschaar. *See* Tribunal (Vierschaar)
viewpoint, 118, *119*, 121, 132
Villalpando, Juan Bautista, 41–3, *42*, 63
Vingboons, Philips, 4, 31, 32
Vinkeles, Reinier, 202, 204, 211
   Amsterdam Town Hall and Weigh House, 205
   Ball in Amsterdam Town Hall in 1768, 206
   Portrait of Petrus Camper, 208
Vitruvius (Marcus Vitruvius Pollio), 41, 43, 63, 97, 101, 210
   on caryatids, 143, 146–50, 161–2, 164–5
   illustrated editions of, 148–50
vivacity, 120, 122–3
Vlaardingerbroek, Pieter, 62–3, 86, 182
Vondel, Joost van den, 7, 8, 9, 17, 85, 184
   Blyde Inkomst der allerdoorluchtighste Koninginne Maria de Medicis, 175–6
   Bouw-zang, 11, 90–3
   Inwydinge (Consecration), 18, 78 n.31, 78 n.35, 84, 87–8, *88*, 93–9, 123
Vos, Jan, 8, 9, 15, 17, 65, 85
   Aran and Titus, 99
   inauguration poem, 99–100, 159
Vos, Philips de, 181
Vossius, Gerardus, 17, 73, 74
Vredeman de Vries, Hans, 150, *152*, 165
   'View on a city with palaces and canal from a bird's eye perspective', 118, *119*

Waag. *See* Weigh House (Waag)
Wagenaar, Jan, 48, 201–5, *201*, 210, 211, 218 n.17, 220 n.36

Warburg, Aby, 69
Warnsinck, Willem Hendrik, 185
wars
   Eighty Years' War, 174
   First Anglo-Dutch War, 6
   Thirty Years' War, 29
   War of Austrian Succession, 184
wealth, 9–10, 174
Weigh House (Waag), 2, 176
   by Berckheyde, 11, *12*, 120, *120*, 121
   by Fokke, *202*, *204*
   by Mommers, *127*
   by Ulft, *126*
   by Vinkeles, 205
Western Church (Westerkerk), 176
Whitehall Palace, London, 33, 50, 107
Wilhelmus (song), 88
Willem II, King of the Netherlands, 184, 186
Willem III, King of the Netherlands, 186
William II, Prince of Orange, 9, 33, 107
William III, Stadholder-King (William of Orange), 70, 106–7, 135, 184
William IV, Count of Holland, 33
William the Silent, Prince of Orange, 88
wisdom, 47
Wittel, Casper van (Gaspare Vanvitelli), 132
   View on St. Peter's Square, 12–13, *13*
Wittewrongel, Petrus, 16
wonder, 14–17, 85–6, 87, 90, 102–4, 123–4
Wotton, Henry, 41, 146

Yosef ben Matityahu (Josephus, Titus Flavius), *Jewish War*, 73

Zaleucus (Seleucus), 47, 148, 156–7, 159, 162, 164
Zoet, Jan, 105
   Triumphant Amsterdam (Het triomfeerende Amsteldam), 106–8
Zuiderkerk (Southern Church), 178

www.ingramcontent.com/pod-product-compliance
Lightning Source LLC
Chambersburg PA
CBHW062137300426
44115CB00012BA/1951